JOAN OF ARC

JOAN OF ARC

Edward Lucie-Smith

W • W • NORTON COMPANY INC •

NEW YORK

Copyright © 1976 by Edward Lucie-Smith
Printed in the United States of America.
All Rights Reserved

First American edition 1977

Library of Congress Cataloging in Publication Data

Lucie-Smith, Edward.
   Joan of Arc.

   Bibliography: p.
   Includes Index.
   1. Jeanne d'Arc, Saint, 1412-1431. 2. Christian
saints—France—Biography. I. Title.
DC103.L96   1977   944'.026'0924 [B]   77-9509
ISBN 0-393-07520-6

1 2 3 4 5 6 7 8 9 0

Contents

List of Plates and Maps

Maps

for Gwenda David

❦ Acknowledgements ❧

My greatest debt of gratitude is to Dr Werner Muensterberger, for reading the complete manuscript of this book as it was written, and for saving me from many errors by his suggestions and advice. Grateful thanks are also due to my patient editor, Peter Carson; to my cousin Terence Charley, for driving me all over France in search of Joan of Arc; to my mother, for typing a complex manuscript both accurately and rapidly; to Masud Khan, Librarian of the International Pyscho-Analytical Library, for allowing me to use the facilities of the Library; to my old friend, Paul de Lisser, at whose house in Jamaica revision of the manuscript was completed; and to the dedicated staffs of the London Library and the British Museum.

❧ Introduction ❧

It has been authoritatively stated that, by the year 1920, no less than 12,000 works had been published about Joan of Arc in France alone.[1] More than fifty years later, the number must have considerably increased. To those in French one must add numerous others, the majority in English and written by English authors. England has always taken a masochistic interest in her defeats.

In the face of this formidable production, an author needs a certain hardihood to come forward and add his own book to shelves which are already overflowing. The reader may well ask why I have had the impertinence to do so.

I cannot claim to have relied upon new source-material. The principal sources for Joan's career were extremely well published in the nineteenth century, notably by that superb scholar Jules Quicherat, to whose memory all students of Joan of Arc must be grateful. Little which is new has come to light since Quicherat's time, but some of the chief texts have recently been republished in editions by contemporary *savants*. The most important of these republications is the new three-volume edition of the *Procès de condamnation* brought out by Pierre Tisset and Yvonne Lanhers between 1960 and 1971. Anyone who has encountered this work will admire the good sense of the editors, as well as their thoroughness.

Nor can I claim that I have a new and dazzling theory about my subject's life and mission. Up to the early years of this century, Joan's biographers were content to retail a more or less standard account of her birth, parentage, career in the wars, captivity, trial and death. More recently, this has been considered to be both naïve and boring. Instead, we have been given Joan the royal bastard, Joan who escaped burning, and Joan the witch. There have also been attempts to bring Joan into line with modern political theory, and particularly with theories inspired by Marxism. In the course of three-and-a-half years' research, I have examined many of these so-called 'explanations' of Joan's career, and I think they are all unconvincing.

Nevertheless, some kind of explanation is needed. Joan has been called 'the best-documented personage of the early fifteenth century', and yet I find, when I read the standard biographies, that none of them shows me a human face. It is only the works of fiction, notably Shaw's *St Joan* and Anouilh's *L'Alouette*, which seem to bring a human being before us. And these fictions are still unsatisfactory, in relation to Joan herself, because one becomes aware of the degree to which their authors, finding themselves unable to cope with the facts, have veered away into inventions of their own.

The trouble is, perhaps, that the facts and the myth are subtly at variance with one another. It was this which seems to have troubled at least one shrewd contemporary observer, Pope Pius II. 'Whether her career was a miracle of Heaven or a device of men,' he remarks in his *Commentaries*, 'I should find it hard to say.' And a little later he sighs: 'It is a phenomenon that deserves to be recorded, although after ages are likely to regard it with more wonder than credulity.'[2]

In some respects Joan's life has the pattern of the Christian myth, and this is one reason why she has achieved such renown. Her death was a death to save France, and in her last moments we find the same terrible desolation which Christ himself suffered upon the cross. The admission she made to her confessor, just before she set out for the Vieux-Marché and death at the stake, that her voices had deceived her, is paralleled by the Saviour's own despairing cry: 'My God, my God, why hast Thou forsaken me?'

Yet Joan moves in another dimension from the Jesus who taught in Galilee and who was crucified at Golgotha. It is difficult to imagine, for example, what our attitudes towards Christ would be if we possessed the full record of his trial before Pontius Pilate. In Joan's case, we possess not only the record of her trial in Rouen, but that of her subsequent rehabilitation.

My aim has been to listen to all the witnesses – to Joan herself, to those who knew her, to the chroniclers who recorded her career, to those who preserved fragments of information about her in other documents, such as the royal accounts – and to try to construct from their testimonies a convincing portrait. I began with no theory, and I end with none. But I think that mirrored in these multiple fragments one does at last find an extraordinary woman – living, suffering, developing. My Joan is perhaps less admirable than the Joan who is to be found in most of the modern literature. She is intensely arrogant, violent (but afraid of her own violence), and not always truthful. She is the prisoner of an obsession, or of a group of obsessions. At the same time she has moments, and more than moments, of ordinary human fear, self-doubt and depression. We may pity, admire and even love her. At the same time, we may feel a sneaking sympathy for those – even those who were supposedly supporters of the same cause, such as Regnault de Chartres, Archbishop of Rheims – who grew to detest her.

Often I have allowed the witnesses to Joan's life to speak for themselves. It is the master of Joan's household, Jean d'Aulon, for example, who describes some of the fighting which ended the siege of Orleans. From his descriptions we see what a chancy thing Joan's first and greatest triumph was, how often success hung on an impromptu decision, or an impulse of chivalric rivalry. Those who wish to see the hand of providence in what Aulon has to tell us are nevertheless at liberty to do so.

Where the main body of the evidence is concerned, I have been very reluctant to discard any scrap of it. If the sources were in conflict, or in apparent conflict, with one another, my aim was to reconcile them, rather than to choose one in preference to another. While certain crucial difficulties remain, and are noticed in the places where they arise, I am encouraged to find how often this method has seemed to yield me good results. Often what seemed to be opposed versions of a particular event have turned out, upon closer examination, to be perfectly congruous accounts of a related sequence of events. The witnesses report what struck them, and their memories seem to fasten upon slightly different moments in a particular drama. Indeed, the inner consistency of much of the documentation seems to have been underestimated by previous historians.

Though Joan did not live in an illiterate society, she lived in one where the written word occupied a position which was both more and less authoritative than the one it has today. It was more authoritative because it was rarer, and people relied upon it less for the same reason. One noticeable thing about the accounts given by the witnesses at the Trial of Rehabilitation is the way in which Joan's personality fills the direct quotations they give. Their recollections of what she said are quite astonishingly consistent with the record of the Trial of Condemnation, which is based on notes which were made on the spot, then welded into a continuous narrative after each day's session. We may reasonably believe that the men and women of the fifteenth century were in some respects better equipped to preserve the truth for us than a similarly varied band of witnesses would be today. Their verbal memories were demonstrably better, and we do well to pay attention to the nuances, as well as the actual content, of their testimony. The way in which a thing is reported can be very nearly as important as the facts.

Believing this, I have made it my business to listen carefully to Joan's contemporaries. Still more so, I have listened to Joan herself. No speech of hers (nor, indeed, of anyone else's) recorded here has been invented by me. Her incomparable pithiness and directness are things which carry across the ages, and which would in themselves serve to justify her apparently undying renown.

JOAN OF ARC

FRANCE in 1429

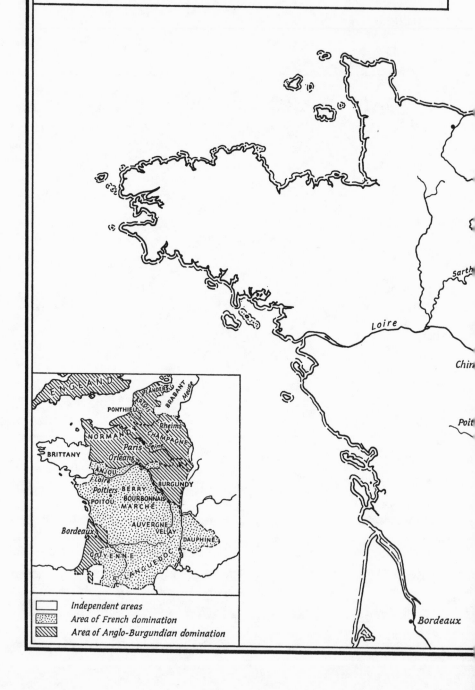

Sarth

Loire

Chir

Poit

Bordeaux

ENGLAND
FLANDERS
BRABANT
Meuse
PONTHIEU
ARTOIS
Rheims
NORMANDY
CHAMPAGNE
Paris
Seine
BRITTANY
Orleans
ANJOU
Loire
Poitiers
BERRY
BURGUNDY
POITOU
BOURBONNAIS
MARCHE
AUVERGNE
Bordeaux
VELAY
DAUPHINE
GUYENNE
LANGUEDOC

☐ Independent areas
▓ Area of French domination
▨ Area of Anglo-Burgundian domination

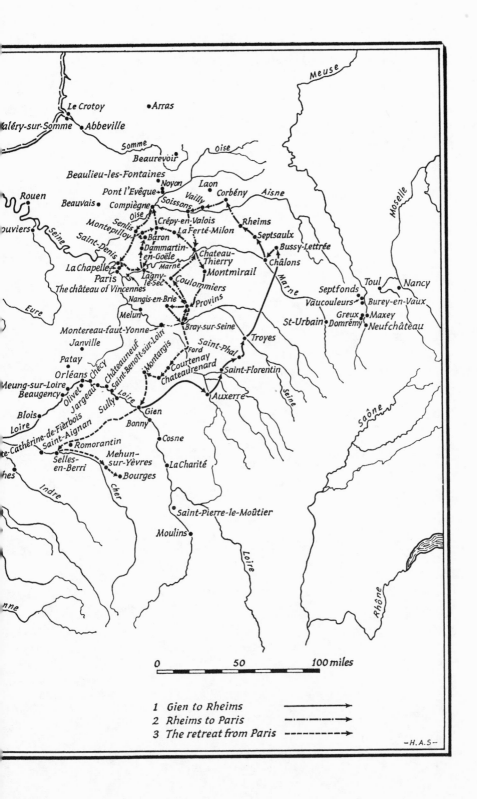

Meuse

Le Crotoy • Arras
aléry-sur-Somme • Abbeville

Somme
Oise
Beaurevoir
Beaulieu-les-Fontaines
Noyon Laon
Pont l'Evêque Corbény Aisne
Rouen Beauvais • Compiègne Soissons Vailly
uviers • Oise Crépy-en-Valois Rheims
Montepilloy Senlis La Ferté-Milon Septsaulx
Saint-Denis Baron Bussy-Lettrée
Dammartin- Chateau- Châlons
en-Goële Thierry
La Chapelle Marne Montmirail Septfonds Toul Nancy
Paris Lagny- Coulommiers Vaucouleurs Burey-en-Vaux
The château of Vincennes le-Sec St-Urbain Greux Maxey
Nangis-en-Brie Provins Domrémy Neufchâteau
Melun
Montereau-faut-Yonne Bray-sur-Seine Troyes
Janville Saint-Phal
Patay Châteauneuf Ford Saint-Florentin
Orléans Checy Saint-Benoît-sur-Loire Montargis Courtenay
Meung-sur-Loire Olivet Jargeau Chateaurenard Auxerre
Beaugency Sully Loire
Blois Loire Gien
e-Cathérine-de-Fierbois Bonny
Saint-Aignan Romorantin Cosne
Selles- Mehun-
en-Berri sur-Yèvres La Charité
hes Bourges
Indre
Cher
Saint-Pierre-le-Moûtier
Moulins
Loire
Saône
Rhône
Eure
Seine
Marne

0   50   100 miles

1 Gien to Rheims   ———→
2 Rheims to Paris   —·—·→
3 The retreat from Paris - - - →

—H.A.S—

I

On the morning of 30 May 1431 Joan of Arc was burnt in the Place du Vieux-Marché in Rouen. Her end was witnessed by 'an almost innumerable throng of spectators',[1] perhaps as many as ten thousand people. They included not only most of the citizens of the town, but others drawn from the surrounding countryside. A contemporary historian says that many people came to Rouen for this purpose as if to a public show.[2]

Though executions were, at this time, always a form of public entertainment, the size of the crowd indicated not only the curiosity aroused by the personality of Joan herself, self-styled or styled as she claimed by her voices *'Jeanne la Pucelle, fille de Dieu'*,[3] but the efficiency of the English occupying power. Tried as a heretic, Joan had made a public abjuration of her errors in the cemetery of the church of Saint Ouen on 24 May. She had then been condemned to perpetual imprisonment. On the following Sunday, 28 May, she was found to have relapsed, and the next day the ecclesiastical court responsible for her trial had met again to condemn her.

The authorities concerned must have made certain that the news of her condemnation and impending execution spread quickly. They wanted Joan's death to be witnessed by as many people as possible – the ignominious end of the supposed miracle-worker who had raised the siege of Orleans, who was held to be responsible for the rout of an English army at Patay, and who had led their enemy, Charles of Valois, to the anointing

1

and crowning at Rheims which seemed to legitimize his claim to the French throne.

Even though ten thousand pairs of eyes saw the flames envelop Joan where she stood chained to the stake on the high plaster scaffold, this was not enough. When her cries ceased 'the fire was raked back and her naked body shown to all the people . . . to take away any doubts from people's minds. When they had stared long enough at her dead body bound to the stake, the executioner got a big fire going about her carcass, which was soon burned up.'[4] Afterwards her ashes were thrown into the Seine.

It ought to have been, as it was meant to be, consignment to oblivion. Joan had excited popular wonder since her arrival at Charles VII's court at Chinon, in the spring of 1429. Her reputation had been a little tarnished by her failure to take Paris, as she promised to do. It had been further dimmed by her capture at Compiègne, while it was being besieged by the armies of the Duke of Burgundy. For just over a year before her death she had been a prisoner, first in Burgundian, then in English hands. During the early part of her captivity, she had made several attempts to escape, all of which had failed.

When she was transferred to English custody, in return for a substantial sum of money, her fate became inevitable, though both she and her judges sometimes seemed reluctant to recognize this. The position was summed up by the Earl of Warwick's remark to her doctors, at a time when she was sick in prison: 'The King does not wish, for anything in the world, that she die a natural death; for he holds her dear, having dearly bought her.'[5] Yet, even on the day of her execution, there were signs that the English plan had misfired. The majority of the spectators were greatly moved. Even if they had not approved of Joan before, they now felt a movement of sympathy towards her. Some of her judges wept. One said, as she died, to the man standing next to him: 'Please God that my soul be in the place where I believe this woman to be.'[6] And it was afterwards reported that the executioner, Geoffrey Thérage, who had been plying his gruesome trade in the city since the year 1407, went that afternoon to the convent of the Friars' Preacher, where he saw two monks who had been amongst the most sympathetic members of the ecclesiastical tribunal. 'I greatly fear that I am damned,' he said to them, 'for I have burned a holy woman.'[7] An English soldier, heard in confession at the same time, claimed that he had 'seemed to see', at the moment when Joan expired, a white dove come out of the pyre and fly towards France.[8] Other witnesses alleged that they had seen the name Jesus written in the flames.[9]

Soon the rumour began to be put about that Joan had somehow escaped burning. In the 1430s an impostor appeared, using the name of Dame des Armoises. She visited Orleans, and was 'very honourably received'.[10] A Norman chronicler was sufficiently doubtful of the true facts of the matter to remark, at the conclusion of his account of Joan's career: 'Finally, they burned her publicly, or another woman like her: concerning which many people were and still are of different opinions.'[11]

Today it is clear that the execution with which the English authorities had intended to write *finis* to a troublesome career, was, instead, the true start of one of the most considerable legends in European history. Like most legends it appears in a variety of guises. The Joan of Voltaire, the Joan of Schiller, the Joan of Michelet, the Joan of Anatole France and the Joan of George Bernard Shaw are all very different from one another. In modern historical literature she has been presented as everything from a great Christian mystic and visionary to the leader of a secret and unorthodox religion. The notion that she escaped burning persists; and some writers have been attracted by the idea that she was not a mere peasant girl at all, but a royal bastard with Valois blood in her veins. Theories of this kind seem to me unprovable.

What is certain is the fact that Joan existed. Her existence is vouched for not only by contemporary chronicles, but by two primary documents which form the basis for any assessment of her life and character. The first of these is the so-called Trial of Condemnation, which forms the record of the proceedings before the ecclesiastical court at Rouen in 1431. The second document, the Trial of Rehabilitation, is more complex. It is the record of three linked investigations, which were designed to quash the proceedings held before Pierre Cauchon, Bishop of Beauvais, and Joan's other judges.

The Trial of Rehabilitation began with two preliminary inquiries: one held before Guillaume Bouillé, a former rector of

3

the University of Paris and Canon of Noyon, in 1450; and another before the Papal Legate, Cardinal d'Estouteville, and Jean Bréhal, the Grand Inquisitor of France, which took place in 1452. This was followed, in 1455-6, by an inquiry on a much larger scale, begun before Jean Jouvenel des Ursins, Archbishop of Rheims, Guillaume Chartier, Bishop of Paris, and Richard de Longueil, Bishop of Coutances. Bouillé heard only seven witnesses; d'Estouteville, twenty-one; and in the course of the final inquiry depositions were taken from over a hundred: in Joan's district of origin, and in Orleans, Paris and Rouen. One witness made a deposition in Lyons. There is, of course, a considerable overlap between the preliminary inquiries and the final one, both as far as the actual witnesses are concerned, and in the content of their depositions. In the record of the final inquiry, which forms the true Trial of Rehabilitation, we find testimony from members of every social class, ranging from peasants to a royal duke. All had known Joan personally, and all were asked to tell what they remembered of her.

From these two documents we can trace the basic outline of Joan's life: her birth at Domrémy, on the river Meuse, which was then one of the frontiers of France; her visit to Vaucouleurs to seek the help of Robert de Baudricourt, the captain of the town and the principal royal representative in the region; her journey to Chinon to see King Charles VII, whom she insisted on calling 'the dauphin' because (though his father was dead) he had not yet been crowned and anointed. From Chinon Joan went to Poitiers, where an inquiry into her *bona fides* took place. This having been carried out to the satisfaction of the investigators, she proceeded soon thereafter to the city of Orleans, then besieged by the English. With her was a royal army. Orleans was relieved in a way which many people thought miraculous, and this success was followed by the taking of Jargeau and Beaugency, and the rout of an English army at Patay.

Joan then persuaded Charles VII to go to Rheims for the ceremony which, in her view, would make him a true king. This object was safely accomplished, and a number of important places were taken on the way, among them the city of Troyes where, in 1420, France had been handed over to the English by a treaty between Henry V of England, Philip the Good, Duke of

Burgundy, and Charles's own mother Queen Isabeau, acting on behalf of her mad husband Charles VI.

After the coronation ceremony at Rheims, Joan wanted to make an attempt on Paris, and Charles VII reluctantly agreed to let her do this. The attack failed, Joan was wounded, and her credit at court was permanently damaged. The royal army retreated towards the Loire. In the winter of the same year, 1429, Joan undertook another campaign, this time against the places held by the famous mercenary captain Perrinet Gressart. She succeeded in storming Saint Pierre-le-Moûtier, but failed against La Charité, which was Gressart's principal stronghold.

The next March, Joan departed from Sully-sur-Loire, where Charles was staying with his favourite, Georges de La Trémoille. She did so without the king's permission, and her aim was to campaign once more against the English and the Burgundians. She went to the town of Lagny-sur-Marne. There, with the help of a small mercenary force under an Italian captain, she defeated and captured the Burgundian freebooter, Franquet d'Arras. She then decided to try and relieve the city of Compiègne, which had just been invested by Anglo–Burgundian forces. Making a sally from Compiègne, she was pulled from her horse and captured by the men of Jean de Luxembourg, the ablest captain in the service of the Duke of Burgundy.

Jean de Luxembourg transferred his prisoner to the near-by castle of Beaulieu, and then, after she had made an attempt to escape, to his principal residence at Beaurevoir. Here Joan leapt from a tower and there is some dispute whether this was another attempt at escape or an attempted suicide. She survived her fall with little injury. Meanwhile, her captor was negotiating her sale to the English authorities in Normandy.

At the end of 1430 Joan was transferred to English custody at Rouen. Here she was tried for heresy and witchcraft by the ecclesiastical tribunal already mentioned. The trial began on 21 February 1431. On 24 May Joan made a public abjuration in the cemetery of the church of Saint-Ouen, and was taken back to her prison in Rouen castle. On 28 May she was found to have resumed male dress in her cell. On 29 May the court was reconvened and declared that she had relapsed into her former errors. Her execution followed.

According to Joan's own account, she was about nineteen

years old[12] at the time when her trial took place. This means that she was born in 1412 or 1413. We may even be able to fix the day and the approximate hour. Three days after the victory of Patay, Perceval de Boulainvilliers, one of Charles VII's chamberlains and Seneschal of Berri, wrote an excited letter to the Duke of Milan, describing the personage of the moment. He says that she was born on the night of Epiphany, as the peasants celebrated in the fields, and as the cocks began to crow.[13] Her birth was thus at the time of the false dawn, about 5.30 a.m. on 6 January, as the revellers were stumbling home after their night of celebration. The place was the village of Domrémy.

Joan's family had a place at the very centre of the social organization of the village. Her father, Jacques d'Arc, was born about 1375, and came from elsewhere. The general belief is that he was born at Ceffonds in Champagne. This was a little village dependent on the Abbey of Montier-en-Der. The serfs of this abbey had a tradition of rebellion against the monks, their overlords. They also had a traditional dislike of the English, who came into their orbit through the marriage of Blanche, widow of the last Count of Champagne, to Edmund, brother of Edward I. These facts have a certain resonance, if we take them in the context of Joan's story.

Despite the fact that he was born elsewhere, Jacques d'Arc played an increasingly important part in village affairs. In 1420 he appears as one of the two lessors of the Château de l'Ile, a strongpoint upon an island in the Meuse, the river upon which Domrémy lay. During the troubled times through which France was passing, the villagers meant to use it as a place to shelter their livestock. In October 1423, when the villagers agreed to pay protection money to a local mercenary captain, Robert de Saarbruck, Jacques d'Arc signed as 'doyen', and was placed in rank immediately after the mayor and the sheriff. Among the ordinary tasks of the doyen were the command of the watch and keeping guard over prisoners. Such duties must have made him seem an important figure to a child during the anxious 1420s, and particularly so to a child who happened to be his own daughter. The doyen also collected taxes and saw to the verification of weights and measures.

By 1427 Jacques d'Arc was a man who carried enough authority in the affairs of the district to be appointed official representative of the people of Domrémy in a suit which had been brought before Robert de Baudricourt, captain of Vaucouleurs. Baudricourt was in effect the king's viceroy, and the supreme power in the region where Domrémy lay.

Joan's mother, Isabelle Romée or Isabelle de Vouthon, came from a village which lay immediately to the south-west of Domrémy. Isabelle's origins were humble. Her brother, Jean de Vouthon, was a thatcher and tiler. Nevertheless another brother, Henri, was curé at Sermaize, which is close to Ceffonds. It may have been he who arranged the marriage between Jacques d'Arc and his sister. And it was apparently Isabelle who possessed a little property, both at Vouthon and in Domrémy where the couple lived. Despite repeated assertions by the witnesses at the Trial of Rehabilitation that Joan's parents were 'not rich', they had about twenty hectares of land in and around Domrémy, of which twelve were arable, and the rest equally divided between pasture and woodland. Rather than living in the miserable earth-walled hovel which was the common habitation of peasants in many parts of France, they had a substantially built, if small, stone house which can still be seen today.

One of the most interesting things about Joan's mother is her surname. Romée was the sobriquet given to those who had made the long pilgrimage to Rome, or at any rate an ambitious pilgrimage of some kind. Historians have usually asserted that Isabelle must have inherited it from her parents, or from some remoter ancestor. In this case, perhaps it came from the distaff side, as Joan told her judges that 'in her country, girls bore the name of their mother'.[14] On the other hand, we do know that Isabelle had a taste for pilgrimages. Her immediate reaction to her daughter's sensational departure for Chinon to see the king was to set out for Puy-en-Velay,[15] where the Jubilee of Puy was being celebrated, as it was whenever Good Friday coincided with the day of the Annunciation (25 March 1429). As it happens, there were special links between the diocese of Toul, in which Domrémy was situated, and the chapter of Notre Dame du Puy. But this can hardly have been Isabelle's reason for going. What led her there must have been the fervour aroused by a place and a cult which were to the France of the fifteenth century what Lourdes is to our own time. Isabelle's journey to

Puy at this particular juncture makes one think of her as a woman who had been affected by the emotional currents which were sweeping through the religious life of the epoch. Joan was later to assert that 'no one taught her her belief, unless it was her mother'.[16] The evidence we have thus seems to show that Joan's parents were contrasted in character. Her father's natural authority in the household would be reinforced by the official positions he assumed; while any emotion lacking from his character would be made up from the mother's side.

When their daughter was born, Jacques and Isabelle chose numerous godparents for her. She may have had as many as seven godmothers and four godfathers altogether. This multiplicity was not at all uncommon at the time. The purpose, in part, was to make up for the lack of written records and for the high rate of mortality. But the godparents also served to bind the child to the community. One of Joan's godmothers was the wife of the mayor; and one of her godfathers, Jean Morel, represented the people of Domrémy in their suit before Robert de Baudricourt at the same time as Jacques d'Arc himself. One of the few certain relics of Joan of Arc is the baptismal font at which she was held. This survives in the much-altered church at Domrémy: a simple, octagonal, stone basin, it must be the most ancient object there. Joan was not the first child of the Arc family to be brought to it, and she was not to be the last. She had two brothers and a sister who were older than herself, and she was followed by a younger brother.

The eldest brother, Jacquemin, plays no part in her story. He seems to have been almost grown up by the time she was born, and by 1425 he was living at Vouthon, probably working the land that came to him from his mother. Then – it is not certain in what order – came a sister, Catherine, and another brother, Jean. Catherine was married to Colin Le Maire, son of the mayor of the immediately neighbouring village of Greux, and died before Joan set out on her mission in 1429. Pierre, the youngest child in the family, born around 1413, was the member of it who took the most substantial role in the events which followed Joan's departure from Domrémy. He accompanied her on her campaigns, and was captured with her on the fatal sortie from Compiègne.

Domrémy, the village in which Joan was born and in which she grew up, occupied a rather special position in the complicated political situation of the time. From the religious point of view, it depended from Greux, which contained the principal church. Greux, in turn, was attached to the bishopric of Toul, which was not a French see but one which belonged to the Holy Roman Empire. The feudal relationship was different. Domrémy lay on the very frontiers of the duchy of Lorraine – the river Meuse formed the boundary. Technically it was a part of the duchy of Bar, but in fact belonged to that portion which was called the *Barrois mouvant* because it 'moved' or depended directly from the French crown. Joan was thus, from her birth, a subject of the French king, ruled directly by the royal administration.

In practice Domrémy was administered from the near-by town of Vaucouleurs, although, to complicate matters still further, this applied to only a portion of the village. The southern part, which included the Château de l'Ile already mentioned, and about thirty houses, formed a seigneury belonging to the Bourlémont family. This seigneury depended from the castellany of Gondrecourt, which in turn depended from the duchy of Bar, itself a fief of the Empire and not of the French crown. Patchwork arrangements of this type were the rule rather than the exception under feudalism. What made Domrémy different was the ease with which the various relationships could be interpreted in national terms, as forming a kind of microcosm of the distressed realm of France.

In Joan's day the Bourlémonts were a declining power. The main line died out in 1412, and the property passed to a niece of the last seigneur. Her husband had other seigneuries elsewhere, and she did not take much interest in the Château de Bourlémont, much less in Domrémy. It was her representative, Jannel Aubri, mayor of the village and husband of one of Joan's godmothers, who in 1420 arranged to let the Château de l'Ile, which was a mere enclosure with a chapel attached to it, for a period of nine years to one Jean Biget and to Joan's own father. It was a wise precaution on their part to rent it – Joan was later to remember helping to drive the cattle there 'for fear of the men at arms'.[17] We gain the impression that, though threatened from time to time by roving bands of marauders, the inhabitants of Domrémy made up for this by an unusual degree of independence from feudal control.

The district that surrounded Domrémy remained loyal to Charles VII in an area which was otherwise Burgundian or English in its allegiances. Robert de Baudricourt, who governed the territory dependent on Vaucouleurs, used many shifts to preserve his little dominion. On the whole he was successful. The district did not suffer nearly as much as many other parts of France from the ravages of warfare. There were constant alarms, but nothing like the repeated *razzias* which the peasants suffered elsewhere.

Occasionally, however, danger came uncomfortably close. Lorraine was a mass of squabbling feudatories, and in July 1419 two of them fought a small battle at Maxey, which was just the other side of the Meuse. Among the prisoners was the husband of one of Joan's godmothers. In 1421 part of the English army penetrated as far as near-by Gondrecourt, and it seems likely that the skirmishers reached the outskirts of Domrémy. The strain of events such as these, was, nevertheless, more psychological than physical. The inhabitants of Domrémy got enough to eat, and they had roofs over their heads. Their lot was easy compared to that endured by many of their contemporaries. We find no sign of the social breakdown which afflicted other parts of France.

2

Joan's childhood has so often been traduced that it is now hard to form any idea of what it must have been like. Yet there is enough material in the main sources to enable us to form an opinion. True enough, the witnesses at the Trial of Rehabilitation often give us the impression that they are reproducing a formula. The questions put to them seem designed to elicit a stock response – testimonies to Joan's sweetness of character and perfect religious orthodoxy. All the same, we probably know more about Joan during her earliest years than we know about any of her contemporaries at the same period of their lives. Some of this material is doubly precious because it comes to us from her own mouth.

The valley of the Meuse is tranquil and beautiful today, and must have been even more so in the early fifteenth century. Then as now the meadows would be pearled with dew in the summer mornings, and the wooded hills scarved with mist. As the heat of the sun grew, the mist would be seen rising from the dense foliage and streaming away to disappear in the blue of the sky.

The idyllic quality of some of the days and seasons which Joan experienced when she was young emerges clearly when we read her own testimony, and that of her fellow-villagers, about the so-called Fairies' Tree which preoccupied her judges in Rouen. To those harsh schoolmen, the Fairies' Tree smelt of witchcraft. To us, it seems a charming instance of the folk beliefs and ceremonies which gave a special poetry to rural life in Europe during the Middle Ages, and which often survived until much later. It grew close to the village – a large weeping beech, particularly well formed and symmetrical. Gérardin d'Épinal, a fellow-villager who was one of the witnesses at the Trial of Rehabilitation, thought it was 'as beautiful as a lily'.[1] The branches swept so low to the ground that they formed a kind of natural shelter, and the tree was also dubbed *'aux Logis-des-Dames'* – the Ladies' House.[2] The tree belonged to the Bourlémont family, and attached to it was a legend about a fairy who, 'in ancient days', had loved one of the seigneurs de Bourlémont.[3] The villagers remembered that the lovers were supposed to have used the great beech as a trysting place. They remembered, too, that the last Bourlémont seigneur had sometimes gone to dance there with his wife.[4] On Laetare Sunday – the Sunday in mid Lent which was a popular festival throughout the Barrois – they too were accustomed to go and celebrate the birth of spring. They danced and sang, and spread a cloth to eat a picnic under the tree.[5] Joan went with the rest, to make wreaths of flowers for the image of Our Lady in the chapel of Notre Dame de Bermont, and to hang garlands in the branches of the tree itself. She 'danced there sometimes with the children, but she sang there more often than she danced'.[6]

If these activities are well authenticated, strangely enough Joan's duties as a herder of sheep are much less so. At Domrémy the herds were chiefly cattle, and it was these that constituted the wealth of the villagers. Yet the idea that Joan was a 'little shepherdess' is now so firmly rooted in the public imagination that it is difficult to combat it. Perceval de Boulainvilliers was one of the first to give it currency. He speaks of her as 'looking after her parents' sheep, while these wandered in the fields'.[7] The error was bred by distance, by the impulse towards courtly hyperbole, and by ignorance of local conditions. But it is also an example of a very medieval kind of allegorical thinking. A keeper of sheep, following in the footsteps of Christ, was likely to be a saviour herself.

At the time of her trial Joan was anxious to play down this aspect of her childhood. Her judges wished to prove that, while guarding the flocks and herds, she had escaped from the supervision of her parents. Her denial that she 'guarded the sheep and other animals' during the period that she lived in her father's house[8] has been taken to refer to her brief sojourn in Neufchâteau, and to be the result of an error made during the compilation of the official version of the trial document. In addition to this, however, Joan is on record as having claimed that she did not usually keep watch over the animals, though she helped to drive them to pasture.[9] She added that she could not recall whether, in her youngest years, she looked after them.[10]

The probability is – and we find it supported by those who knew her as a child – that she took her turn at a common duty which did not occur so very often, and only at one season in particular. Every family, after the hay harvest, was allowed to graze a certain number of head of cattle, according to the amount of land they owned. The beasts were guarded on a rota system, by someone from each household in turn. It was the kind of job which could be delegated to children, and Joan certainly undertook it, but not, as she pointed out 'when she was bigger and had reached the years of reason'.[11] One of her godmothers also said that Joan watched over the animals,[12] and her childhood playmates were later to recollect seeing her with her father's beasts, her distaff in her hand.[13] But we must not imagine her spending the greater part of every day in some remote and lonely spot, surrounded by a herd of sheep.

For a peasant girl who lived in Domrémy, there were many other jobs to be done, and Joan did not shirk them. Her contemporaries remembered her as a hard and willing worker.[14] Some of the tasks she undertook required strenuous physical effort. For example, she sometimes went ploughing either with her father,[15] or with one of her young companions.[16] These exertions must have helped to build up the reserves of physical strength which others later marvelled at. Joan sewed and span, and was proud of her skill at these occupations – she told her judges that in this respect 'she did not fear comparison with any woman in Rouen'.[17] Her physical dexterity, too, was to be a subject for comment once she became famous. She also carried out all the ordinary household duties which were expected of a girl of her class and kind. In all this she did nothing out of the ordinary in terms of the community to which she belonged.

There came a point, however, when those who surrounded Joan began to notice that she was increasingly different from the rest. She was intensely pious – 'so pious', her childhood friend Mengette declared, 'that her comrades and I said she was too much so'.[18] When she heard the bell sound for mass, and she was in the fields, she would immediately return and go to church in order to hear the service said.[19] When evening came, she listened keenly for the compline bell, and, if she was still in the fields, would fall to her knees and say her prayers.[20] On occasion the churchwarden Perrin Drappier would forget to ring for compline. Joan, though normally gentle, would then become perturbed and would scold him. She even offered to give him some wool if he would be more conscientious about his duties in this respect.[21] Within the church she could sometimes be seen prostrated before the crucifix; or with her hands joined and her face and eyes lifted towards the image of Christ and that of the Holy Virgin.[22]

Every Saturday, she would go on pilgrimage to the little chapel of Notre Dame de Bermont, which lay above the road between Domrémy and Neufchâteau. She apparently started this custom in the days when her sister Catherine was still alive; and the sisters would go there with other young people, taking candles with them to light before the image.[23] Later, Joan developed the habit of slipping away to this chapel on her own, at times when her parents thought she was busy ploughing or working elsewhere in the fields.[24] By this time her contemporaries were aware of her tendency to draw apart from them.[25] They teased her for her piety,[26] and half-jestingly complained that she now refused to dance.[27]

Perhaps the most significant sign of the crisis through which Joan was passing was the frequency with which she went to confession. Joan's own evidence conflicts with that of the people who knew her in her childhood and adolescence, perhaps for good reason. When the subject was raised by her judges, all she would say was that she 'confessed her sins every year to her parish priest, or, if he was unable to hear her, to some other priest'.[28] She was thus giving the court to understand that her religious practice was strictly in line with that expected of most of the laymen of her time, and that she was careful to make the obligatory confession before the equally obligatory Easter communion which marked her as a member of the Church.

Her fellow-villagers recalled the matter differently. A modest estimate was that she 'confessed at Easter and at the other solemn feasts'.[29] Others thought that she confessed whenever she got the opportunity, and that opportunities were not lacking. Mengette said, for instance, that she often saw Joan on her knees before their parish priest.[30] Joan herself was to remark, though in another context, that 'one cannot cleanse one's conscience too much'.[31] While these frequent confessions made the ecclesiastical court suspect her orthodoxy, at the time those who looked after her spiritual welfare approved of her attitude, and did not find it strange. Her parish priest, Messire Guillaume Fronté, was heard to say that he had never met a better Catholic, and that there was none better in his parish.[32] Today, though without siding with those who condemned her, we may legitimately ask what it was that drove such a pure and blameless girl to these repeated purgings of conscience? One answer, perhaps, is that she was disturbed by the changes she found taking place in her own body, now that she had reached puberty, and by desires she scarcely understood.

The true secret she was keeping from her family and friends, however – and it seems that she did not tell her priest about it either, even under the seal of confessional – was the fact that she had begun to hear voices. Her description of the way in which these voices first came to her is justly famous:

When she was thirteen years of age, she had a voice from God to help her to know what to do. And on the first occasion she was much afraid. And this voice came about the hour of midday, in the summertime, in her father's garden. . . She heard the voice upon the right side, towards the church, and she rarely heard it without an accompanying brightness. . . And, after she had heard this voice upon three occasions, she understood that it was the voice of an angel.[33]

Since Joan's voices were to govern her conduct for the rest of her career – she herself said: 'Everything that I have done that was good I did by command of my voices'[34] – it is necessary to look at this fascinating subject in more detail.

In the first place, we must note that Joan's voices and apparitions were not unique. It is perhaps surprising to learn how many people are from time to time visited by visual or auditory hallucinations. Towards the end of the last century, for example, the English Society for Psychical Research conducted a census of hallucinations based upon a very large sample – nearly 16,000 people from English-speaking countries, and over 27,000 altogether. 9·4 per cent of the respondents from English-speaking countries said that they had experienced hallucinations of one kind or another, and affirmative replies from the whole sample amounted to as much as 11·96 per cent. In the English table of results, more than half (52 per cent) of hallucinatory experiences occurred when the subjects were aged between fifteen and thirty – that is they began with puberty, and declined after young adulthood.[35] However, the census-takers noticed the rarity of auditory hallucinations compared to visual ones, and of hallucinations affecting several of the senses compared to others.[36]

Joan's voices and visions tend to fit a pattern which is quite familiar to twentieth-century doctors, and which is extensively recorded in medical literature. One specialist remarks, for example, that on their first appearance hallucinations are experienced as inexplicable, and as something foreign to the subject's own concept of himself or herself. They therefore have a quality of the uncanny, and arouse feelings of awe, or alternatively of dread, horror and loathing.[37] There is a marked similarity here, to Joan's description of how the voices came to her; and also a similarity to the account she gives of her first meeting with St Michael: 'The first time, she was in great doubt if it was St Michael who came to her, and this first time she was much afraid; and she saw him a number of times before she knew it was St Michael.'[38] When adolescents suffer from delusions of this type, even today, they often present themselves in religious terms.

The more bizarre details given in the trial document, especially in the section of Posthumous Information, which is sometimes dismissed as being in large part a fabrication, are also closely paralleled in the accounts offered by present-day patients. Joan is said to have told one of her judges that she once beheld a multitude of angels 'in the guise of certain very tiny things'.[39] In addition, she told another judge that her apparitions came to her on some occasions 'in great multitudes and in very small dimensions'.[40] These descriptions precisely match modern cases, where the subject sees the multitudinous personages of his vision much reduced in volume, but extraordinarily brilliant in hue, as if the shrinkage had led in turn to a condensation of the colours.[41]

The manner in which Joan's voices and visions manifested themselves, and the relationship they seemed to establish with her, also have close similarities with the situations that doctors encounter today. One reason for her withdrawal from her friends at Domrémy was that the voices which now preoccupied her were more clearly heard in solitude. When she was a prisoner in Rouen, Joan was to complain that 'the tumult of the prisons and the noise made by the guards' prevented her from hearing St Catherine.[42] Yet the voice was capable of drawing attention to itself, often with great insistence, at moments when Joan's attention had every cause to be focused elsewhere. There is a terrible pathos in the answer she made to her judges during the séance of 27 February 1431. Asked if she heard the voice in the room where the trial was being held, she replied that she had, but 'she did not understand the voice properly, and understood nothing she could repeat, until she had gone back to her chamber'.[43]

One reason why, at Domrémy, she took such a close interest in the churchwarden's dutifulness, or lack of it, in ringing for compline and the other offices was that the bells served as a kind of trigger-mechanism for the manifestations. She was to say in her last hours that she heard her voices 'above all when the bells sounded, at the hour of compline and of matins'.[44] As her relationship with them strengthened, however, she began to feel able to consult them at will, at times when there was some problem to be resolved, and soon felt confident of being able to summon them if she needed them. 'Often,' she said, 'they came without being called, and at other times, if they did not come, she would ask God to send them. . . She had never had need of them and not had them.'[45]

But who and what were these advisers with whom Joan had been provided? She mentions three saints in particular: St Michael (the first to come to her), St Catherine and St Margaret. They spoke to her in French – 'a better French than yours', as she rudely told Séguin Séguin, a member of the commission appointed by Charles VII at the start of her mission.[46] When asked by her judges in Rouen if St Margaret spoke to her in English, she replied with equal tartness: 'Why should she speak

English, when she does not belong to the English party?'[47] Because her saints 'spoke very well and marvellously',[48] Joan had no difficulty in understanding them after the first few occasions. In addressing Joan in the only tongue she knew and by gradually becoming more distinct to her, they again followed a pattern of auditory hallucination which is well known to specialists.[49]

All the saints who came to Joan had some connection either with her own personal situation, or with the situation in which France then found herself; and all were particularly suitable as guides in what was to be her mission. St Michael appeared to her in the guise of *'un très vrai prud'homme'*[50] – or, as we might say, a good deal more tamely, as 'a fine-looking gentleman'. He was the obvious patron for any kind of patriotic endeavour – in the early fifteenth century he had virtually replaced St Denis as the patron of France, and the Valois kings paid special regard to him. Charles VII, when Dauphin, had a particular reverence for this saint, and in 1419 ordered that his image should be painted upon the standards of France. At the time when Joan's visions began, Mont Saint-Michel was one of the symbols of French resistance to the English, and one of the few successes that Charles VII could show at this period was the naval victory won by his supporters before the stronghold in June 1425. In addition to all this, St Michael was the patron of the Barrois, from which Joan's mother came.

St Catherine and St Margaret were announced by St Michael as Joan's other councillors.[51] Both were high-born virgins and martyrs. Catherine was the name of Joan's sister, who may still have been alive when the visions began. She was also the patroness of Maxey, just across the Meuse from Domrémy. Perhaps more important in Joan's mind, however, was the fact that St Catherine was the bride of Christ. When Joan 'having her ring on her hand and upon her finger' touched Catherine as she appeared to her in visible form,[52] it was near to being a repetition of the mystic marriage which the saint herself had undertaken.

St Margaret was represented in an elegant statue in the church at Domrémy. It is still there, and, judging from the style, must have been fairly newly installed in Joan's time. But it seems that Joan attached less importance to her. She is much less often mentioned, and usually appears as a kind of coadjutor of St Catherine's, just as she often accompanies the latter in representations of the virgin surrounded by saints.

It is apparent, from some of Joan's replies, that there was a certain inconsistency about the way in which her visions appeared to her. Where St Catherine and St Margaret are concerned, it is fairly evident that they manifested themselves not as full length figures but as heads with glittering crowns – 'she saw them always in the same form, and their forms were very richly crowned. . . About their robes she knows nothing'.[53] And again: 'What aspect did she see? – She saw their faces.'[54]

About St Michael she was even vaguer – she said that he did not have a crown and that she knew nothing of his clothing.[55] Asked if he was naked, and if he had hair, she produced two of her magnificently impertinent retorts. To the first question, the answer was: 'Do you think God has nothing to clothe him with?'[56] And to the second: 'Why should it have been cut off?'[57] Yet at last she admitted that she did not know whether St Michael had hair or not.

Questions about the actual appearance of her saints made her extremely uneasy, just as she was uneasy, and also irritated, at being questioned about what they said. There seem to have been two reasons for her disquiet. The first was that questions about her voices seemed to her a violation of privacy – they were an attempt to meddle with revelations which had been made to her directly and by divine agency. The second was that she felt threatened, because her voices and visions had a curious habit of slipping out of focus, and she did not like to admit to this. When, for example, she was asked if she saw other parts of her three saints except their faces, she burst out angrily: 'I have told you all I know about that, and rather than tell you all I know I would prefer you cut off my head.'[58]

Despite this, she believed unwaveringly in her counsellors, and to her they were very real. She even asserted that she had embraced St Catherine and St Margaret, who had a beautiful perfume about them.[59] Her experience of this sweet odour is, curiously enough, one of the things which links her to the religious mystics, such as St Theresa of Avila, from whom she otherwise differs in many details. When asked by her judges whether she saw St Michael and the angels corporeally and in reality, she replied – and we can still catch the passionate accent of the answer – 'I saw them with the eyes of my body, as plainly as I see you; and when they left me, I wept, and longed for them to take me away with them.'[60] On another occasion she declared, with reference to her saints: 'I have seen them with my own eyes and I believe that it is they as firmly as I do that God exists.'[61]

It remains to ask what commands her voices laid upon Joan. At first, following a pattern which is familiar to modern experts on auditory hallucinations, they seem to have confined themselves to brief phrases and injunctions of a fairly general kind. St Michael told Joan 'to be a good girl and God would help her'.[62] But he told her too – and we may guess that some small space of time has been telescoped in the reply – that 'she would come to the aid of the King of France'.[63] Then, elaborating once more, 'the angel told her of the pity which was in the kingdom of France'.[64] One gets a closer view of the process of gradual amplification and clarification from another of Joan's replies:

Questioned about the teaching which this voice gave her concerning the salvation of her soul:
She said that it taught her to lead a good life; and to go to church; and it said to Joan that it was necessary that she, Joan, should go into France. . . She confessed further that this voice said to her two or three times a week that she, Joan, must leave and go into France; and she also admitted that her father had known nothing of her departure. She said, also, that the voice told her that she would go into France; and that she could no longer remain where she was; and that this voice told her that she would cause the siege laid before Orleans to be raised. She said then that the voice had told her that she, Joan, should go to the fortress town of Vaucouleurs, to find Robert de Baudricourt, captain of that place, and that he would give her people who would go with her; Joan then replied that she was a poor girl and did not know how to ride a horse or to make war.[65]

This answer is sequential, and covers a period of over three years, from the moment when the voices first announced themselves in the summer of (probably) 1425, until the time in December 1428 when Joan left Domrémy for Burey-en-Vaux, on the way to Vaucouleurs.

If 1425 was probably the year in which Joan first began to hear her voices – assuming, that is, that she was born early in 1412 – it was also a year which brought a traumatic shock to the inhabitants of Domrémy. In July 1425, an Anglo–Burgundian band drove off the cattle which belonged to the village, and also those which belonged to Greux. By good luck, they were recovered, but Domrémy, church included, seems to have been burnt and plundered by the soldiers. A witness deposed that 'when the said town of Domrémy was burnt, on feast-days Joan always used to go and hear mass in the town of Greux'.[1] So the bright light that came with Joan's first vision, and which nearly always accompanied her visions afterwards, on this first occasion may have hovered beside a blackened shell. The damage cannot have been too serious, however, since the font and the statue of St Margaret survived intact.

An incident of this kind must have brought home the desperate reality of the war. Not that Domrémy, though it was situated on the very frontiers of the kingdom, had ever been isolated. It lay on the road that linked the two major blocks of territory ruled by the dukes of Burgundy. Near by, Neufchâteau specialized in the import of wines from Burgundy and especially Beaune to the territories of the lower Meuse and Flanders. Cloth from Ypres and Ghent travelled the other way. And news followed trade in both directions.

Another source of information, much of it highly coloured,

must have been the beggars and broken men from the wars who drifted up and down the length of the Meuse valley. Joan was tender-hearted towards unfortunates such as these – one of her fellow-villagers remarked that she would 'sleep beneath the hood of the hearth, so that the poor might sleep in her bed'.[2]

The politics of the kingdom were, in this region, reflected all the way down the geographical and social scale. If the people of Domrémy thought of themselves as members of the party of Charles VII, which they did – Joan only knew of one Burgundian there 'and she would willingly have seen his head cut off, but only if it pleased God' – then upon the other side of the Meuse the people of Maxey were Burgundian in their sympathies.[3] There were fights between the children of the two villages and, though Joan denied having taken part in these, she remembered seeing 'certain people of the village of Domrémy who had fought with those of Maxey, and sometimes returned much battered and bloody'.[4]

The war was thus very much within the compass of a child's experience and a child's imagination, and there was probably no need for the voices to tell Joan which side to take, though she later said that 'after she understood that the voices were for the King of France, she did not like the Burgundians'.[5] In this, as in so much else, her counsellors were expressing her own desires and impulses. But what was it that drove her to translate her feelings into positive action – the voices themselves, or some force in her own life of which the voices were a disguised expression?

There are certainly two, and possibly three, views which can be taken of Joan's voices and their origin. The first is that they were divinely inspired, and that Joan was the God-appointed means of rescuing the kingdom of France from its difficulties. This is the religious and, in France at least, the patriotic view. The second is that Joan's visions, her actions, and therefore ultimately her whole life and character, are susceptible to purely rational explanations, and that her career involves no disturbance of the natural order. The third is that, though Joan's career is explicable in terms of common experience, her impact on the history of her time was not a matter of coincidence or accident, but was divinely ordained.

Following the principle that it is necessary to exhaust the

possibilities of the natural world before accepting any kind of supernatural explanation, we must now ask in what ordinary soil the roots of Joan's visions might possibly be found. The thing to look at is her family situation, more especially because hallucinations of the type from which she suffered are often, today, associated with unresolved family conflicts.

Joan's relationship with her parents was not entirely smooth. If we examine what she has to say about them, and especially about her father, we get an impression of stress and conflict, which was in turn a cause of emotional disturbance to both parties. Her judges at Rouen gave Joan a difficult time about her failure to tell her parents either about her visions or about her impending departure. Her explanations are somewhat lame. She says that concealment was not imposed upon her by her voices, but that she did not want to reveal what they told her for fear of the Burgundians – an indication, this, of her growing sense of her own importance – 'and especially because she much feared that her father would prevent her from making her journey'.[6] The dialogue then continued as follows:

Asked if she believed she had done well in leaving without the permission of her father and mother, when one ought to honour one's father and mother, she replied that in all other things she had entirely obeyed her father and mother, excepting for this departure; but later she had written to them about it and they had pardoned her.

Asked if, when she left her father and mother, she thought she was committing a sin, she replied that, because God commanded it, it had to be done. She said in addition that, because God commanded it, she could have had a hundred fathers and mothers and could have been a king's daughter, but would nevertheless have gone.

Asked if she had asked her voices whether she should tell her father and mother about her departure, she replied that as far as her father and mother were concerned, the voices were quite content that she should tell them, had it not been for the pain it would have caused them if she told them about her departure; and as far as she was concerned, she would not have told them for anything. *Item*, she said that the voices left it to her to tell her father and mother or to keep silent.[7]

We see how she gradually finds herself lured into greater and greater candour about her fixed determination to tell her parents nothing, and we note that it was her father's reaction in particular that she feared. But as far as Joan's relationship to her parents is concerned, there are two incidents which seem highly significant, and one phrase that stands out. One of these incidents is private and interior; the other is public and in a sense official.

The first is the story of a prophetic dream – dreamt not by Joan but by her father. Joan's judges had heard about it, and asked Joan for an explanation:

> To this she replied that, when she was still in the house of her father and mother, it was several times told her by her mother that her father said that he had dreamt that the said Joan his daughter would go away with the men-at-arms; and her father and mother took great care to guard her and held her in great subjection. . . She had heard it said by her mother that her father said to her brothers: 'Truly, if I thought that thing would happen which I am afraid of where my daughter is concerned, I would want you to drown her, and if you did not do it, then I would drown her myself.'[8]

To a modern psychoanalyst such a dream might have quite complex implications. To 'go away with the men-at-arms' meant, in a fifteenth-century context, that Joan was doomed to become a soldiers' trull. If her father's subconscious was ready to place her in such a situation, it implies a wish to possess her himself. The dream, therefore, has a strongly incestuous element, combined with a degree of sadism. This is a rape fantasy, as well as an incest fantasy. But, combined with this, there might also be a feeling of inferiority. The peasant, though a considerable figure in his own community, recognizes his own helplessness when faced with the swaggering violence of the mercenary bands which threaten not only his daughter, but his life and his livelihood. But the way in which the story is presented is in many respects almost as interesting as its content. We note that Joan has no direct communication with her father – information about the dream comes to her only through her mother. And the phrase that leaps to the eye is the one that summarizes her parents' attitude towards her – they kept her, she says, 'in great subjection'. The words seem to carry with them a burden of resentment of which the speaker herself is unconscious.

The second incident, though public, has mysterious elements. It is the matter of a suit for breach of promise brought before the officiality at Toul – that is to say, before the ordinary ecclesiastical court of the diocese in which Joan lived. Joan's judges thought that it was she who brought the suit, and that it was the young man who had refused to marry her. He did so, according to them, because of the company she kept while she was at Neufchâteau.[9] Joan maintained that, on the contrary, it was she who had refused to marry her suitor.

Joan's visit to Neufchâteau in Lorraine was due to an Anglo–Burgundian invasion similar to that of 1425. In late June or in July 1428, the population of Domrémy were forced to flee *en masse*, taking their cattle with them. Neufchâteau was an obvious refuge, as it was traditionally the market-town for Domrémy, and the men of Neufchâteau gave the inhabitants of Domrémy cattle to feed in the summer months. At Rouen, the ecclesiastical court would have liked to make out that Joan went to Neufchâteau on her own, without the permission of her father and mother, and had there worked as a maidservant at an inn frequented by young women of loose morals and by soldiers. They thought it was here that she learned how to ride and also something of the profession of arms.[10] Joan vigorously denied this, though she admitted that she had indeed spent fifteen days in the town, in the house of a woman called La Rousse.[11] At the Trial of Rehabilitation, the witnesses combined to support her story. What really makes the brief visit to Neufchâteau important, in the context of Joan's life, is its link to the suit for breach of promise.

Such a suit can only have originated in a determined attempt on the part of her parents to marry her off. And the point is that Joan resisted. She herself tells us that she 'obeyed them in all things, except in the matter of the case at Toul concerning marriage'.[12] She was prepared to bring the family dispute right out in the open before the court. She 'swore before the judge to tell the truth', and the truth was that 'she had not made this man any promise'.[13] Her parents, and especially her father, must have been astonished at her resistance. According to the social customs of the time, he could have expected his daughter to accept a match which he himself favoured, however repugnant it might be to her. Though he did not yet know of Joan's vow of virginity, made to the voices the first time they spoke to her,[14] Jacques d'Arc must have begun to realize that he, though *doyen* of the village, was no longer master in his family.

Indeed, the plan to marry Joan off may have arisen, not only because she was now the right age, but in response to unformulated family tensions which made it uncomfortable to have Joan in the same house. Jacques d'Arc's dream seems to confirm this. It hints that his incestuous feelings, on some deep level, were reciprocated by his daughter. If his reaction was to avert the peril by putting her into the hands of another man, hers was more powerful still. Dangerous emotions of this kind, and her repression of them, were just the forces needed to create, not only her voices themselves, but her ever-increasing determination to carry out their commands.

But there is one further aspect of the form which her mission took which attracts attention, in the context of what we know about her family. Though Charles VII was, in fact, considerably older than herself, it often seems as if Joan thought of him as a child to be guided and protected. This makes us think about her relationship with her younger brother Pierre, later to be her close companion of her campaigns and destined to be captured with her at Compiègne. It may be that Joan's relationship with her father and with her brother Pierre took the form of 'double displacement'. The incestuous feelings she originally felt for her father were transferred to her brother, and thence to the king, who shared some part of both their characteristics, being a father-substitute because he was royal, and a replacement for Pierre because he was in need of the help that Joan might bring him.

When Joan returned from Neufchâteau to Domrémy, her mission was already fully formed in her mind, as was her resolution to put it into effect. She would 'go into France' and rescue the king, sublimating any guilt she might feel towards her real father and brother by her services to this substitute. Running through her head was the prophecy which she was soon to quote to her cousin-by-marriage, Durand Laxart,[15] and to her hostess at Vaucouleurs, Catherine Le Royer: 'Have you not heard that France, lost by a woman, will be saved by a virgin?' To Catherine she added: 'a virgin from the Marches of Lorraine'.[16] She thus both adopted and adapted a traditional saying. In place of a world lost by Eve and saved by Mary,[17] she proposed to substitute a kingdom lost by the 'bad' mother of Charles VII, Queen Isabeau of Bavaria, and saved by none other than herself. It is interesting that the queen shared a christian name with Joan's own mother.

Though she had as yet told no one of her task, and despite the need to conceal her plans from her parents, she could not resist dropping a few hints to her fellow-villagers. To Gérardin d'Épinal she said: 'Friend, were you not a Burgundian, I would tell you something.'[18] Disappointingly, perhaps, he misunderstood her, and thought she was referring to the possibility of a marriage to one of her childhood friends. The idea may, indeed, have been put into his mind by the case at Toul. To Michel Lebuin, speaking on St John's Eve – that is, on 24 June 1428, and in the very midst of the scare which took the inhabitants of Domrémy to Neufchâteau – Joan was more specific. 'There is,' she told him, 'between Coussey and Vaucouleurs, a young girl who, before a year is out, will have the King of France crowned.'[19]

4

The ruse Joan adopted to escape her parents' vigilance was simple. She asked Durand Laxart to tell her father that she, Joan, had gone to help Durand's wife, her cousin, in childbed.[1] Laxart himself was fifteen years older than Joan and, following local custom, she therefore addressed him as 'uncle'. He was a simple labourer, and he lived at a village called Burey-le-Petit, now Burey-en-Vaux, only a small distance to the south-west of Vaucouleurs, which was the place that Joan must go to in order to confront Robert de Baudricourt, who alone had power to send her to the king.

Durand Laxart was Joan's first real confidant, and her first convert. He seems to have put up surprisingly little resistance to her plans. Joan remembered that 'she then said to her uncle that it was necessary that she go to Vaucouleurs and her uncle took her there'.[2] She made no bones about the reason why she wished to go, as Laxart's own account makes plain: 'I myself went to fetch Joan at her father's house and took her to my house. And she told me that she wanted to go to France, to the dauphin to have him crowned. . . And she told me also that I was to go to Robert de Baudricourt that he might have her taken to the place where the lord dauphin was to be found.'[3]

She stayed with Laxart, according to her own account, for only eight days;[4] then later lodged with a woman called Catherine Le Royer in Vaucouleurs itself.[5] It does not seem likely that she made an interim return to Domrémy, though some authorities imply that this took place. The exact date when she left her native village is also in dispute, but the best guess seems to be that it happened in December 1428.[6] In the beginning, Joan's approaches were badly received. Having brought her to Burey, Laxart duly went off to see Baudricourt, but received no encouragement. 'This Robert several times told me that I should send her back to her father's house, having first soundly boxed her ears.'[7]

Robert de Baudricourt was not the kind of man who would readily listen to mystagogues and fantasists. He was a professional soldier, who sprang from the Lorraine nobility. His father was chamberlain to Robert, Duke of Bar. He had been captain of Vaucouleurs since 1420, and had remained consistently loyal to the dauphinist government. As a result, he had suffered from English confiscations. Since Vaucouleurs was isolated from the other areas controlled by Charles VII, he was, for long periods of time, abandoned almost completely to his own resources. He defended the territory which had been entrusted to him by means of a long series of expedients, compromises, diplomatic ruses and tricks. The Anglo–Burgundian invasion of 1428 was almost his closest shave, and cannot have improved his temper. Like many men of his type, he was not scrupulous. He was a notorious plunderer, and he had a bad reputation with women. Some were to wonder, indeed, how Joan's vaunted virginity survived his sexual proclivities 'for the Sire de Baudricourt did not willingly leave any girl in such a state'.[8]

It is not surprising that Baudricourt's initial reaction was negative. But there is no reason to think that his intentions towards Joan were actively hostile. Though one chronicler says that he thought she would make good sport for his men-at-arms,[9] and though he may even have uttered some coarse jests on the subject, it seems obvious that he knew that to mistreat her would be impolitic. Jacques d'Arc was already known to him, through the lawsuit of 1427; and there were probably people in Vaucouleurs, some of them 'gentry', to whom Joan's parents were also known personally. Bertrand de Poulengy, who was a squire, says that he 'several times' went to her parents' house,[10] and it is plain that this would have been before, rather than after, the departure for Chinon. Yet it cannot have been a promising first encounter, when Joan at last managed to confront Baudricourt herself. She was later to claim that she recognized him thanks to her voices, though she had never seen him before.[11] However, it is unlikely that she needed much guidance as both her father, and, more recently, Laxart, must have described him to her.

Joan presented herself to Baudricourt wearing a 'poor and worn' red dress.[12] Long red frieze dresses of this type were the everyday costume of the peasant girls of the region. Her speech, however, was by no means consonant with her humble attire:

I am come before you from my Lord, so that you may tell the dauphin to be of good heart, and not to cease the war against his enemies. Before mid Lent the Lord will give him help. In fact, the kingdom does not belong to the dauphin, but to my Lord. But my Lord wants the dauphin to be made king, and to rule the kingdom. Despite his enemies, the dauphin will be made king; and it is I who will take him to the coronation.

Somewhat stunned, Baudricourt demanded: 'Who is your Lord?' and Joan replied: 'The King of Heaven.'[13]

But if Baudricourt was sceptical, others were not. To Laxart, Joan began to add other converts. One was a member of the garrison, the squire Jean de Nouillonpont, who ran into her, evidently not for the first time, soon after her arrival at Vaucouleurs. Nouillonpont was already a patriot. He recounts his exchanges with Joan thus:

I said to her: '*Ma mie*, what are you doing here? Must the king be chased out of his kingdom, and we be English?' To which she replied: 'I have come here, to this royal town, to speak to the Sire de Baudricourt, so that he may take me, or have me taken, to the king. But he pays no attention to me or to my words. However, before mid Lent I must be with the king, though I wear my legs down to the knees; for no one in the world, neither kings, nor dukes, nor the daughter of the King of Scotland,* nor any others, can recover the kingdom of France. And there is no help but me, though I should prefer to spin beside my poor mother, seeing that that is my estate. But I must go, and I will do it because my Lord wishes me to do it.' I asked her who her Lord was, and she answered: 'It is God.' Then I gave Joan my sworn word, taking her by the hand, that with God's

*Margaret of Scotland became engaged to Louis, Charles VII's son, later Louis XI, on 30 October 1428.

help I would take her to the king. At the same time I asked her when she wanted to leave. 'Better now than tomorrow, and tomorrow than later.'[14]

She talked in a similar strain to Henri Le Royer.[15]

People were beginning to be impressed by her burning desire to accomplish the task which had been laid upon her. 'Joan's desire [to leave] was very strong,' said Catherine Le Royer. 'Time weighed upon her as if she had been a pregnant woman, because she was not taken to the dauphin. And from that time both I and many others believed in what she said.'[16] She also charmed the townspeople by her evident piety and by her quiet demeanour. Her hostess recalled that 'she liked to spin, and span well', and that Joan and she used to sit and do so together.[17] When not busied with tasks of this kind, Joan was, as usual, in church. A young clerk attached to the castle chapel describes her frequent attendance there:

She heard the morning masses and remained long in prayer. I saw her also in the crypt chapel of the church, on her knees before the Virgin, her head sometimes bowed, sometimes lifted towards heaven.[18]

Eventually Joan could endure her own impatience no longer. 'When she saw that Robert would not have her taken to the place where the dauphin was, she took some of my clothes and said she would start.'[19] Laxart and a man called Jacques Alain agreed to accompany her, and they rode with her 'as far as Saint-Nicolas' – probably the shrine of Saint-Nicolas-de-Septfonds, rather than that of Saint-Nicolas-de-Port near Nancy, which was further off, and which in any case lay in the wrong direction. Joan no doubt wanted to pray there, since St Nicolas was the protector of travellers against robbers – a protection she and her companions might soon need. But at this point Joan had a change of heart, deciding that 'it was not honest to go away in such a fashion',[20] so the party returned once more to Vaucouleurs.

This abortive expedition raises two interesting questions, though one carries greater weight than the other. They are that of Joan's horsemanship, and that of her assumption of male dress.

At her trial Joan was to say with some emphasis that she did not know how to ride when the voices laid upon her the task of raising the siege of Orleans.[21] She therefore claimed to be ignorant of this accomplishment in, or after, October 1428. By the time she got to Chinon, her horsemanship was to be the subject of wonder and admiration. The Duke of Alençon, a connoisseur of such matters, specifically mentions it.[22] Joan's disclaimer must obviously be treated with a certain reserve, as an instance of her unconscious tendency towards myth-making. The truth of the matter is that Joan seems to have learned how to ride in the high war-saddle of the knight with remarkable swiftness and ease. It is one example among many of her athleticism and physical dexterity. But saddles of this type were designed to give the rider all the help a mere contrivance could provide. Their whole purpose was to keep him steady in his seat, and to brace him against the shock of opposing weapons, particularly lances. They were made so as to support the small of the back and grip the thighs. Joan may have found more difficulty with an ordinary riding saddle. But from her youth she had been brought up with animals, and may well have ridden the farm-horses, and even the cattle, bareback when she was a child. And the brief ride to Saint-Nicolas-de-Septfonds was to be only the first of a whole series of journeys which would have accustomed her to riding, and to doing so astride in male attire. When she reached the court of Charles VII she had already had a good deal of practice in basic horsemanship – otherwise she could never have got there.

Joan's assumption of male dress is much more important, not least because her resumption of it in Rouen, after her abjuration, provided her judges with part of the evidence they needed to say that she had relapsed, and must now be condemned to the stake. At her trial, the clothes she wore provided the subject of more than one question. Responding to these, Joan was usually stubborn, and sometimes evasive. Asked who had ordered her to put on men's clothing, she replied: 'It is a little thing and of small importance. I did not don it by the advice of the men of this world; I donned it only by the command of God and the angels.'[23] Asked, on another occasion, if it was St Catherine or St Margaret who had ordered her to change her dress, she refused to reply.[24] Asked, a third time, why she insisted on wearing men's clothing, she replied: 'Because I do so by the commandment of God and in his service, I do not think I do ill: and as soon as it please God to order this, then I shall cease to wear it.'[25]

Her mode of dress meant so much to her that she even refused to change it in order to be allowed to hear mass and to take communion. The day before Palm Sunday, which in 1431 fell on 25 March, she asked her judges to allow her to hear mass 'because of the solemnity of the days and of the season'. On Palm Sunday itself, Cauchon reported on her attitude:

We asked her if, should we allow her to do this, she would lay aside men's clothing and put on women's dress, such as she had been accustomed to wear in the place of her birth and such as the women of her country wore. To which Joan replied by asking to be allowed to hear mass in the men's clothing she was wearing and asked too that she might receive the sacrament of the Eucharist at the feast of Easter.

We then asked her to reply to the question: whether she would put off men's dress, should this be permitted to her? But she replied that she had not taken counsel on that, and could not as yet put on women's clothes.

And we asked her if she wished to take counsel from the saints as to whether she should again wear such clothes. To which she replied that she could well be permitted to hear mass in her present state, something she most urgently desired; but she could not change her dress and even the decision was not within her power.[26]

After her abortive adventure with Laxart and Jacques Alain, when she appears to have taken the initiative of wearing men's clothes herself, it was Jean de Nouillonpont who prompted her to think of wearing them on her next journey, which was to see the Duke of Lorraine at Nancy. Nouillonpont must obviously have known of the guise in which Joan had chosen to travel before:

I asked her again if she wished to travel in women's clothes. 'I would willingly put on men's clothing.' So for the time being I gave her the clothes and leggings of one of my men.[27]

For the third and biggest step – the journey to Chinon – men's clothes must have seemed the natural and necessary choice, for they would serve as a disguise as well as a protection, and this time the people of Vaucouleurs clubbed together to have a full set of male clothing made for her, in place of the borrowed garments she had hitherto been wearing.[28] Yet, in putting on male dress, Joan undoubtedly discovered something that corresponded to a deep-seated need within herself. It was the revelation of a hitherto unknown aspect of her own nature, and having found this, she was never afterwards able to deny it. Wearing men's clothes, though not originally prescribed by her voices, became one of the imperatives laid upon her, which no earthly power could make her disobey.

Several ideas can be put forward concerning Joan's transvestism. The first is that she was uncertain of her own sexual identity. While those who knew her reported that she was in every external respect female – the Duke of Alençon admired her beautiful breasts[29] – we have evidence from her squire Jean d'Aulon that she did not menstruate.[30] This condition, though not completely unusual in a healthy girl of Joan's age, must have had considerable psychological impact upon her.

Joan's clothes were also a means of taking on a new social, as well as a new sexual identity. She did not long remain in the plain dress she assumed at Vaucouleurs. We soon hear of her dressed in the manner of a young nobleman. The Bourgeois of Paris – an admittedly hostile source – speaks of her wearing a scalloped hood and fashionable scarlet hose.[31] One chronicler describes her as being clad in 'very noble garb of cloth of gold and of silk with much fur'.[32] These descriptions are confirmed by two of the seventy articles of accusation which were presented to Joan at her trial. Article XII claims that Joan wore 'a shirt, breeches, a doublet with leggings joined to the doublet by twenty laces, high slippers laced on the outside, a short robe to the knee or thereabouts, a scalloped hat, tight boots, long spurs, a sword, a dagger, a mail tunic, a lance and other arms with which she armed herself after the manner of the men-at-arms'.[33] Article XIII carries the description further, saying that Joan was 'sometimes clad in magnificent and sumptuous habits of precious cloth, gold and also furs. And not only did she wear short tunics, but also tabards, and robes open at every side; and the thing is notorious, as she was taken in a gold *huque*, open on every side'.[34] This *huque*, a kind of surcoat, with floating panels of cloth, seems to have been a splendid garment indeed, worthy of any knight. Another source tells us that it was made of *'velours vermeil'.*[35] We must probably imagine a magnificent red velvet pattern against a gold background, typical of the precious stuffs made at the time. Joan scarcely bothered to challenge the descriptions which were given of her dress, and it is clear that, for much of her career, she dressed not only as a man, but in the very height of masculine fashion.

Was it pure vanity which made her do this? Her judges obviously concluded that it was, and this conclusion was shared by others. But we must remember that throughout her career Joan placed great emphasis on the notion of hierarchy, of everything being in its proper place, and of every man knowing what category he belonged to, and behaving according to the rules of that category. On the other hand, she always claimed that she herself was exceptional, because she had been chosen by God for her mission, and was guided by his saints. Her clothes – their richness as well as their masculinity – were a way of making the difference visible. They were a silent but conspicuous assertion of her claim to be someone to whom no common rules applied.

After the fiasco of her abortive trip to Saint-Nicolas-de-Septfonds, matters began to look up. Help came to her in the form of a summons from Duke Charles of Lorraine in Nancy. Duke Charles was not a particularly admirable character. He comported himself more like a brigand than a great prince. He had been for some years separated from his wife and had long kept a mistress by whom he had five bastard children. His only legitimate child, Isabeau, the prospective heiress to his dukedom, was married to René of Anjou. Though not yet forty, Duke Charles was now in failing health (he would die in 1431), and he was searching desperately for a reprieve or a means of recovery. Hearing of Joan's claims to a miraculous mission, he immediately sent for her.

Baudricourt probably thought that the duke's summons provided an ideal opportunity for seeing what stuff Joan was made of, before he committed himself to sending her to the king. At any rate, there can have been no question of her leaving without authorization on this occasion. It seems likely, indeed, that Baudricourt, already aware of Joan's stubbornness, found it wise to lure her into going to see Duke Charles in return for an opportunity to settle legal business still outstanding at Toul, and for a further opportunity to visit the greatly venerated shrine at Saint-Nicolas-de-Port, which was far more famous than the little hermitage at Septfonds. Joan therefore set out to see the Duke of Lorraine, though she saw no particular relevance in doing so. With her went Jean de Nouillonpont, who turned back at Toul,[36] and with her too may have gone Laxart and Jacques Alain.

When she arrived in Nancy she gave Duke Charles short shrift. To her judges Joan said that 'the duke questioned her concerning the recovery of his health, but she said to him that she knew nothing about that; and she told the duke little about her [intended] voyage'.[37] Later she was more expansive. A witness afterwards reported:

I have heard Joan say that the Duke of Lorraine, who was sick, wanted to see her, and Joan had been to speak with him, and had told him he was behaving badly and that he never would recover his health if he did not mend his ways, and she exhorted him to take back his good spouse.[38]

The duke took her rebuke patiently. He presented her with the sum of four francs, which she showed to her uncle Laxart;[39] and also a black horse.[40] Perhaps it was one he could no longer ride himself. Emboldened she asked the duke 'to give her his son and men to take her into France, saying she would pray for his recovery'.[41] To this she received no positive response. The 'son' she meant was undoubtedly René, not one of the duke's bastards.

Though she regarded it as an irrelevance, the trip was useful to Joan in several ways. It enabled her to see a large and prosperous city for the first time. It gave her her first experience of court life. She tasted the freedom which even princes were prepared to allow to the God-inspired. And her demeanour seems to have convinced Baudricourt that there were arguments for taking her seriously. In fact, she had embarked on the perilous career which was first to raise her to the heights, and then to dash her into the depths. In our own day, Joan of Arc would probably be regarded as deranged. Her visions, or hallucinations, and the course of action which they would drive her to try and impose upon those surrounding her, would render her incapable of taking her place satisfactorily in a society such as the one which we now possess. In the middle ages, people had a stronger belief in the supernatural, and therefore a much greater tolerance of individuals who claimed to be in touch with it. Those who did so, however, took great risks in return for the respect they were accorded. For the supernatural realm was the place where the battle between good and evil, God and the devil, was continually fought out, and it was all too easy to mistake the partisans of one for the partisans of the other. As all men knew, the servants of darkness were continually striving to pass themselves off as the ministers of light.

When Joan returned to Vaucouleurs, there was one final scene to be played out. Joan had been to see the captain; now he came to interview her at her lodgings, bringing with him the curé of the town. They interviewed Joan privately, but the latter afterwards told her landlady Catherine Le Royer what took place.

The curé had brought his stole, and in the captain's presence adjured her, saying: 'If you are a thing of evil, depart from us; if you are good, approach.' Then Joan dragged herself towards the priest and remained at his knees. All the same, Joan said that the curé had not done well, seeing that he had heard her confession.[42]

Baudricourt had at last decided to give way to Joan's importunities, and to send her to the king at Chinon. The continuing enthusiasm of the townspeople may have influenced him as much as anything else, though Joan was afterwards to codify the gradual shift in his attitudes towards her into the ritual three requests of a fairy-story – two rejections, followed by a third and final acceptance of her mission.[43]

Having made his decision, he put it into effect with his usual efficiency. Joan was to have six companions. Two of them were already her partisans – the squires Jean de Nouillonpont and Bertrand de Poulengy. These two were followed by two servants or pages. With them went Colet de Vienne, and a servant of his, called Richard the Archer. Colet seems to have been a kind of royal messenger, one of those who served to maintain communications between the court and the isolated putpost of Vaucouleurs. It is probable that he came from Champagne, and was given this employment because he already knew the region.

Having chosen the members of the party, Baudricourt then made them swear on oath that they would lead Joan well and surely.[44] Since she was already equipped and mounted, he presented her with a sword, the one thing that seemed to be lacking.[45] He left the two squires to pay the expenses of the journey.[46] His parting words to Joan were more resigned than enthusiastic. 'Go, go,' he said, 'and come what may.'[47]

The little party set out for Chinon on the first Sunday in Lent – 13 February 1429.[48] As Joan was making ready, someone came up to her and said:

'How can you make such a journey, when there are men-at-arms on all sides?' She replied, 'I am not afraid of the men-at-arms, for my road lies open before me: and, if there are men-at-arms upon it, I have God, my Lord, who will well know how to open the road so that I can go to messire the dauphin. I was born to do this.'[49]

With this last rebuke to a sceptic, Joan and the others rode up to the citadel, and out through the Porte de France, which formed part of the defences, and which is still to be seen. Their first night's stop was to be at the monastery of Saint-Urbain; their last really secure night's lodging for some time.

5

It was merciful that Joan knew so little about the ruler she had set out to rescue or the court that surrounded him. Biographers of Joan of Arc consistently distort the character of Charles VII. They never manage to explain, except by reference to the career of their heroine, how a so apparently feeble prince survived innumerable perils, to die thirty years after Joan herself, in 1461, after a total reversal of his fortunes. Yet it must be admitted that this ultimately successful king was a difficult man to idealize.

He was born on 22 February 1403, at two in the morning, at the Hôtel de Saint-Pol, at that time the principal royal residence in Paris. He was the eleventh child of his parents, and, when he was born, two older brothers stood before him in direct line of succession to the throne. His father was Charles VI, King of France, and his mother was the German princess, Isabeau of Bavaria. His heredity was conspicuously unfortunate, and even his legitimacy was not entirely above suspicion.

At the time of Charles's birth, his father had long been subject to recurring fits of madness, which paralysed the government of the kingdom. The first attack was in 1392, when the king went berserk during a military expedition, and killed four of his attendants. From 1392 until his death in 1422, Charles VI suffered forty-four separate attacks, lasting from three to nine months, with lucid intervals between each. Modern doctors would probably see in him a case of severe schizophrenia. The chroniclers of the time report many symptoms which are characteristic: he was sometimes dangerously violent, sometimes buffoonish; he would rip his clothes; he suffered from hallucinations, such as the conviction that he was made of glass and must carry pieces of iron in his clothes to protect himself; he refused to eat and sleep at regular hours, and had to be bathed and have his linen changed by force; he believed he was persecuted by his physician; and, when supposedly lucid, he would 'suddenly tremble and cry, as if pricked with a thousand points of iron'.[1] After 1393 his signature became disorganized in a way that is supposedly typical of schizophrenics.[2]

His wife Isabeau had much to endure. In her youth she was a pretty woman, a brunette who lacked a queenly air because she was noticeably short in the leg – this physical defect she passed on in exaggerated, knock-kneed form to her son. Her marriage had been, on her husband's side at least, a marriage for love, and before his first major seizure, they seem to have been happy together. When the king went mad, things altered. Her husband constantly humiliated her. During his bouts of madness, he not only spoke harshly to her, but sometimes actually struck her. Nevertheless, they continued to live together as man and wife, and she went on producing children whose legitimacy no one dared, at least at the time, to doubt.

At first, Isabeau's compensations were relatively harmless. She was ostentatiously pious. Like Marie Antoinette after her, she liked to play at the rustic life, and in 1398 a model farm was set up for her amusement. Her greatest faults during these years were her extravagance and her frivolity, a thirst for amusement which had to be satisfied whatever the circumstances. Isabeau, though not deranged like her husband, was strongly phobic. She was terrified of thunder, which seemed to bring out deep-rooted guilt feelings, and eventually carried this fear so far that she had a specially designed conveyance to protect her from the danger. Her accounts record 'a chariot serving for the thunder'.[3] Nor was thunder the only thing that frightened her. She had a terror of disease, and would never visit any place where there were rumours of infection. In addition, she was agoraphobic – a trait she shared with Charles VII. Her agoraphobia gave her a particular fear of bridges. Her accounts show that wooden railings were erected on the one at Corbeil, because she would not cross a bridge without a balustrade. Similarly, Charles VII refused to go over any wooden bridge on horseback 'be it never so well built'.[4]

At first she was a devoted mother to her numerous children. By 1405, however, there were complaints that she systematically neglected them. The dauphin, Louis of Guyenne, told his father (then in a lucid interval) that he had not seen his mother for three months. Her accounts for 1404 and 1405 confirm that she was then often absent from Paris. From 1404 onwards, she and the king's younger brother Louis of Orleans had become intimate friends, and by 1405 this intimacy led many people to think they had become lovers. In July 1405, for instance, they spent several days alone together at the Château de Saint-Germain. A little later, they spent two months at Melun. When Louis was assassinated by agents of Duke John the Fearless of Burgundy, on the evening of 23 November 1407, he was coming away from the Hôtel Barbette, where he had supped with the queen.

If Charles VII was illegitimate, then Louis of Orleans was his father. Doubts of his birth only began to be aired some years later, and Charles's own fears seem to have been aroused by his mother's conduct in 1417, when she was the centre of a dissolute court at Vincennes. Rumours circulated at this period that 'in the queen's household, divers dishonest things were done'.[5] Isabeau herself gave countenance to the idea that her son was a bastard when she decided to denounce him after the murder of John the Fearless at Montereau in 1419. But the Isabeau of this period was a much degenerated being, both morally and physically. Physically she had become grotesquely fat. By the end of 1409, she had already reached a point where it was considered doubtful, because of her obesity, whether she could any longer act as regent of the kingdom, should the need arise. She also became gouty, and in 1415 had to have a wheelchair made in order to get about. And there is evidence, from pilgrimages made on her behalf, that she was a sufferer from menstrual troubles.

It is doubtful, even from the most favourable descriptions, whether her rejected son, Joan's dauphin, ever possessed much in the way of physical attractions. He was, we are told, 'thin and weak', with 'feeble foundation and a strange walk without proportion'.[6] Fouquet's brilliant portrait, with its dull eyes and pendulous nose, fills in details of his appearance which contemporaries were too polite to mention. Yet there is no doubt that he had seduction of a kind. The graciousness of his manners is often mentioned, and it is a quality which emerges from some of his exchanges with Joan. The trouble was that he often seemed to attract loyalty merely in order to betray it.

His character was a strange mixture of the fixed and the mutable. He was conspicuously loyal both to long-established councillors and to long-serving professional soldiers. These learnt, however, that there were always moments when the king would leave them in the lurch. His favourites, as opposed to his servants, found him intensely changeable. The Burgundian historian, Georges Chastellain, who gives us the most detailed literary portrait, speaks of the 'frequent and diverse mutations about his person . . . when anyone was lifted high and near to him, right to the summit of the wheel, then he began to chafe, and at the first opportunity offered, would cast him down again'.[7] Chastellain accuses him of mutability, diffidence and, 'worst of all', envy.[8]

Changeability, however, was a quality to be found, not only in Charles's relationships with other people, but in the deepest recesses of his nature. It can be detected in quite simple matters, such as his pattern of everyday behaviour. He is, for instance, usually described as being sober at table. 'He took only two meals a day. He spoke and drank little.'[9] Yet we also find him condemned for 'drenching his passions with drunkenness and debauchery, stupid with self-indulgence and slothfulness'.[10] At an extremely low point in his fortunes, after the battle of Verneuil in 1424, he is spoken of as being easily led away to 'feasts, dances and pleasure'.[11]

His frequent ineffectiveness was linked to what everyone recognized as high intelligence. 'Monseigneur the dauphin,' says one of those who knew him, 'even when he was young, always possessed good sense and understanding.'[12] Chastellain tells us that, in addition to having 'good and lively manners', he was 'a great historian, a good raconteur, a good latinist, and was wise in council'.[13] We know of his interest in medicine, and also of his fascination for anything to do with artillery. Both of these might be described as 'advanced' subjects in the intellectual terms of the time. Perhaps the most noticeable thing about

Charles VII, both at the period when Joan met him and later, was his large collection of neurotic symptoms. In addition to being unable to ride over a wooden bridge or lodge in a room with a plank floor – as we shall see, there was good reason for the latter tic – he could not bear to be stared at, and was upset by the presence of an unfamiliar face in a familiar group. If he had to eat in public, as was the accepted royal custom until long after his time, he was put out of countenance if people looked at him too directly, 'and could not eat and at last fled away'.[14] He found great difficulty in confronting large gatherings – we read of him, on an occasion when a sizeable group of petitioners came to see him, retreating to a smaller room and slamming the door in their faces. He had a particular fear of assassination, and 'was not assured amidst a hundred thousand, but frightened of one man he did not know'.[15]

Some of these phobias were due less to inherited temperament than to the experiences of his youth and young manhood. Charles VII had a harsh schooling as a monarch. When he was still a child, the political situation was dominated by the rivalry between the brilliant, ruthless Louis of Orléans and the latter's cousin, John the Fearless, Duke of Burgundy. Louis succeeded in cutting off, to his own profit, the flow of royal money which had hitherto nourished the Burgundian dukedom. John replied by having Louis murdered in 1407. Power thenceforth oscillated between the Duke of Burgundy and his partisans, and a rival group who came to be known as the Armagnacs, after their leader, Bernard VII, Count of Armagnac. In 1415, England entered the game. Henry V invaded France and won the crushing victory of Agincourt.

The young Charles, not yet dauphin, much less king, was soon drawn into the politics of the kingdom. He was betrothed to Marie d'Anjou, daughter of Louis II, Duke of Anjou and titular king of Sicily, and of his intelligent, beautiful and strong-minded wife, Yolanda of Aragon. His bride's parents took charge of him, and this meant he was in the hands of the anti-Burgundians, to whom, at that moment, the duke of Anjou and his wife were allied. In 1416, Charles, still only fourteen years of age, was made Captain General of Paris, and Duke of Touraine. From 3 September onwards he began to appear regularly at the Royal Council. And six months later his last surviving brother died, and he became dauphin, and heir to the throne.

Almost immediately he had a quarrel with his mother, and the breach was never healed. Isabeau, who had long ago reconciled herself to the Duke of Burgundy, despite the murder of Louis of Orleans, was living at Vincennes amid a dissolute court which included at least two men who were later to be her son's favourites. One was Georges de La Trémoille. The Count of Armagnac, who then had possession of Paris and the king, contrived to have Isabeau arrested, and stripped of the wealth she had accumulated, much of it stockpiled secretly in various churches. As a result, the dauphin had an acrimonious confrontation with his mother. She seems to have held him largely responsible for her misfortune. Isabeau soon escaped from captivity, and threw in her lot with John the Fearless, once and for all. In May 1418 Paris fell to the Burgundians, and a horrible massacre ensued, on the scale of that in 1792: perhaps 5,000 people were killed. The Count of Armagnac was among them. The dauphin escaped, and became the leader of the party that opposed the Burgundians, who in turn were soon to ally themselves to the English. He conceived a distaste for Paris which was to last for the rest of his life, and he also absorbed a tactical lesson. The city, unique in its immensity and the size of its population, could not be conquered by military force alone. There must be strong popular support of the kind that existed in 1418 if any attempt on it was to succeed.

Before the end of the year, the fifteen-year-old Charles had set up an alternative government in the Loire region. It had its own *Parlement* at Poitiers, and its *Chambre de Comptes* at Bourges. In order to ensure that continuity was maintained, he provided for the vacancies that now existed in all the great offices of state. His claim was to be the custodian of the traditions of the monarchy.

After a good start, he compromised himself almost fatally by conniving at the murder of John the Fearless of Burgundy, which took place in his presence on the bridge at Montereau in September 1419. This act of folly threw the dukedom of Burgundy into the English camp, and led directly to the Treaty of Troyes, signed on 21 May 1420. Isabeau agreed to an arrangement which disinherited her son and made Henry V of England heir to the kingdom: Henry married Isabeau's daughter Catherine.

From 1420 to the arrival of Joan of Arc at Chinon in 1429, Charles had extremely varying military fortunes. His forces beat the English at Baugé in 1421, but lost to them at Cravant in 1423 and again at Verneuil in 1424. Verneuil was a serious setback, and more or less deprived him of the power to take the military initiative. The general who defeated Charles's army was John, Duke of Bedford, one of Henry V's brothers, who had been appointed regent for the infant Henry VI in France after the King's premature death. Bedford was to become not only Charles's, but Joan's chief opponent, and he was a man of great ability.

Charles's difficulties, in the years from 1420 onwards, were due, not only to the superiority of English troops and tactics, but to financial and psychological factors which were in some respects linked. By 1421, his finances were showing signs of the chaos into which they were soon to fall. In April of that year, for instance, a butcher of Bourges refused to supply the court any longer because he had not been paid.[16] The dauphin's increasing poverty could be attributed to a number of causes. In the first place, he was anxious to maintain the traditions of the monarchy, and this meant maintaining the pattern of his father's court – itself notoriously extravagant – and the prerogatives and franchises of the officers of his household, the household of the queen (Charles was at last married to Marie d'Anjou in 1422) and, later, that of his son. More than this, the dauphin maintained the convention of ostentatious generosity which always weighed upon the finances of medieval monarchs. In particular, he was careful to compensate the princes of the blood who remained faithful to him, and large pensions were given to those who were with his armies.

Generous to his associates, Charles also did not stint himself, despite the continuing decline in his resources. It was a time of particular luxury and exaggeration in dress. Around 1420, just as the financial rot was setting in, Charles's accounts show with what splendour he clothed himself. His robes had long hanging sleeves in the fashion of the time, and were covered with silver-gilt ornaments. He was quick to indulge in a passion for fine horses, buying from travelling merchants and from friends. His love of horsemanship had not yet fallen victim to his agoraphobia. Some years later, at his very lowest financial ebb in 1428, Charles continued to eat off gold and silver plate,[17] though there might be days when the viands were rather scanty. At this point, things had indeed become difficult for the royal household. It was a sign of the times that the dauphin was having his old doublets renovated by getting new sleeves put on them.[18]

It was not only Charles's extravagance, but the utter mismanagement of his finances which had brought him to such a pass. The lands of the royal domain were constantly being pledged or sold, which meant a continuing fall in income. The king, when pressed for funds, was ready to borrow from almost anyone. In April 1423, needing a loan to make an urgent payment, he turned to one of his own cooks. This was perhaps less dangerous than his habit of borrowing from his favourites, which in turn tended to put him deeper and deeper in their power. His relationship with Georges de La Trémoille, the reigning favourite of Joan's time, affords an outstanding example. Between January and August 1428, for example, La Trémoille advanced Charles no less than 27,000 livres. The castellany of Chinon, one of Charles's favourite residences, had to be given as a pledge. In military terms, the lack of money to pay their wages meant that Charles's troops were poorly disciplined, and plundered friends and enemies alike. His Scottish mercenaries were particularly feared.

Yet basically Charles was much better off than his English opponents, though by no means as rich as the rulers of Burgundy, who had the wealth of the Low Countries to draw on. The region he ruled over was largely agricultural, but agriculture remained the basis of economic life in France. Other enterprises were also possible. Somewhat after Joan's time, the financier Jacques Coeur was to prove that it was perfectly feasible to create a widespread trading empire with Bourges as a base. Charles probably got one third to two thirds more in revenue than his English opponents, in the course of a normal year. In addition, he was not faced with the difficulty that continually harassed his rival, the much better organized John, Duke of Bedford, which was that of how to support an army of occupation from lands not productive enough to sustain it. The English-occupied territories were in any case much more thoroughly devastated by the war. The financial ills Charles suffered from, though acute, were in part what we should now call 'cash flow' problems, rather than total want of money or any possibility of getting it.

Charles's financial attitudes were bound up with his own life and with his feelings about the direction it was taking. His personality underwent a drastic change around the end of 1422. Until then, he had been full of energy in disastrous circumstances. Now things changed radically. He suffered a kind of breakdown. He had been putting a tremendous strain on his mind and spirit, and at this point two incidents occurred which had a devastating effect.

In October 1422, he went to La Rochelle, his only port and outlet on the sea. The town had been menaced by conspiracy, and Charles was there in order to restore confidence. He arrived on the tenth of the month, and next day a large assembly was held under his presidency in the great hall of the bishop's palace. The building was structurally unsound, and the floor collapsed under the weight of the crowd. Many people were injured and some killed. Charles, fortunately for himself, was seated at one end of the room, in a throne under a kind of arcade. He therefore fell less heavily than the rest, sliding downwards and receiving only bruises. But his cousin, Pierre de Bourbon, who was standing behind him, was among those who were killed. Charles seems to have been shaken by this accident, though he attributed his escape to St Michael.

No sooner had he returned from La Rochelle to his castle of Mehun-sur-Yèvre, near Bourges, than he got news of his father's death. His reaction was emotional. The Burgundian chronicler Monstrelet says that he was 'sad at heart and wept abundantly'.[19] The monarchy, of course, continued, and to symbolize this Charles wore mourning for only one day. Yet it is significant of his state of mind that he did not assume the title of king until nearly a week after the news was received, and made no plans for any kind of coronation ceremony. Many people, including Joan, continued to call him the dauphin, and his followers dauphinists.

It is from the end of 1422 onwards that we find established the pattern that Joan was to find when she came to Chinon in 1429. The king no longer led his armies in person. And in general he behaved like a spectator, able to appreciate his situation but without the will to act. He knew that his people were oppressed, and was, says the poet Martial d'Auvergne, 'marvellously full of pity'.[20] He was aware of the excesses committed by his troops, but unable to prevent them. His commands were often disobeyed or simply ignored, and he himself alternated between depression and desperate frivolity.

With the king deprived of the power to act, his court was full of intrigue. There was a peace-party and a war-party. The peace-party wanted an accommodation with Burgundy, and its membership included many members of the high aristocracy, among them the queen's mother, Yolanda of Aragon, less irreconcilably opposed to the new Duke of Burgundy, Philip the Good, than she had been to his father. The adherents of this faction had strong ties, both of blood and marriage, with the Burgundian court. The war-party thought in terms of foreign alliances – with the Spanish kingdoms, with Lombardy, and above all with Scotland. Many of its members were adventurers and opportunists, out to make their fortunes through the war. The most striking feature of the court, and of Charles's relationship with it, was not so much the existence of these factions (the king sometimes roused himself sufficiently to play one off against the other), as the need which the monarch felt to submit to the domination of some favourite. The existence of this favourite often seemed more important than his precise identity. All Charles's favourites had an exceedingly insecure tenure, and when they fell, the king soon forgot them. The manner of their going was often both violent and squalid. While each favourite lasted, however, he seemed to enjoy an absolute sway over the king. Charles was not overtly homosexual – in middle age he was to be notorious for his mistresses, especially the beautiful Agnes Sorel – but his relationship to these men was profoundly dependent. It often seemed that the worse he knew their characters to be, and the more arrogantly they behaved, the greater the fascination they had for him. All his feelings of unworthiness, all his guilt about his inability to act and to rule his people as a good king should, were summed up in his submission to them. Often they seemed chosen to remind Charles of some painful episode in his past, and at least three were reputed to have been among his mother's lovers.

At the time when Joan arrived at Chinon the ruling favourite was the formidable Georges de La Trémoille. La Trémoille had been born around 1385, and was thus considerably older than Charles. He had been brought up in the household of John the Fearless, and Burgundian influence stood him in good stead during the years when Burgundy dominated the royal government. By 1410 La Trémoille was already a member of the Council of Charles VI, and in 1413 he became Grand Chamberlain of France. In 1416 he married the widow of the Duke of Berri, who was Countess of Boulogne in her own right, and his claims to this strategic territory caused a falling out between him and John the Fearless. But he did not swing into the dauphinist orbit until the early 1420s, and by 1422 he was a member of Charles's Council.

In 1427 there was a palace revolution, which brought to power Artur de Richemont, a famous warrior who was brother of the Duke of Brittany. Through the influence of Yolanda of Aragon, and against Charles's wishes, Richemont became Constable of France, and was put in charge of the military affairs of the kingdom. Charles grew to dislike this blunt, coarse soldier as he disliked no other man. It was Richemont, in turn, who installed La Trémoille in a position close to the king. Charles's reaction to this, when Richemont first put the proposal to him, perfectly summarized his attitudes and mental state:

And the king was not content that La Trémoille should remain with him, and monseigneur the constable said to him that he was a powerful man who could serve him well. And the king said: 'My dear cousin, you give him to me but you will repent of it; for I know him better than you.'[21]

La Trémoille immediately put the king's prophecy into effect by having Richemont banished from court. He retained his sway over Charles until 1433. Though no stranger to the violence of the age, he was nevertheless a man of some subtlety, whose managerial talents might have been exercised in a better cause. His durability was probably due to three factors in particular: an imposing personality, a skilful manipulation of alliances, and an even more skilful use of money. As to the first, we know that he was fat, but find him described in a near-contemporary source as 'one of the handsomest men one could wish to meet,

49

and a bold knight'.[22] His fatness actually saved his life in 1433, when he was seized by a band of conspirators at Chinon. He was stabbed in the head and belly, but the fat kept the dagger directed at his stomach from reaching any vital organ. His private alliances were widespread, and he took the care to embody them in formal treaties. In 1428 he signed one such treaty with the Duke of Alençon. In 1429, Gilles de Rais agreed to serve him 'until death and with his life'.[23] But it was La Trémoille's fortune which provided the necessary backing for his power. He always seemed to have ready money when no one else did. He lent large sums to the king, he was also willing to make loans elsewhere. Among those who borrowed from him were men captured with Joan on her fatal sortie from Compiègne. La Trémoille helped them with their ransoms. For example, he made a loan of 500 *écus* to the master of her household, Jean d'Aulon.[24]

One of the reasons that Charles clung to La Trémoille was that he saw in that massive bulk, that dominating personality, a shelter from the demands which were made upon him by the princes of the blood. He mistrusted their ambitions far more than he disliked La Trémoille's corruption. His favourites exercised power only upon an *ad hoc* basis, and did not strive to build a dynasty that threatened Charles's own. And at the same time the king found ways of circumventing the dominance he allowed to the favourite of the moment.

A striking thing about Charles, as Joan was to discover, was that he was apparently capable of manipulating his own phobias and compulsions, while seeming to surrender to them completely. He was like a sick child who knows how to get round the adults who in theory govern every detail of his life, and his court had an appropriately stifling, sick-room atmosphere. Charles's humiliating relationship with La Trémoille undoubtedly satisfied a present emotional need. Yet it remained as much political as it was personal. It enabled him, quite coldly and consciously, to buy the time during which the monarchy could be reconstructed on a more centralized pattern. Charles's weaknesses were day-to-day matters. His strength was in the long term. He was a more formidable and less pitiable figure than legend makes him out to be.

Joan's journey to Chinon was not a comfortable one. The winter of 1428–9 was exceptionally wet in the Meuse region, and all the rivers were in flood. The first part of the route led through territories which had been devastated by the war. Joan and her companions would have encountered deserted farms and villages, and fields so much overgrown that it was difficult to recognize that they had once been cultivated land. Instead of going along the river valleys, they were compelled by the direction they were taking to cross them. They also had to cross the rivers themselves, either by bridges, where these existed and it was safe to use them, or else by such fords as they could find. At the fords, it would have been necessary to swim the horses across if the water became too deep. With this, and the February rain, they must often have been drenched and shivering. Probably each member of the party had a spare horse, otherwise it is hard to see how they managed to make such good time in the conditions they met with. The whole journey from Vaucouleurs to Chinon took only eleven days.[1] Before they even reached Auxerre they had crossed no less than six rivers, large and small.

The first stage of the journey, which was considered the most dangerous, was made by night.[2] Even after this, they did not dare to enter the towns. For Joan this was a special deprivation, for she wanted to hear mass. She said as much to both Jean de Nouillonpont and Bertrand de Poulengy, but for the most part they remained deaf to her hints. 'For fear of being recognized,' says Bertrand, 'we only heard it twice.'[3] At night they often slept in the open, or perhaps in a deserted house. On these occasions, Joan lay between the two members of the party whom she knew best, keeping on her doublet and hose. Despite this close physical propinquity, she aroused no spark of carnal desire in her companions. 'I feared her so much that I would never have dared to make advances to her',[4] said Nouillonpont. Poulengy's feelings were precisely the same:

I was young then and yet I had neither desire nor carnal movement to touch woman, and I should not have dared to ask such a thing of Joan, because of the goodness which I saw in her.[5]

As they rode they conversed. Some members of the group were not as thoroughly converted to Joan and her mission as Poulengy and Nouillonpont. In fact they thought her presumptuous. Before they set out indeed, one or two of them had had the idea that they would put Joan to the test. 'But once they were on the road, escorting her, they were ready to do anything she wanted, and were as anxious to bring her before the king as she was herself to get there. They could never have denied her anything that she asked.'[6]

A source of anxiety, in addition to the ever-present dangers that surrounded them, was the kind of reception they were likely to get when they arrived at their destination. 'But Joan repeatedly told us not to be afraid, and that once we came to the town of Chinon, the noble dauphin would give us good countenance'.[7] Finding her audience increasingly sympathetic, Joan talked fairly freely about her visions – more freely, perhaps, than she had spoken to anyone as yet, excepting Baudricourt, who had not really wanted to listen. Nouillonpont recalled these conversations:

Making my way beside her, I asked her if she would do what she said, and the Maid always told us to have no fear and that she had a mandate to do this, for her brothers in Paradise told her what to do; and that for four or five years already her brothers in Paradise and her Lord, to wit God, had been telling her that she must go to the war to recover the kingdom of France.[8]

He added: 'I had great confidence in what the Maid said, and I was fired by what she said and by love of her – a divine love, as I believe.'[9] Poulengy agreed. 'She was for me an emissary of God',[10] was his verdict at the Trial of Rehabilitation.

When they got to Auxerre, they at last felt bold enough to enter the city in order to hear mass in the cathedral, despite the fact that the place gave allegiance to the Duke of Burgundy. 'At this time,' Joan said, 'I frequently heard my voices.'[11] No doubt their activity had been stimulated by the emotion, exertion and danger of the journey. The risk the party took in entering Auxerre was not altogether sensible. People noticed, and later remembered that they had noticed, a small group of men, as they thought from Lorraine, who passed through Auxerre in late February 1429, and who claimed to be merchants. These witnesses even recalled that the party had included two young peasants, one of whom might have been sixteen or seventeen years old.[12]

It was at Gien, where Joan and her companions crossed the Loire into firmly dauphinist territory, that their sense of discretion began to crumble more conspicuously. Somebody talked. The likelihood is that it was Joan herself. This time she provided more than the hints which she had given at Domrémy. The Bastard of Orleans, soon to know Joan personally, was besieged in Orleans at this time, but communication with the outside world was by no means completely cut off. He remembered how there arrived 'news or rather rumours, that there had passed through the town of Gien a young girl commonly called the Maid, claiming that she was on the way to the noble dauphin to raise the siege of Orleans and to take the dauphin himself to Orleans, there to be crowned'.[13]

The Bastard, or Dunois as we shall call him henceforth, though he did not become Count of Dunois until later, was the illegitimate son of Louis of Orleans, and had been brought up with Louis's legitimate children. Since his half-brothers were prisoners in England, he represented the family interests. He had already proven himself to be an able soldier. Like many of his contemporaries, Dunois was superstitious, and made use of astrologers: 'they governed him in his high enterprises'.[14] Naturally, he was curious. The citizens of Orleans were also much excited by the rumour from Gien. To satisfy himself and to satisfy them Dunois actually sent a mission to the king, to discover if there was any truth in what he had heard. His emissaries arrived at Chinon in time to witness the initial confrontation between Joan and the man she had come to save. And they afterwards made a report on the subject to a public meeting in Orleans.[15]

Joan's declaration of her mission at Gien probably accounts for an incident which is otherwise puzzling. There are two contradictory accounts of this, both of which are at best third hand. One version has it that an ambush was laid for the little band, with the purpose of capturing Joan and robbing both her and her companions. 'But at the moment when [the men-at-arms] were about to do so, they found themselves unable to stir from their positions.'[16] The other version states the ambush was a trick, played upon Joan by some of those escorting her.[17] It is at any rate clear, in either case, that the would-be assailants were dauphinists, and not English or Burgundian soldiers. Neither story seems very likely. Joan and those with her had little worth taking, and they were escorted by the equivalent of a king's messenger. Granted Charles's notorious inability to impose his authority, or even to protect those who served him, an ambush for purposes of robbery would seem a curious enterprise. Still more curious would be the failure to carry it through. The theory that the whole thing was nothing but a practical joke falls because Joan's party was so small. It would have been impossible for two or three members of it to detach themselves without being missed, and we hear nothing of an increase in her escort once she had crossed the Loire. The truth may well be that someone at Chinon, perhaps La Trémoille, wanted to know what stuff Joan was made of, and staged a mock ambush for the purpose. It was realistic enough to give her companions a scare. Joan was not frightened. 'When [her escort] wanted to run away she said to them: "Do not flee, in God's name! They will do us no harm." '[18] From Sainte-Cathérine-de-Fierbois, Joan sent to announce her arrival to the king.[19] One of the claims she made in her letter was that she would recognize Charles 'among all others'.[20]

The chapel of Sainte-Cathérine-de-Fierbois which, with the surrounding hamlet, made the last stage before Chinon, was a well-known place of pilgrimage at this period. It had known increasing popularity since the wars began. To it, in particular, came those who had been taken prisoner, and who had afterwards regained their liberty. They arrived to give thanks to St Catherine for her intervention on their behalf, and often they left the chains they had been forced to wear, or items of their equipment, as votive offerings. There were many stories of miracles performed on behalf of poor soldiers by 'Madame Sainte Kathérine'.

A few years before Joan's arrival, the growing fame of the place had led the celebrated warrior Marshal Boucicaut to build an almonry beside the church. The building, though somewhat altered, can still be seen, and it was here that Joan lodged. But, as we might expect, she spent most of her time in the chapel itself. It was not merely that the shrine was dedicated to one of her 'voices', and therefore might seem a good place to receive guidance, but there was also the fact that she had been starved of the comforts of religion during her clandestine journey. To make up for lost opportunity, she heard three masses in one day.[21]

King and Council found great difficulty in deciding whether to receive Joan or not. The question was still unresolved when Joan arrived in Chinon itself, and saw the château, which was really three castles in one, sprawled on its high ridge above the town. Like Loches, the castle at Chinon is really a kind of city within a city. The main approach is through a great gatehouse, which leads into the central enclosure, in the midst of which are the ruins of one of the three chapels within the castle complex. The castle was immensely strong. Even now, when it is in a state of ruin, one looks over the broken parapets, and sees a sheer drop upon every side. Perhaps for this reason, it was a favourite residence with the nervous Charles VII. Here he could be in his realm, and yet not of it. The Royal Lodging which contained his apartments (the rest of the court was much less comfortably housed) was an almost separate building, of fairly recent construction, which stood on one side of the main enclosure. The main part of the town of Chinon lay immediately below. From his window, Charles could look down on the thickly clustered buildings, the river and the bridge. They seem incredibly remote when one looks out of the same opening today.

Similarly Joan, as she entered the town and rode over the bridge, could look up and see, high above her, the shelter

Charles had chosen for himself. Its remoteness gave the measure of the distance which still lay between her and him. She had left Sainte-Cathérine at daybreak, and she entered Chinon around noon. She stopped at an inn, and after dinner she again sent to announce her coming to the king.[22]

It was at last resolved that the Council, rather than the king, should interview her. Joan confronted them with typical recalcitrance:

She began by saying that she would say nothing, except directly to the king. But it was put to her that it was in the king's name that she was being asked to explain the motive for her mission. 'I have,' she said, 'two things as a mandate from the King of Heaven – one to raise the siege of Orleans; the other to take the king to Rheims for his sacring and coronation.'[23]

Characteristically, too, the explanation, though forthright, was not quite complete, as her mission already had more items in its programme than these two. Joan told the councillors as much as she thought would be good for them. Once she had been heard, the debate broke out once more:

A certain number of councillors declared that the king should put no faith in this girl. The others were of the opinion that, since she said she had been sent by God, and had things to say to the king, the king should at least hear her.[24]

Still hesitating, Charles asked some of the churchmen attached to the court to interview her. This too was done. 'At last, not without difficulty, it was agreed that the king ought to listen to her.'[25] The decisive impetus was given by a reminder of Baudricourt's sponsorship.[26]

Joan had arrived in Chinon on 23 February,[27] and almost two days had passed in these wrangles. On the evening of the second day, preparations were made for her reception in the great hall of the Royal Lodging. Here, not only Charles, but those in attendance upon him, would have a chance to look at this new phenomenon.

As she passed over the drawbridge into the castle, an untoward incident took place. Joan was insulted by one of the guards. 'Isn't that the Maid?' he shouted. 'Jarnidieu!* If I had

* *Je renie Dieu*: I deny God.

her for a night, she wouldn't remain a maid.' Joan later told her confessor, Jean Pasquerel, that she had answered: 'Ha! In God's name, you deny Him, when you are so near to death!' Within the hour, the man fell into the water and was drowned.[28] This edifying story must be taken with a large pinch of salt. Joan deeply resented insults to her virginity, just as she was always enraged when her enemies called her a whore. Pasquerel, an emotional man, preserves some tall tales besides this one. They are never things which he witnessed himself, but things which Joan related to him. The story of the guard's death, immediately and unshriven, bears a suspiciously close resemblance to the death of the English commander William Glasdale at Orleans. He, too, fell in the water and was drowned, after insulting Joan in much the same way. The anecdote is a piece of wish-fulfilment, based on what happened to Glasdale later on. It can also be taken as a symbol of Joan's inner tensions, as she approached this moment of crisis. In psychoanalytic terms, 'falling into the water' can be interpreted as an attempt at intercourse, water equalling womb. The would-be assailant is castrated (i.e. killed) for his presumption. The dangers of sex were still stirring in Joan's mind.

The Royal Lodging, which Joan was now approaching, was built upon a simple plan. It had a guardroom and a great hall (it is likely that the latter was richly hung with tapestries, despite the king's poverty), and behind these a range of smaller rooms, the *chambrettes* which the agoraphobic king much preferred. The king's apartments were joined to the great hall by a wooden gallery. He could emerge by a door near the great fireplace which dominated the rear wall of the hall itself.

When she arrived, Joan was received with no little ceremony. She was led by the hand into the hall by Louis de Bourbon, Count of Vendôme, a prince of the blood and grand master of the king's household.[29] This courtesy – that of a lord to a lady of equally high birth – was not precisely in her honour. Joan had offered to submit to a test – to pick the king out. The test was now to take place, and this, rather than Joan herself, was the reason why the gathering was conducted with so much pomp. For the men of the age, such a proof must be given in due form. A ritual was therefore devised to contain it. The size of the gathering which waited to receive her was, however, a tribute to the curiosity she had already aroused, in Chinon as well as in Orleans. Joan afterwards estimated that more than three hundred knights were present. The scene was illuminated for her by 'some fifty torches, not to mention the spiritual light'.[30] It must have been hot and smoky as well as crowded. The hall at Chinon, though a larger than average room, would not qualify as vast.

Charles himself was not present when Joan entered the hall. It was an age when etiquette was becoming both increasingly elaborate and increasingly rigid. One royal lady, when paying a call upon another, knew exactly how low a curtsey she ought to drop, and also how many of her hostess's ladies-in-waiting she ought to kiss.[31] We may therefore assume that normal court procedure was followed, and that the monarch and his suite would not have arrived until everyone else was assembled. Indeed, it is more than probable that Charles was still, at the eleventh hour, hesitating whether to confront Joan or not. Meanwhile, the subject of the test was first of all shown one of the king's cousins, the Count of Clermont, and was told that he was the king. The most elaborate account of what followed, which is not, however, first hand, runs as follows:

But she at once said that it was not the king, and that she would know him well if she saw him, although she had never till then seen him. And afterwards a squire was brought, and they feigned that he was the king, but she well knew that it was not he.[32]

After this preliminary pantomime, Charles at length timorously emerged, to confront his would-be saviour. Obeying his instincts, as well as the plan that had been agreed, he lurked behind the ranks of his courtiers, some of whom were far more flamboyantly dressed than he. Alerted by the stir which his entry inevitably caused, Joan approached him and doffed her hat. 'God give you good life, gentle king,' she said. Charles replied: 'Joan, it is not I who is king.' Then, pointing to one of the more gorgeous of the great lords who were present, he added: 'There is the king.' And Joan then answered: 'In God's name, gentle prince, it is you and none other.'[33] She later claimed that she 'knew him among the others' by the counsel of her voices, which revealed him to her.[34]

It is unnecessary to make a miracle out of what must, after

all, have been very simple. How could Joan have failed to recognize Charles, despite the fact that she had never seen him before, and despite the lack of splendour of his costume? His small eyes, drooping nose, knock knees and shambling gait must all have been described to her a score of times by different people. For nearly five years her emotional life had been centred upon him, so she must certainly have tried to find out as much as she could. Then too, the reactions of those about her would surely have alerted her, once she arrived in the hall, to the monarch's identity. A secret of that kind cannot be kept among three hundred people.

Among those who witnessed the confrontation was the soldier-courtier Raoul de Gaucourt. Joan was later to have dealings with him on her campaigns. Gaucourt, like many others, was impressed by the way in which Joan behaved herself, and it is he who reports what were probably Joan's next words: 'Very noble Lord dauphin, I am come and am sent by God, to bring succour to you and your kingdom.'[35]

After this, Charles and Joan drew aside and began to talk privately together. They must have made a remarkable picture. Joan was not as richly dressed as she was to be in future. Her garments were those she had been given at Vaucouleurs, and which she had travelled in. We are told that they consisted of a black doublet, with leggings attached, while over the doublet she wore a short robe of *'gros gris noir'* – *gris* can be fur or linen, but this was more probably coarse linen stuff rather than black fur. On her head she had been wearing a black hat, but she took this off to salute the king, 'making the customary reverences, as if she had lived constantly at court'.[36] In contrast to the king's pallor, Joan had a healthy country look. We hear that she was 'sturdy and well made',[37] but not tall. She had black hair, which was already cut in the curious masculine fashion of the time, in a kind of pudding-basin, but above the ears. She was ruddy complexioned.[38] One observer later noted 'something virile' about the way she carried herself, though he also reported that her voice was sweet and womanly.[39]

For once forgetful of the eyes focused upon him, Charles continued his dialogue with Joan. This, naturally, was eagerly observed by the throng surrounding them, though the spectators, out of respect, had withdrawn from earshot. As they watched, they saw a sudden change come over Charles's face. His mood of depression lifted, and 'he was seen to be joyful'.[40] Joan had won her second battle. Having first conquered Baudricourt's resistance, she had now succeeded in making a favourable initial impression upon the king.

7

What did Joan say to the king, both during this crucial first interview, and in the course of the conversations which were held soon afterwards in his private apartments? Students of Joan of Arc have devoted an immense amount of energy to the matter of the 'King's Sign' or the 'King's Secret'. They have been led to do so by Joan's own assertion, before her judges in Rouen, that the king had a sign before he wished to believe her.[1]

Having made this statement, she then refused to reveal what the sign was. At one moment she claimed that she had promised St Catherine and St Margaret to remain silent on the subject, but 'without their requiring it. And Joan made this promise at her own request, for too many people would have asked her about it, had she not made this promise to the saints aforesaid.'[2] This, at any rate, offers an interesting insight into the nature of Joan's voices and her relationship with them. On another occasion, Joan told her judges that she refused to answer on the subject of the sign given to her king 'because the churchmen forbade her to tell it'.[3] When the tribunal at Rouen pursued the matter, it was rewarded with an elaborate story which the judges did not believe; and which Joan herself afterwards admitted to be false.[4]

Sources close to Joan insist upon the sign. Pasquerel, her confessor, says that Joan told the king something about himself 'which none knew or could know but God'.[5] It is clear that this is not the assurance of his legitimacy which Joan gave to

Charles at the very start of their interview: 'I say to you on behalf of Messire [i.e. on behalf of God] that you are true heir to France, and king's son.'[6] Since this was known to Pasquerel, and presumably to others, it cannot have been regarded as private. We must, however, admire Joan's forthrightness, and perhaps her shrewdness, in going directly to this delicate matter. Her confident assertion that Charles was legitimate immediately prejudiced him in her favour. But it did not contain the true secret. If there was one, she did not utter it at the first meeting.

Jean d'Aulon, who became the master of Joan's household and who was very close to her, also believed in a sign. He deposed that, after she was presented at court, 'the said Maid spoke to the King our Lord secretly, and told him certain secret things – what they were I do not know'. As a result of this, Charles sent for some of the members of his Council, among them Aulon himself, and told them that 'the Maid said to him that she was sent by God to help him recover his kingdom, which was then largely occupied by the English, his ancient enemies'.[7] Dunois apparently agreed with Aulon. He told the historian Thomas Basin, who recorded it years afterwards, that he had it as a fact from the king that there had been a sign or secret. Joan had revealed 'things so secret and hidden that none save [Charles] could have had knowledge of them, save by divine revelation'.[8] This may seem to be supported by Dunois's confident assertion at the Trial of Rehabilitation of his own belief that 'Joan was sent by God, and that her deeds in war were the fruit of divine inspiration rather than of human agency'.[9] The belief that Joan had made some revelation of particular importance in her interviews with Charles was widely held elsewhere. The Venetian merchant Pancrazio Giustiniani mentioned in one of his newsletters that 'he [the king] had from her [Joan] revelation of great things'.[10] The story has already taken almost definitive form in the Chronique de la Pucelle:

One day she wished to speak to the king in particular, and said to him: 'Gentle dauphin, why do you not believe me? I tell you that God has pity upon you, your kingdom and your people: for St Louis and Charlemagne are on their knees before Him, praying for you; and I will tell you, if you please, such a thing that it will give you to know that you must believe me.' However, she was content that a few people should be there, and in the presence of the Duke of Alençon,

62

the Seigneur de Trèves, Christophe de Harcourt, and Master Gerard Machet, [the king's] confessor, whom he [the king] made swear, at the request of the said Joan, that they would reveal and say nothing, she told the king something important which he had done, very secret: whereby he was much astonished, for there was none who could know it, save God and himself.[11]

All that is lacking here is the exact substance of the secret itself, and this is supplied to us by other sources, the chief among whom is Pierre Sala. What Joan did, according to him, was to tell the king of a secret prayer he had uttered. Sala claims to have had the story from a chamberlain and intimate of Charles VII:

In the time of the great adversity of King Charles VII, he found himself so low that he no longer knew what to do. . . The king, in his extremity, entered one morning alone into his oratory, and there made a humble petition and prayer to our Lord in his heart, without utterance of words, in which he petitioned devoutly that if so it was that he was true heir descended from the noble House of France, and that the kingdom rightfully belonged to him, then it should please God to keep and defend him, or, at worst, to grant him the mercy of escaping death or prison, and that he might fly to Spain or Scotland which were from time immemorial brothers-in-arms and allies of the kings of France, for which reason he had chosen them to be his last refuge.[12]

The only trouble is that this anecdote was not written down until the early sixteenth century. Another late chronicler tells us that the prayer divined by Joan was uttered at Loches, on the All Saints' Day immediately preceding her arrival in Chinon,[13] and a third gives a vivid description of how the king 'rose from his bed in his shirt, and, at the side of his bed, spontaneously knelt on bare knees, tears in his eyes, hands joined',[14] to make the prayer in question.

Unfortunately, the more detailed and specific this account of the 'King's Sign' becomes, the more hopelessly unconvincing it seems, not merely in practical terms but in those of human character. Let us examine the practical difficulties first. One of the most intractable of them is to be found in the testimony of the Duke of Alençon, who is said by the *Chronique de la Pucelle* to have been present when Joan made her crucial revelation to

the king, although he was not in Chinon at the time when Joan
first arrived there:

I was out shooting quail when a messenger came to tell me that
there was come to the king a maid who affirmed she was sent by God
to drive out the English, and to raise the siege which was laid by the
English in Orleans. That was why, on the morrow, I went to the king
who was then in the town of Chinon and I found Joan talking with
the king. When I drew near, Joan asked who I was and the king
replied that I was the Duke of Alençon. Thereupon, Joan said: 'You
are very welcome. The more of the blood royal there are together, the
better it will be.' And on the morrow Joan came at the king's command, and when she saw the king she bowed, and the king took Joan
into a chamber and I was with him and the lord of La Trémoïlle whom
the king kept with him, telling the rest to withdraw. Then Joan made
several requests of the king, among others that he should give up
his kingdom to the King of Heaven; and when he had made this gift,
she said, the King of Heaven would do to him as He had done to his
predecessors and restore him to his former state. And many other
things, which I do not remember.[15]

It is plain from this account that no secret of the kind described
was revealed in Alençon's presence, either then or later. The
duke is not concealing anything – there are simply a few details
which he admits he has forgotten. Indeed, if the king's prayer
was the secret to which so much importance was attached, it
seems curiously trivial. The revelation of it, either at the time
of Joan's trial, or later, during the Trial of Rehabilitation,
would have done little or nothing to damage Charles VII.
Everyone who surrounded him was aware of the depths to
which not only his, but the general morale had sunk. Margaret
La Touroulde, later one of Joan's hostesses, waxes eloquent on
the universal depression among the dauphinists at this time.

When Joan came to the king at Chinon, I was at Bourges where the
queen was. At that time there was in his kingdom and in those parts
in obedience to the king such calamity and lack of money that it was
piteous, and indeed those true to their allegiance to the king were in
despair. I know it because my husband was at that time Receiver
General and, of both the king's money and his own, he had not four
crowns. And the city of Orleans was besieged by the English and
there was no means of going to its aid. And it was in the midst of
this calamity that Joan came, and I believe it firmly, she came from

God and was sent to raise up the king and the people still within his allegiance, for at that time there was no help but God.[16]

Joan may indeed have guessed, or divined, that the king had had thoughts of the kind which appear in the prayer as we now have it. And she may have told him what she guessed. We have already seen, from her first encounter with him, and perhaps also from her dealings with Baudricourt, that she was keenly attuned to tiny, largely unconscious gestures and signals. But the secret itself, if it existed, must surely have been something very different. In what direction should we look? I believe that Joan herself gave the clue or clues during her trial, and that she was not as discreet as she is usually said to have been. She told her judges, for example, that 'before her king put her to work he had numerous apparitions and fine revelations'.[17] She also said that 'her king and several others saw and heard the voices which came to her, Joan, and that Charles de Bourbon [Clermont] was present and several others'.[18]

Joan was notoriously reluctant to share her visions – they were personal to her, proof that she had been singled out by God to perform a unique task. This is one reason, quite apart from its irregular form, why a charter of nobility granted to one Gui de Cailli, which alleges that the recipient once shared a revelation with the Maid, must be regarded as suspect.[19] But Joan seems to have made an exception for the possessors of the blood royal. As her remark when she was introduced to Alençon indicates, she attributed great virtues to those who possessed it. This notion of the sacredness of the blood royal was not peculiar to her. It was widespread during the Middle Ages, and persisted until much later. It forms one of the leading ideas of Shakespeare's *Richard II*. For Joan, Charles was not only the subject of a driving obsession, he represented the blood royal raised to its highest power. She considered him a 'child of God' in the special sense in which she applied that description to herself. It is therefore quite likely that she tried to persuade Charles that he saw and heard a part at least of which she herself experienced, and, given the suggestibility of his character, equally probable that she succeeded at least momentarily in convincing him that he possessed a share of her own visionary gifts. This is the light in which one must examine the long and circumstantial story she told her judges about the angel with the crown. Her judges had been pressing her hard on the subject of the king's sign, and she had so far failed to satisfy them, either evading their questions or point-blank refusing to answer them. Now, on 13 March 1431, she suddenly gave way. Asked 'What was the sign that she gave to her king?', she first of all retorted with another question: 'Are you content that I risk perjuring myself?' On the face of it, she was asking if she must ignore the oath she said she had taken to her saints, but the implications, at a deeper level, are disturbing. It is almost as if she was asking formal permission to lie. She then went on:

The sign was that the angel certified [her revelations or her mission] to the king, by bringing him the crown and saying to him that he would have the whole of the kingdom of France entirely with the help of God and by means of Joan's labour, and that he should put Joan to work, that is to say by giving her men-at-arms, otherwise he would not be so soon crowned and anointed. . .

How did the angel bring the crown and did he put it on the head of the king?

The crown was given to an archbishop, to wit the Archbishop of Rheims, as it seemed to her, in her king's presence; and the archbishop received it and gave it to her king; and Joan was present. And this crown has been placed in the treasury of her king.[20]

To this basic outline, Joan then proceeded to make a number of very circumstantial additions. The sign was given at Chinon, she said, and it was late at night, in the month of March or April – i.e. some time after her first arrival at Chinon, and perhaps when she was there for a second visit after she had been to Poitiers. The angel had come to her in her lodgings in the town, and had accompanied her to the castle. It had been seen by Alençon, La Trémoille and Bourbon, in addition to the king. Later, the angel had left her in a little chapel – probably that dedicated to St Martin, in the section of the castle to the west of the Royal Lodging.[21]

Her judges did not believe Joan, and on the face of it there is no reason why we should do so either. In the end, she actually admitted that 'she herself had been the angel'.[22] Yet there is the very strongest reason to believe that this extremely tall tale contains at least a core of truth. Alençon reports that soon after

Joan arrived at Chinon she was urging the king to put his kingdom into the hands of God, and to receive it back from God again. The demand was foreshadowed by what she had already said to Baudricourt. It is certain that, being who she was and what she was, she meant the request in a very literal sense, and would not rest until it was granted. A curious passage in a chronicle seems to confirm that a ceremony embodying this concept took place:

One day, the Maid asked the king for a present. The prayer was granted. She then asked for the kingdom of France itself. The king, astonished, gave it to her after some hesitation, and the young girl accepted. She even asked that the act be solemnly drawn up and read by the king's four secretaries. The charter having been written and recited, the king remained somewhat astonished when the girl said, showing him to those who were by: 'Here you see the poorest knight in his kingdom'.

And a little later, in the presence of the same notaries, acting as mistress of the kingdom of France, she put it into the hands of all-powerful God. Then, at the end of some moments more, acting in the name of God, she invested King Charles with the kingdom of France; and she wished a solemn act to be drawn up in writing of all this.[23]

In its symbolic essence, this is another version of the story of the angel bearing the crown. But not only symbolism was involved. Joan's consciousness that she was telling at least part of the literal truth is reflected in her assertion that Regnault de Chartres, Archbishop of Rheims, would confirm her story. 'He would not dare', she claimed, 'to say the contrary of what I have told you.'[24]

There was indeed material here for heresy hunters; enough, perhaps, to inspire a tacit conspiracy to hush up any news that the king himself had turned visionary in Joan's wake. There must also have been a strong impulse to ignore the curious ritual which Joan had succeeded in imposing upon Charles, as unworthy of the dignity of the monarchy. Matters such as these do, therefore, have a claim to be regarded as the real 'secret' between the king and Joan of Arc. Even after Joan's rehabilitation it was embarrassing to think about them or to mention them.

But, despite the heavy weight of evidence in favour of the existence of a sign, the truth probably is that there was no specific moment at which something hidden was revealed, and which forged the link between Joan and the King. To insist that there was indeed such a moment is to take far too mechanical a view of human personality. The legend of the 'King's Sign' is evidence, not only of the workings of the medieval mind in a general sense, but also of the urge to supply what happened between Charles and Joan with a rationale. Her tenacious obsession was foiled and baffled by his elusiveness and mutability. Suspecting himself to be unworthy, he felt the need to be dominated by men of bad character, who would drag him down to their own moral level. Joan's idealization of him irked Charles, and perhaps bred a sense of panic in her presence. He could not serve as the surrogate father with whom she wanted to have an intimate though spiritual bond. It was not only that Charles himself was still young, and possibly young for his age. The fact was that he too was still in need of a father. This is well demonstrated by the procession of his advisers, many of whom took conscious advantage of the king's impressionability. Possessed of the same needs, Joan and Charles were like two children playing a game, seeking but never finding, trying to make each vouchsafe the security which neither could provide for the other.

As far as Charles was concerned, Joan might dress as a man, and behave as one, but she remained a woman, and this did not suffice him. He was not homosexual, but, hazily defined, one can see passive homoerotic traits operating in his willing submission to forceful men who were more interested in the symbolic stature of Charles as king than in his person. Charles's kingship was what interested Joan too. She instinctively projected onto Charles her own masculine strivings under the guise of religiously inspired thrust. In the circumstances, his submission to her could not be as complete as it was to his male favourites.

Despite his initially favourable reaction, when he first spoke to her in the hall at Chinon, Charles's conduct towards her immediately after this lapsed into something characteristically ambiguous. He could not quite make up his mind whether to treat Joan as a major prophet or as a kind of curiosity, something not very far from a performing monkey. And if he was trying to find a category into which she could conveniently be fitted, so too were those who surrounded him, who now had to accept her as a new and possibly important factor in their lives. Joan, however, would not have struck them as being entirely without precedent. It was an age, not only of astrologers and magicians, but of prophets and visionaries of every sort, from the noblest to the most tawdry. Many of these were women, and the role of prophetess was one of the few which allowed a woman to play an active part in great affairs.

Charles VII's grandfather, Charles V, generally accounted the most intelligent and successful of the Valois kings, had been advised by Catherine de la Rochelle, whom he brought to Paris. Other holy women of the fourteenth and fifteenth centuries included Marie, called the Gasque d'Avignon, of whom we shall hear more in a moment (she acted as a kind of forerunner or John the Baptist to Joan of Arc), and the Franciscan reformer St Colette of Corbie, whom certain authorities have also tried to connect to Joan's story. There were also international celebrities, such as St Catherine of Siena and St Brigit of Sweden. This last, who died in 1374, had her prophecies concerning France approved by the Council of Constance, and was canonized in 1415. In the annals of the time we find mention of other *Pucelles* or Maids. They included the Pucelle de Lyon, the Pucelle de Schiedam, and the Pucelle de Rome. Sometimes these visionaries fell foul of the Church, instead of being accepted by it. One such was Catherine Sauve of Montpellier, burned in 1417.

Having decided that Joan's claims merited further investigation, Charles moved her from her lodgings in the town into the castle itself. This had the double advantage of cutting off her contacts with outsiders, who might perhaps be manipulating her; and of making her conveniently available for further investigation and study. The lodging assigned to her was a chamber in the Tour du Coudrai. This was the donjon of the earliest and westernmost part of the castle, easily accessible from the Royal Lodging over a little bridge. In recent years, it had not apparently been much used. If Joan had known something of the previous history of the rooms she occupied, she might have shuddered. In 1308, it served as the place of imprisonment for the principal officers of the Templar Order, after they had been arrested by King Philip the Fair on trumped up charges of heresy and sorcery. These prisoners left their graffiti in the room, including a cross with the instruments of the Passion, and a stag pursued by a hound. The latter was the work of the unfortunate Grand Master of the Templars, Jacques de Molay, who was subsequently burned. It was his curse which was popularly supposed to have snuffed out the Capetians, the line of kings who had preceded the Valois. Molay signed the design with his name, and added the inscription 'I beg God to pardon me'. These designs must have been visible to Joan, unless they were covered by tapestries at the time.

Joan herself was put in the charge of the king's majordomo,[25] and she was given a page to look after her. This page, Louis de Coutes, then aged fourteen or fifteen, was of good family, and had previously served Raoul de Gaucourt, who numbered the captaincy of Chinon among his offices. Louis lived in the Tour du Coudrai during the daytime. At night, women were assigned to stay with Joan, as was only seemly. He remembered, later, that Joan's lodgings were the scene of comings and goings on the part of various notables, though he was not allowed to stay and listen to what was said. He also recalled the ardour of Joan's prayers, and the fact that she sometimes wept as she prayed.[26]

Though Joan was under surveillance, her relationship with Charles grew increasingly informal, as we can see from Alençon's deposition. The duke adds one charming detail: 'After the meal the king went to walk in the meadows, and Joan ran a tilt with a lance, and when I saw how she handled the lance and tilted, I gave her a horse.'[27]

Despite the impression she had made upon him, Charles, who had an innately bureaucratic turn of mind, decided that Joan's credentials must be thoroughly examined by what seemed to him the appropriate authorities. The calculating coolness which was so strangely intermingled with the compulsive side of his character made the king think that, if this girl received the Church's approval, her effectiveness would be greatly increased and he himself would be to some extent protected from accusations of heterodoxy. These examinations were just getting under way when Alençon arrived, and he was present at what seems to have been the first of them. Joan gave what were, by now, almost a stock set of answers. She had been asked these questions before, when it was a question of whether she should be allowed to see the king at all. Later, relaxing in Alençon's company, she lost some of her wariness, and informed him that she 'knew more and could do more' than she had as yet said.[28] She was always indiscreet when she wanted to impress people with a sense of her own importance, secretive when she remembered that men's judgements mattered little to one who had received her mission directly from God.

8

From Chinon, Joan was sent to Poitiers. Here she was examined by a committee of churchmen appointed by the king. The record of this examination is lost, and is one of the principal gaps in the documentation of Joan's career. This repeated questioning made Joan impatient. She told her confessor Pasquerel that

She was not content with so many interrogations, that she was being prevented from accomplishing what she had been sent for, that she was in haste to act, and that it was time.[1]

On the other hand, she was also rather proud of the way in which she had dealt with this group of learned doctors; and she tended to think of the examination at Poitiers as something which gave her a clean bill of health thenceforth from the point of view of religious orthodoxy. To her judges at Rouen she said that she had been 'interrogated for three weeks by clerks at Chinon and Poitiers. . . And the clerks of her party were of the opinion that there was nothing but good in what she did.'[2]

The fact that the questions put to her, and the answers she gave to them, were written down evidently impressed her mightily. Like all illiterate people, Joan had the greatest respect for the written word, and she was inclined to feel that, once a thing had been put into writing, all arguments regarding it could be thought of as settled. Thus we find her referring the

Rouen tribunal to the proceedings of the earlier one upon several occasions, saying 'send to Poitiers, where I was interrogated previously',[3] or 'that is recorded in the register at Poitiers',[4] or, again, 'that is written at Poitiers'.[5] In fact, her examination seems to have followed much the same lines as some of the subsequent questioning at Rouen, especially with regard to certain crucial points, her voices, her mission and her insistence on wearing men's clothing. The crucial difference was that at Poitiers the men examining her were on the whole prejudiced in her favour, while at Rouen they were even more strongly prejudiced against her. Even so, both examinations were conducted by men of the same stamp, schooled in the same disciplines.

The commission at Poitiers was both large and distinguished. There seem to have been some seventeen or eighteen members, though it is unlikely that all were present at the same time. They included the Archbishop of Rheims, two other bishops, and the confessors of both the king and the queen. Among those who played a particularly prominent role were the king's confessor, Gérard Machet, who had been both Rector and Vice-Chancellor of the University of Paris, and Séguin Séguin, Dean of the Faculty of Poitiers University. The sessions of this examining body took place at various places. We hear of a meeting 'in the house of a woman called La Macée', and of interrogations conducted at the house where Joan lodged.[6] Joan's host was Jean Rabateau, one of Charles's privy councillors, and advocate-general before the *Parlement* of Poitiers. His house was called the Hôtel de la Rose.

With men of the type who had been deputed to examine Joan, some lively exchanges were inevitable. For instance, one of the examiners said to her: 'According to what you say, the voice told you that God wishes to deliver the people of France from the calamity in which it finds itself. But if God wishes to deliver the people of France, it is not necessary to have soldiers.' Joan replied: 'In God's name, the soldiers will fight, and God will give the victory.'[7] Séguin Séguin, 'a very sour man' according to one chronicler, though his deposition reveals that he had a sense of humour, remembered that the following dialogue took place between himself and Joan at one stage of the examination:

'Do you believe in God?'

'Yes, better than you.'

'But God does not wish that you be believed, unless some sign appears showing that we should believe in you. We cannot advise the king, upon your simple assertion, to trust in you and put soldiers in danger. Have you nothing else to say?' 'In God's name, I have not come to Poitiers to give signs. But take me to Orleans and I will show signs why I am sent.'[8]

Looking back, Joan had some reason to be pleased with the way in which she had acquitted herself. One of her own retorts particularly stuck in her mind. Later on she told 'how she had been examined by some clerks and had said in answer to them: "There is more in Our Lord's books than in yours." '[9] Indeed, she seems rather to have played on the striking contrast which her lack of book-knowledge made with their learning. On one occasion, she greeted the clerks who came to see her with the words: 'I suppose you have come to examine me. But I don't know A from B.'[10] Nevertheless, she confounded them with the readiness of many of her replies. One of the examiners at Poitiers later told an acquaintance that Joan 'replied with great wisdom, like a great clerk'.[11] In the circumstances, it was the highest compliment he could pay. There is a passage in a contemporary chronicle which seems to catch very well the atmosphere of these interviews:

There were assembled several notable doctors of theology and others, bachelors, and they entered the room where [Joan] was, and when she saw them she went to sit at the end of the bench [i.e. in the humblest and therefore most respectful position], and asked them what they wanted. Then it was said by the mouth of one of them that they came to her because it was said that she had said to the king that God had sent her to him; and they showed by fine and sweet reasons why she should not be believed. They were there more than two hours, when each of them spoke in turn; and she replied to them; whereat they were greatly astonished, that a simple shepherdess, a young girl, should so prudently reply.[12]

But we must also note that the 'fine and sweet reasons' for not believing Joan were sometimes put only for form's sake. From the beginning several of the examiners were prepared to believe in Joan and her message. One was Gérard Machet, who remembered an old prophecy that 'a Maid would come to help the

King of France'.[13] Another was a professor of theology called Jean Érault, who recalled the prophecy made by Marie, the Gasque d'Avignon, to Charles VII some years previously. What this lady had said was

that the kingdom of France would undergo great sufferings and would sustain many disasters. She spoke too, of having had frequent visions concerning the desolation of France. In one of them Marie saw many pieces of armour which were brought before her, which frightened her. For she was afraid that she would be forced to put this armour on. But she was told to fear nothing, and that it was not she who would have to wear this armour, but that a Maid who would come after her would wear it and deliver the kingdom of France from its enemies.[14]

Érault, of course, firmly believed, that 'Joan was the Maid of whom Marie d'Avignon had spoken'.[15]

This story illustrates particularly clearly the intellectual and emotional climate of the time. In 1413, even the relatively level-headed University of Paris had appealed officially to all those who possessed the gift of prophecy 'among devout persons and those who lived the contemplative life' for their help in disentangling the troubled state of the kingdom.

Meanwhile, Joan fascinated not only the learned doctors who examined her, but the townspeople. She converted the great functionaries to her cause – the 'presidents and counsellors of *Parlement*' – and she greatly moved the women, 'ladies, damoiselles and townswomen', who flocked into her presence, speaking to them 'so gently and graciously that she made them weep'.[16] At other times she was to be seen engaged in more warlike exercises, 'going with the men-at-arms to the fields and coursing with the lance as well as any, and riding black chargers, so bad tempered that none dared to ride them'.[17]

It is uncertain quite how long Joan's examination at Poitiers lasted. She herself put its duration at three weeks. Perceval de Boulainvilliers says that it went on for six.[18] The difference may perhaps be accounted for by the other inquiries which were going on at the same time. Gérard Machet questioned those who had brought Joan from Vaucouleurs, either before he left Chinon or soon after his arrival in Poitiers. They stressed the miraculous smoothness and rapidity of their journey to seek the king.[19] Joan's background was investigated: 'The king sent to [her] native land, to know from whence she was.'[20] It is likely that in this case the men who undertook the inquiry were mendicant friars, who could travel anywhere without much fear of molestation.

Joan's manner of life was closely observed, and it was afterwards believed that she had been tested in various secret ways. For example, it was said that she was offered an unconsecrated host but 'detected immediately that it was not the body of Christ, while the priest had the true host in concealment'.[21] Whether this particular ruse was tried on her we do not know (the source is prone to enthusiastic exaggeration), but it is at least clear that no fault could be found in her way of living. Efforts were also made to get a kind of guarantee from outside authorities. Charles may even have tried to wrest such a certificate from Pope Martin V. At any rate, we hear that he wrote to the Pope about her.[22] And he did obtain endorsements from two eminent theologians, who wrote treatises about Joan. There was one last test which Joan had to pass before the king would put her to work, and this was a test for virginity. This was undertaken by a very eminent personage indeed, Yolanda of Aragon, the Queen of Sicily. Yolanda was, next to her own daughter, Charles's queen, the woman who ranked highest at the Valois court. She was assisted by three ladies of the court.

The said Maid was seen, visited and secretly looked at and examined in the secret parts of her body, but after they had seen and looked at everything which ought to be looked at in such a case, the said lady [Yolanda] said and related to the king that she and the said ladies found that she was certainly a true and entire maid, in whom could be found no corruption nor mark of violence.[23]

Joan, of course, was longing more fervently than ever to begin her task. Even on the way to Poitiers she had known that her stay there would be frustrating. While riding from Chinon, she exclaimed: 'In God's name, I know well that I will have much to trouble me at Poitiers where you are taking me; but Messires [the Saints] will help me, so let's get on, for God's sake.'[24] Now Charles himself had followed her to the city, and she was pestering him daily to let her begin. What did she truly believe her task was? Like many of the topics connected with

Joan and her career (the 'King's Sign' is another example), this question has become formalized to a quite extraordinary extent. Séguin Séguin gives one of the most convincing accounts of her mission, and bases it upon what she said to him in the presence of the other members of the tribunal:

And then she prophesied to me and those others present four things which were then still to come and which fell out as she foretold. First she said that the English would be defeated, and that the siege they had laid to Orleans would be raised and that the town of Orleans would be freed of the English but that she would send them a summons first. Then she said that the king would be anointed at Rheims. Thirdly, she said that the city of Paris would return to the king's rule, and then that the Duke of Orleans would come back from England.[25]

Séguin adds: 'I have seen all these things come true.'

Did Joan, however, believe that she would accomplish all four of these tasks herself? Her most fervent admirers, reluctant to fault her in anything, have preferred to limit her actual mission to the two things she in fact accomplished – the relief of Orleans and the coronation at Rheims. Unfortunately any number of pieces of evidence exist to contradict this thesis. One is her famous letter of summons to the Duke of Bedford. Another is her statement to her judges in Rouen: 'When I have done that for which I have been sent by God, then I shall put on women's clothes.'[26] This implies that, at the time when she was tried, her mission was still not fully accomplished. The extended version of Joan's mission acquired an extremely widespread currency throughout France.[27] The only piece of evidence to put in the scales against this is Joan's answer to the seventeenth of the seventy articles of accusation that were read to her on 27 March 1431. She said then that

She had brought news from God to her king: that Our Lord would give him back his kingdom of France, would have him crowned at Rheims, and would rout his adversaries.[28]

The vagueness of the answer is sufficiently accounted for, not only by the imprecision with which the article itself is framed, but by Joan's unwillingness to admit that her voices could in any way have misled her.

What we must also allow for is her extreme youth and her

total lack of education. Fifteenth-century ideas about geography were, on the whole, vague. When Joan found herself on the wrong side of the river from Orleans, she was surprised as well as angry.[29] She clearly had not the slightest notion what crossing the sea to rescue the Duke of Orleans might involve, though she is reported to have said that he was 'in her charge, and if he did not return from thence, she would have much trouble in going to seek him in England'.[30] Her actions before Paris are significant because they indicate that she lacked a specific plan. When she said to the tribunal in Rouen that she had not gone to Paris by the revelation of her voices, but 'at the request of the gentlemen who wished to make a skirmish or feat of arms',[31] though her own intention had indeed been to go further and 'get over the ditches', she was telling a curious kind of half-truth rather than an outright lie. Having set the current of events in motion, she then allowed herself to be carried along with it, trusting that all would turn out as her voices had predicted. Attempts to set her up as a great strategist are not to be taken seriously.

Her letter to the Duke of Bedford, composed at Poitiers but not dispatched till later, shows that she was at least anxious to stick to the correct forms of contemporary warfare, at least as she understood them. She did not want to go and make war against the English unless she had sent a summons to them first.[32] So she dictated her message to one of the most sympathetic of her examiners in Poitiers, Jean Érault.[33] According to the text preserved by the *Procès de condamnation*, this letter ran as follows:

JHESUS MARIA

King of England, and you, Duke of Bedford, who call yourself regent of the kingdom of France; you, William de la Pole, Earl of Suffolk; John, Lord Talbot, and you Thomas, Lord Scales, who call yourselves lieutenants of the said Duke of Bedford, acknowledge the summons of the King of Heaven, and render up to the Maid who is here sent by God, the King of Heaven, the keys of all the good towns you have here taken and violated in France. She is come here by God's will to reclaim the blood royal. She is very ready to make peace, if you will acknowledge her to be right by leaving France and paying for what you have held. And you, archers, companions of war, men-at-arms and others who are before the town of Orleans, go away into your own country, by God; and if you do not do so, expect news of the Maid who will come to see you shortly, to your very great injury. King of England, if you do not do so I am chief-of-war, and in whatever place I reach your people in France, I will make them quit it, willy-nilly. And if they will not obey, I will have them all slain; I am sent here by God, the King of Heaven, to drive you, body for body, out of the whole of France. And if they do obey, I will be merciful to them. And do not think otherwise, for you do not hold the Kingdom of France from God, the King of Heaven, son of Saint Mary, as King Charles, the true heir, will hold it; for God, the King of Heaven, wishes it so, and this is revealed by the Maid, who will enter into Paris with a goodly company. If you will not believe the news sent to you by God and the Maid, we will strike into whatever place we find you, and make such great 'hayhay' that none so great has been in France for a thousand years if you will not yield to right. And believe firmly that the King of Heaven will send more strength to the Maid than you will be able to bring up with all your assaults, against her and her good men-at-arms; and on every horizon it will be seen who has the better right from the King of Heaven. You, Duke of Bedford, the Maid begs and requires of you that you do not allow yourself to be destroyed. If you grant her right, you may still come into her company where the French shall do the greatest feat of arms that was ever done for Christianity. And make answer if you wish to make peace in the city of Orleans; and if you do not do so, may you be reminded of it by your very great injuries. Written this Tuesday of Holy week.[34]

Both its tone and some of its details make this letter immensely interesting. We need not doubt that it is entirely Joan's own work. She herself told her judges that she dictated it, though she also showed it to some members of her party before it was sent. She specifically denied that it was the work of any other person.[35] If this does not suffice, then we have the evidence of a witness who was present when the letter was being composed. Even the style supports the supposition that the letter to Bedford accurately represents her thoughts at this particular period. As one of the best of Joan's biographers has noted, it shows the characteristic 'repetitions used by illiterate people when most in earnest'.[36]

Those familiar with Joan's legend may find this a surprisingly aggressive document, with little trace of meekness about it. The offers of mercy which it contains are made very much as afterthoughts. But Joan's attitudes towards violence were always ambiguous, and in this she was the child of her times. On the one hand, she could praise the sword she took from Franquet d'Arras as 'good for giving fine strokes and slashes'.[37] In almost the next breath, she was asserting that she liked her standard 'forty times more' than her sword.[38] At Poitiers, just before the letter was dictated, she told Séguin Séguin and her other examiners that 'she did not wish to use her sword and did not wish to kill anyone'.[39] Her enemies, of course, found it hard to credit this. One hostile chronicler claims that she 'killed and struck with her sword the men-at-arms and others'.[40] Another hostile source tells us that 'when any of her own men displeased her she struck them with great blows of her staff',[41] and her dislike of the prostitutes who followed the army could certainly break out into physical violence.

Joan seems to have been uneasily conscious that some phrases in her letter could be misconstrued. When it was read back to her in Rouen she challenged three in particular. For 'render up to the Maid', she wished to substitute 'render up to the King'. She also denied using the words *chef de guerre* (chief-of-war) and the slightly mysterious phrase *corps pour corps* (body for body*).[42] These denials seem to have been part of a general plan of defence. She did not want to admit that she had taken direct military command at any point during her campaigns, probably because the deaths which ensued in the course of them would then seem all the more obviously her responsibility. But it is in fact likely that the copy of her letter presented to her at Rouen was accurate.[43]

All the same, Joan's military status was always uncertain, because she herself was unique. Even in the loose structure of a fifteenth-century army she had no obvious place, though her reputation tended to make people count her among the leaders, and she certainly expected that she would be invited to take part in any council of war. The ambiguous designation *chef de guerre* was commonly applied to her, largely because no other label could be found which seemed remotely applicable.[44]

Joan's use of the words JHESUS MARIA in the superscription to this and other letters was also a matter in which her judges at Rouen took an unfriendly interest.[45] The Anglo–Burgundians

* It does not seem to have quite the same meaning as *corps à corps*: hand to hand.

thought she was using it in a presumptuous and perhaps blasphemous way to give a sacred colouring to what were essentially lay matters. The superscription, as it happens, was not peculiar to Joan herself. It was employed by the Franciscan reformer St Colette of Corbie in the letters she wrote to convents she had founded or reformed, and also in the correspondence she exchanged with members of the Third Order of St Francis. Members of the Order used it, in turn, when they wrote to her.[46] These facts have been used as the foundation upon which to build a seductive theory that Joan herself was connected in some way with the Third Order, and that she was influenced by St Colette. Despite a tenuous tradition that the two ladies met, there does not seem to be nearly enough evidence to prove it. What the words suggest, in a more general sense, is Joan's connection with the popular, highly emotional current in fifteenth-century religion inherited from her mother. The supposition is further strengthened by the exchanges on the subject of Joan's rings which also took place at the trial. We learn that one of these rings had the words JESUS MARIE written upon it and that she wore it 'for pleasure and honour of her father and mother'.[47] The ring clearly meant much to her; and because she valued it, it attracted notice. Some people even thought it might have occult powers. A chronicler reports: 'She wore on her left hand a ring which she looked at almost continually, as an eye-witness told me.'[48]

The letter to Bedford is dated 'Tuesday of Holy Week' – 22 March 1429. Its composition seems to have marked the triumphant conclusion of Joan's examination. The examiners' verdict was that 'in view of our urgent need and the peril of the city of Orleans, the king might well make use of [Joan] and send her to that city'.[49] Charles himself was almost certainly in Poitiers to receive these conclusions in person – his presence there is recorded on 11 and again on 23 March.

Joan, however, was still forced to linger. She did not leave until around 10 April. And when she at last departed, it was not directly for Orleans, where she longed to be. First she must go back to Chinon, and it was then that she seems to have used her greatly increased authority to impose the ceremony of the surrender of the kingdom upon the king. It was probably during this brief return that she went to see the wife and mother of the

Duke of Alençon at the abbey of Saint Florent, near Saumur.[50] She found the ladies in a state of some anxiety about the coming campaign. Alençon had been made prisoner at Verneuil in 1424, and the ransom he had had to pay then had almost destroyed his fortune. If he were to be captured now, he would never be able to raise the money to ensure his release. Joan did her best to reassure his womenfolk, and promised that she would bring Alençon back to them safe and sound. It was after this, a chronicler tells us, that she became closer to Alençon than she was to anyone else. Just as she called the king *'mon dauphin'*, so, too, she addressed Alençon as *'mon beau duc'* (my fine duke).[51] The possessive in Joan's case is always significant as it indicates that she had incorporated the individual concerned into the realm of her fantasies. Henceforth she would extend to Alençon the same protection as she gave to her youngest brother Pierre.

In Poitiers, meanwhile, the memory of Joan's visit remained. In later years, some thought they remembered her leaving, in armour, with her sword at her side and her standard in her hand.[52] The memory was a romantic fiction, because the armour had not yet been made or the standard painted. But henceforth one of the towers in the city wall would be called the *'Tour de la Pucelle'*.

After her second visit to Chinon, Joan went to Tours and stayed there in the house of one Jean Dupuy. Dupuy was a distinguished man and one of the principal councillors of Queen Yolanda. His wife had been lady-in-waiting to the queen, Yolanda's daughter. Here preparations were made for her part in the war.[1] She was given a retinue, and was henceforth treated as being little inferior to a prince. She had men 'for the service of her person' and others 'to conduct her'.[2] The most important of them was Jean d'Aulon, who now became the master of her household, and who was to accompany her through all her campaigns, and was finally captured with her at Compiègne. He is the most interesting and reliable witness to the whole of Joan's military career. One appointment was made by Joan herself. This was that of a confessor. His name was Jean Pasquerel, and he was a mendicant friar, serving as *lector* in the convent of Tours, but had recently been on pilgrimage to Puy for the Jubilee. At Puy he had met not only Joan's mother but 'some of those who had brought Joan to the king',[3] and naturally there was a good deal of talk about this new prodigy: 'As they knew me slightly, they told me I ought to go with them to Joan, and they would not let me go until they had taken me to her.'[4] Pasquerel's name had also been mentioned to Joan – evidently he had impressed them as the kind of religious adviser she needed and would find sympathetic. When the priest was eventually brought into her presence,

Those who had brought me spoke, saying, 'Joan, we have brought you this good Father; did you know him well, you would love him much.' Joan replied that she was well pleased and that she had already heard tell of me, and that on the next day she would like to confess to me. The next day I heard her confession and sang mass before her, and from that hour I followed her always and remained with her until Compiègne, where she was captured.[5]

It is also probable that Joan's brothers, Jean and Pierre, rejoined her at this point. Pierre was to become a regular member of her military household. He was with her at Orleans, during the preparations for the march to Rheims and during the march itself, and was finally among those captured with her.

In Tours Joan was being equipped for battle. The king had a suit of armour made for her.[6] This must have given her much pleasure, as fine arms delighted her throughout her career.[7] In any case the present was a sign of her new status and of the confidence which was now placed in her, as well as marking a definitive separation from the peasant girl she had once been. A full suit of armour, not only because of its connotations, but because it was so expensive, was the thing which most conspicuously set the knight apart from the rest of those who surrounded him. Joan was also offered a sword, but for this she insisted on sending back to Sainte-Cathérine-de-Fierbois. She asked for a weapon which she knew to be concealed at a particular spot within the church:

How did you know this sword was there?
I knew it was there from my voices. I had never seen the man who went to look for it. I wrote to the churchmen of the place to ask for the sword, and they sent it to me. It was not deep in the earth. It was, as I think, behind the altar; but I am not certain whether it was in front of the altar or behind it.[8]

Joan added that, when the sword was found, it was rusty, but 'the clergy rubbed it, and the rust readily fell off'.[9] She also said that she had a great liking for this weapon 'because it had been found in the church of St Catherine, whom she loved well'.[10]

What did the sword look like, and what was the true story of its discovery? Neither of these questions is particularly easy to answer. As far as its appearance goes, we learn from one of Joan's interrogations that there were five crosses upon the sword, and the *Journal du Siège* informs us that these were upon the blade, near the hilt.[11] Another source tells us that the weapon was 'everywhere imprinted and covered with *fleurs de lys*'.[12] It has been suggested that the five crosses were those of the kingdom of Jerusalem – several families in the Loire region were entitled to include this device among their arms.[13] In fact, another plausible theory would be that they were simply armourer's marks. Whatever its history, and whatever its precise form of decoration, one thing at least is clear, and that is that Joan's sword was almost certainly one of the ex-votos which had been deposited in the chapel.

Since we know that Joan spent a considerable length of time in the building, it is hard to take the claim that she had never seen it before very seriously – and, indeed, if we take the trouble to look at her statement, we notice that it falls somewhat short of making such an assertion. However, it is quite probable, given her state of mind while she was waiting to learn how her letter to Chinon had been received, that the weapon registered its presence upon her preconscious rather than her conscious mind. When the impulse came to send for it, it must indeed have seemed like the prompting of her voices which inspired her to do so. In the earlier part of Joan's career, her sword gained a considerable reputation as a supposedly magical or fetishistic object. Those opposed to Joan suspected darkly that it was used in the rituals of the black art – necromancers were supposed to make considerable use of a sword or swords in their ceremonies – while those on the same side as she were firmly convinced that its discovery was miraculous. One of those who were especially impressed by Joan's prescience in knowing where the weapon was hidden was the king himself. It was he who organized the search for it, and he presented Joan with a sheath. Other sheaths – one of crimson velvet and one of cloth-of-gold – were given to Joan by the churchmen of Sainte-Cathérine-de-Fierbois and by the people of Tours.[14] In the end, thanks to its very celebrity and the faith which people put in it, the sword from St Catherine's chapel was to do Joan a great deal of damage.

One thing which Joan had made in Tours, in addition to her armour, was her standard. The design was suggested to her by the counsel she received. Pasquerel tells us that

She said that now was the time when action was necessary, also that she had asked the messengers of her Lord – that is to say of God – who appeared to her, what she ought to do. And they had told her to take up the standard of her Lord. And therefore Joan had her standard made, with the image of Our Saviour painted on it, sitting in judgement among the clouds of the sky, and with him an angel painted holding a *fleur-de-lys* in his hand, which the image was blessing. I was at Tours where the standard was painted.[15]

The standard became the most celebrated of all the objects associated with Joan – more famous even than her sword, and certainly more celebrated than her ring. We possess a number of other descriptions of it, some more precise than Pasquerel's. The *Morosini Chronicle* reports that the standard was white and that the Saviour appeared 'in the manner of a Trinity', with one hand raised in blessing and the other holding an orb. There were two angels, not one, and they knelt to either side.[16] Joan told her judges that the whole field was sewn with lilies, and that the material was *boucassin* – a kind of fine, transparent linen. The words JHESUS MARIA, which she put on her letters, appeared on either side of the main image, above the two angels.[17] Another source adds that the Saviour was seated on a rainbow and showing his wounds.[18] The symbolism was that the risen Christ would not only bless the king's cause, but would condemn Charles's enemies as the enemies of God. Christ was usually thus represented in pictures of the Last Judgement.

On the reverse side of the standard there was another design, which consisted of an azure shield, perhaps supported by two angels,[19] and bearing a white dove. The dove held a scroll in its beak, and on the scroll were the words '*de par le Roi du Ciel*' – 'on behalf of the King of Heaven'.[20] This device, though not apparently authorized by Joan's voices, was a reminder of her claim to have a mandate directly from God himself. The fact that the ground colour of the standard was white also has a bearing on the problem of whether or not Joan had been appointed *chef de guerre* in any official sense. In the early fifteenth century the standard of an army commander was always white, while the standards, pennons and banners carried by his followers might be of various colours. The emblems they bore were chosen by the captains to whom they belonged, so in specifying what the design was to be Joan conformed to the usual custom. But by carrying a white standard she at least seemed to be laying claim to the right to command, though to her the primary significance of the choice of colour may have been that it emphasized her identification with the Virgin *immaculata*, wholly without stain.

For Joan, the standard seems to have had a psychological function as well as being the public proclamation of her mission. She revealed what this function was when she told her judges that 'she herself carried the standard when she attacked her adversaries, to avoid killing anyone'.[21] This implies that she had a considerable fear of carrying out her own aggressive impulses. In addition to her standard, Joan also had a smaller and more manageable pennon made. It was decorated with an annunciation scene – the Virgin with an angel presenting a lily.[22] This never achieved the fame accorded to the standard itself, not only because it seems to have had no claims to be the product of divine inspiration, but because it was probably destroyed, or damaged past restoration, quite early in Joan's career.[23] Both the standard and the pennon were paid for by the king, as part of the expenses for equipping Joan, and we find payments for them recorded in the accounts of Hémon Raguier, the royal treasurer. The total cost was twenty-five *livres tournois*, a quarter of the sum paid for Joan's suit of armour, and we discover from the relevant entry that the name of the painter was 'Hauves Pulnoir'.[24] It has been conjectured that he was a Scotsman, and that his real name was Hamish Power.

Joan always kept a soft spot for the man who had created her standard, and early in 1430 we find her writing to the city of Tours, asking them to give Hamish Power a hundred *écus* for his daughter's wedding. The city fathers cautiously refused, saying that 'the town's money should be used for repairs to the town, and not otherwise', but they still agreed to honour the girl with a prayer in the name of the town and with a present of bread and wine.[25] The record of the town council's deliberations on the subject casts a number of curious sidelights on Joan's career, and on her relationship to those who surrounded her. We note, for instance, that she, like other great personages of the period, felt free to ask for favours which they regarded almost as rights. And we also seem to get a glimpse of the degree to which her prestige was to decline when the triumph of the coronation had been followed by two conspicuous failures – before Paris and before La Charité. La Charité's successful resistance to Joan would have been a recent memory at the time when her letter to the city fathers of Tours was written.

While Joan was at Tours Alençon had been put in charge of organizing the relief expedition to Orleans, though he was not to accompany it. He was asked to collaborate with Queen Yolanda in doing this, and from his account of the matter we form the impression that he had some difficulty in extracting the necessary sums from the depleted royal treasury.[26]

The point of concentration was not Tours but Blois, further upstream and nearer to Orleans. It was here that many carts were laden with wheat, and here, too, that herds of cattle and sheep were gathered together.[27] In the circumstances of the time, meat could only be taken to Orleans on the hoof. The news from the beleaguered city was increasingly grave. Dunois left his command and came to Blois to confer with the dauphinist captains. He 'told them Orleans was about to be lost'.[28] And to Blois Joan herself came, to join the relieving army.[29] She had to wait there for two or three days while the victuals were made ready.

Joan was not pleased by the condition of the army. In her view, the expedition upon which it was about to embark was nothing less than a crusade, and the soldiers must conduct themselves accordingly. Her understanding of morale, though instinctive, was acute, and she hastily commissioned Pasquerel to have a banner made in addition to the standard and pennon which she already had. Instead of floating out from a pole, this, as a religious rather than military rallying point, hung from a crosspiece, and was like the banners regularly carried in religious processions. The image was that of the crucified Christ. During the few days they were at Blois, Joan,

Twice a day, morning and evening, caused all the priests to assemble, and, when they were met together, they sang anthems and hymns to Saint Mary, and Joan was with them and she would not allow the soldiers to mingle with the priests until they had confessed. And she exhorted all the soldiers to confess so that they might attend the assembly. And at the assembly all the priests were ready to hear those who wished to confess.[30]

Joan added her own harangues to those of the priests, and she took the sacrament accompanied by the members of her suite.[31] She also had her standard publicly blessed at the church of Saint-Sauveur – a particularly suitable place for the ceremony, in view of the image which it bore.[32] To complete the work of purification, Joan made the soldiers get rid of their camp-followers (throughout her career she conducted a vendetta against the loose women who followed the armies), and she also made them leave all their baggage when they set out.[33] The fact that she was able to impose these stringent rules on the undisciplined troops of Charles VII demonstrates the degree of ascendancy which she had already achieved. From Blois, she sent the commanders of the English army besieging Orleans the letter of summons she had composed and dictated at Poitiers. It was dispatched in due form, in the hands of two heralds.[34]

When all was at last ready, the relieving army set off, heading for Orleans 'by the Sologne way', which placed them on the opposite bank of the Loire from Orleans itself. Ahead of the army went the priests whom Joan had assembled, surrounding the banner she had had made for them. They sang the *Veni Creator Spiritus* 'and many other anthems',[35] while Joan exhorted the soldiers to put their trust in God. The date was 27 April 1429.

10

The English high command had been in two minds about attacking Orleans. If Charles VII was in straits, the war was nevertheless reaching a condition of stalemate, and some major effort was needed if Henry V's dream of an English monarchy in France was ever to be realized. The alternatives that presented themselves were an attack on Angers, and one on Orleans. If Angers fell, the English could link their conquests in northern France to their possessions in Guyenne and Gascony, and they would also cut Charles off from La Rochelle, which was his only major seaport. If Orleans fell, however, they struck far more directly at the heart of his kingdom, because the city commanded the Loire. Though Bedford seems to have been in favour of attacking Angers, the choice fell on Orleans. A strong argument in favour of the enterprise was geographical. Orleans was only sixty miles from Paris, and the besiegers could easily be supplied and imprisoned from there.

The siege began in October 1428, and the leader of the English forces was Thomas Montacute, Earl of Salisbury, the ablest general the English possessed. Within a few weeks he was killed by a stray cannon-shot, and this dealt a heavy blow to the besiegers, who were in any case small in number to attack a city of 30,000 inhabitants. Salisbury had about 4,000 men, later to be supplemented by 1,500 Burgundian troops. His intention was probably to storm the place, and before he was killed he succeeded in taking the fortification at the end of the

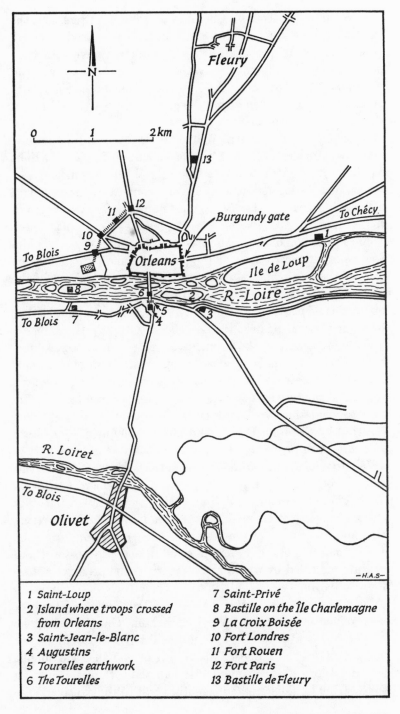

THE SIEGE OF ORLEANS

1 Saint-Loup
2 Island where troops crossed from Orleans
3 Saint-Jean-le-Blanc
4 Augustins
5 Tourelles earthwork
6 The Tourelles
7 Saint-Privé
8 Bastille on the Île Charlemagne
9 La Croix Boisée
10 Fort Londres
11 Fort Rouen
12 Fort Paris
13 Bastille de Fleury

bridge, called the Tourelles because of its twin towers, and the earthwork defending it. The Orléannais were forced to break down an arch of the bridge itself. This impressive structure, built in the twelfth century, consisted of nineteen arches, and was about 350 yards long. The Tourelles stood on the eighteenth of these arches, counting from the city, and was separated from the bank by a wooden drawbridge.

Salisbury's successor was William de la Pole, Earl of Suffolk, and with him the pattern of the siege changed. It was now to be a regular investment, but, since the English had insufficient men to conduct a close siege, they had to content themselves with elaborating a ring of *bastilles* or forts around Orleans. Some of these, such as the Bastille des Augustins, were constructed around semi-demolished churches and other buildings. The aim was not so much to prevent the passage of individuals or even of small bodies of men – these were slipping in and out of the city throughout the siege – as to prevent the arrival of large quantities of provisions. The size of the population could thus be made to work against the defenders.

In February 1429, the French were preparing a major effort to raise the siege, under the leadership of the Count of Clermont. Bedford's riposte was to raise a new army, stripping his garrisons in Normandy and elsewhere, and also (as an interim measure) to send the English forces a large convoy of foodstuffs, escorted by Sir John Fastolf and about 1,500 men. Since Lent was rapidly approaching, the victuals consisted in large part of salted herrings and other 'lenten stuff'. Near Orleans, this convoy collided with the advance guard of Clermont's relieving force. Clermont was soundly defeated in the so-called Battle of the Herrings. Not surprisingly, this had a markedly lowering effect on the morale of the besieged. Their reaction, during the second half of February, was to send an embassy to the Duke of Burgundy, led by the famous captain Poton de Xantrailles.[1] Philip the Good was delighted to be given such an opportunity to meddle. On 4 April, when he came to Paris to meet Bedford, he brought some of the envoys with him. The settlement he proposed was that the siege should be lifted, on condition that he himself, in the name of his cousin of Orleans, should put governors into the place, and that half the revenues should go to the King of England and the other half to the captive Duke of Orleans for his maintenance. In addition to this, the English should go in and out of the city as they liked, and the commune should give 10,000 *écus* a year to the regent for war expenses.[2]

Bedford, normally coolly rational, was given to occasional violent flashes of temper. He had alienated Artur de Richemont forever, by striking him in the course of a quarrel. Now he was angered by Philip the Good's attempt to bear off the spoils of an expensive enterprise which had also cost him his best general. He told the Duke that 'he in no wise intended that lands which belonged to the crown of France should fall into other hands than those of the king'.[3] And he added that he would be 'very angry to have beaten the bushes that others might take the birds'. Philip's reaction to this abrupt refusal was to withdraw all Burgundian forces from the siege.

Xantrailles had returned to Orleans on 2 April, probably to report on Burgundy's terms; now he was followed back by his colleagues, who arrived on the seventeenth, accompanied by a trumpeter belonging to the Duke of Burgundy. The latter's mission was to command all the Burgundian troops to depart, which they did 'in great haste'.[4] By this time both sides were becoming weary of the whole business. The siege was costing the English régime in France sums which it could ill afford – 40,000 *livres tournois* a month. In the first week of March, Bedford ordered all his officials, whatever their rank, to make a forced loan of a quarter of a year's salary to be used for the operations at Orleans. Those who refused would forfeit six months' pay. The regent also gave up part of his own emoluments.[5] There were increasing numbers of desertions among the besieging troops – these had begun as early as Salisbury's arrival in 1428.

The ring of forts constructed by the English was now more or less complete. In addition to the Tourelles and its protecting outwork, there were three on the south bank – reading from east to west they were Saint-Jean-le-Blanc, the Bastille des Augustins and the Fort Saint-Privé. On the north bank, again reading from east to west, were the somewhat isolated Bastille Saint-Loup, the Bastille de Fleury, Fort Paris, Fort Rouen, Fort Londres and La Croix Boissée. Just south of La Croix Boissée was the main English camp, constructed round the church of Saint-Laurent. A further *bastille*, on the Ile Charlemagne in the river just downstream from Orleans, ensured communication from the right, or north, bank, to the left or southern one. The biggest gap in the encirclement was towards the north-east – the besieged had more or less free use of the so-called Burgundy Gate and of the road that led towards Gien. It was thus, for example, that they got such rapid news of the coming of Joan of Arc. And they were able to go in and out without interference at a much later date even than this. On 28 April, for example, the very day on which Joan herself appeared on the left bank, the captain Florent d'Illiers, coming from Châteaudun, entered Orleans without opposition, accompanied by 400 men. The previous day sixty men had arrived with a herd of pigs.[6] They, too, managed to enter without a fight. It has been conjectured that the English, thanks to the long duration of the siege, had settled down too much within the elaborate fortifications they had built.

Nevertheless, it was still the besiegers who had the advantage, though it was a much narrower one than was commonly supposed. What was aiding them was the universal expectation, perhaps even more widespread among the dauphinists than it was amongst the followers of the Regent, that sooner or later the city must fall. This expectation seems to have possessed Charles VII himself, although, as his principal biographer points out, he was far more energetic in the defence of the city than tradition asserts. Not only did he make great efforts to pay his troops, but he kept in constant communication with his captains, sent his own surgeon to tend the wounded, and scoured his kingdom for artillery experts to aid the besieged.[7] Yet the prevalent anxiety was difficult to fight off. As we have seen, it had taken a grip, not only on Charles and his courtiers but on Dunois, whose appeal to the relief-expedition to make haste had about it an urgency which reflected the psychological, as much as the physical, condition of the city he had been asked to defend.

II

Joan was later to say that the relieving army consisted of 'ten to twelve thousand men'.[1] The besieging force, despite the defection of the Burgundian contingent, may now have swollen to just short of 7,000, while the size of the garrison seems to have fallen a trifle, from an initial figure of about 2,400, perhaps because Clermont had siphoned off a few of the sick and the faint-hearted when he left in February. The number of fighting men within the city was in any case constantly fluctuating, as small contingents arrived and others departed.

In Alençon's absence there seems to have been no single recognized commander, but in addition to Joan and her suite, the army contained a number of other captains. Some were amongst the most experienced soldiers that Charles possessed – they included men such as Ambroise de Loré and Louis de Culant. Also with the relieving army was the young Gilles de Rais.[2] Waiting at Orleans was the most famous captain of them all, La Hire.

La Hire and Gilles de Rais make a fascinating contrast, and Joan's association with the two of them tells us much about her own attitudes, and about her effect on those who surrounded her. Gilles's lurid reputation has attracted the greater share of attention, but in many ways La Hire seems more significant. 'La Hire' was a nickname. It derived either from the implement used for ramming down paving stones, or from the Latin *ira* (anger). The former seems more likely as the main derivation in view of the fact that La Hire had been lamed, in 1421, by the fall of the chimney-piece in the room where he slept. His lameness must have given him a characteristic stumping walk, which would easily explain the sobriquet. It would also account for his preference for fighting on horseback. If he had an air of suppressed rage, it may have been due to the need to deny his physical defect. His real name was Étienne de Vignolles, and he had been born in the Bigorre in Gascony, around 1390, and had offered the dauphin his services in 1418. None of Charles's soldiers was more feared by his enemies. The Bourgeois of Paris calls him 'the worst and most tyrannical and most pitiless of all the Armagnac captains'.[3] La Hire was a striking figure, who attracted attention wherever he showed himself. Like many soldiers of fortune, he had a taste for extravagant clothes. For example, he had a robe made for himself which was covered with little bells that tinkled at every movement.[4] This was extreme even for the fashions of the time. He was famous for the appalling blasphemies which he constantly uttered, and for the extreme lightness with which he took his religious duties.

One story will serve to illustrate the latter trait. In 1427, when La Hire was taking part in the expedition for the relief of Montargis, he decided that it would be prudent to obtain a general absolution. He sought out a chaplain and asked for it. The chaplain told him to confess his sins. La Hire replied that there was no time for this, as it was essential to attack the enemy promptly. He was prepared to confess, simply, that he had done 'all that men of war were accustomed to do'. The chaplain was forced to accept this, and gave the absolution required. His penitent thereupon prayed: 'God, I pray Thee that Thou wilt today do for La Hire as much as Thou wouldst wish La Hire to do for Thee, if he were God, and Thou wert La Hire.'[5] If La Hire spoke frankly to God, he also spoke with equal frankness to earthly superiors, such as the king. After the Battle of the Herrings, he returned to Chinon, where he found Charles trying to relieve his depression with feasts and pleasure. His comment was: 'Sire, I never saw a prince who more joyously lost what was his than you.'[6]

Yet this hard-bitten campaigner was, with Alençon, one of the first to accept Joan's mission, while others murmured at her presumption. Their relationship soon became almost intimate.

To everyone's astonishment, La Hire confessed his sins at Joan's instigation, and made an effort to moderate his language. Joan permitted him to swear by his staff or baton of command, which involved no blasphemy. It is evident, I think, that Joan's influence over La Hire was based upon a recognition of certain qualities they had in common – a reckless plain-spokenness, a belief in the exercise of common sense in military matters (Joan's faith in this was based upon innocence, La Hire's upon experience). And there was also Joan's admiration for La Hire's masculine soldierly qualities, and her identification with them despite the apparent 'evil' of his life.

There is no evidence that she felt any such personal liking for Gilles de Rais; and it can be claimed that her influence over Gilles was in the last analysis catastrophic. Gilles was to become a mass murderer of children – the original upon whom the legendary Bluebeard was based. Naturally enough, since he and Joan were not only contemporaries, but companions-in-arms, an attempt has been made to present them as equals but opposites, absolute evil face to face with absolute good. The records of Gilles's life, which include a trial-document directly comparable to that which contains the record of Joan's trial at Rouen, make it plain that this is based upon a romantic misconception.

Gilles belonged to the highest nobility. He was the grandson and heir of Jean de Craon, the most powerful vassal of the Duchy of Anjou. His upbringing, as he afterwards recognized, did not encourage him to put any restraint upon his appetites. His family connections drew him early towards the court of Charles VII. One of his close relations was La Trémoille, the favourite, and it was La Trémoille who got him made a marshal of France at the tender age of twenty-three. In April 1429, just after Joan's arrival, and before the campaign of Orleans, Gilles bound himself by a solemn oath to be La Trémoille's man. During the campaign itself, his chief function was probably to act as the favourite's representative and informant, though it is clear that La Trémoille never thought very much of him. In 1435, after his own disgrace, he laughed at the idea that he was exploiting his cousin. 'It is good to advance him in being bad', was what he said.[7]

The notion of evil exercised an early attraction over Gilles.

In 1426, before he ever met Joan, he was already trying to invoke the devil.[8] The first murders of children, however, seem to date from 1432, and therefore took place when Joan herself had already disappeared. Gilles's trial makes it clear that he was unbalanced, and that his crimes were pathological. The verdict today might well have been 'guilty but insane'.

It is curious to reflect that, if he had never met Joan, he might not have suffered for them at all. What brought Gilles down was the way in which he squandered his fortune, which was immense enough in all conscience, but still not sufficiently large to withstand the inroads which he made upon it. Georges Bataille, who is the author of the best modern study, remarks:

> The necessity to shine is in him like a delirium: he cannot resist the chance to dazzle; he finds it necessary to stupefy with an incomparable splendour.[9]

Gilles, unstable as he was, encompassed extremes of devotion and piety as well as extremes of crime. He lavished money, for example, upon his private chapel, and maintained a choir of children who travelled with him as he moved from castle to castle. Some of these children became his victims. Though he deserted Joan after her failure before Paris, Gilles's part in the relief of Orleans became, for him, one of the main emotional events of his life. The city soon began to commemorate its deliverance with the *Mystery of the Siege*, and in September 1434 Gilles arrived in Orleans to enlarge this spectacle for his own glorification. He stayed for the best part of a year, and the money he lavished on theatrical representations put his finances upon a slippery slope from which they never afterwards recovered. It was the efforts of his relatives to prevent him from wasting what they regarded as theirs as much as his; and the even more strenuous efforts made by overlords such as the Duke of Brittany to exploit this situation to their own profit, which set Gilles on the path which led him before his judges.

The case of Gilles de Rais reminds us that Joan's power lay, not merely in the effect of the actions suggested to her by her voices, but in her potential as a catalyst. That power was about to be spectacularly demonstrated.

The relieving army marched for two full days after it left Blois, sleeping each night in the fields. Its progress was impeded by the provisions it brought with it. These were loaded on to sixty carts and 435 pack animals.[10] Joan did not take her armour off to sleep, and, since she was not used to its weight, she became correspondingly exhausted.[11] Her confidence never wavered for a moment, despite her fatigue. She was, she said later, 'sure of relieving the siege of Orleans, by a revelation that had been made to her'.[12]

On Friday 29 April, news at last reached Orleans that substantial help was on its way:

The king was sending by the Sologne way victuals, powder, cannon and other equipment of war under the guidance of the Maid, who came from our Lord to revictual and comfort the town and raise the siege – by which those of Orleans were much comforted. And because it was said that the English would take pains to prevent the victuals, it was ordered that all take up arms throughout the city.[13]

Dunois went to greet the newcomers, and received no very cordial welcome from Joan herself. She was incensed to find that the army was on the wrong side of the river from the town it had come to succour. 'Was it you,' she said, 'who advised me to come here, on this side of the river, instead of going straight to where Talbot and the English are?' Both the tone and substance of the question give us some clue as to why Joan was admired, obeyed and even worshipped, more often than she was liked or trusted. Dunois replied that he and others had indeed given this advice. Joan then burst out:

In God's name, the counsel of the Lord God is wiser and surer than yours. You thought you had deceived me, but it is you who have deceived yourselves, for I am bringing you better help than you ever got from any soldier or any city. It is the help of the King of Heaven. It does not come through love of me, but from God himself who, on the petition of Saint Louis and Saint Charlemagne, has had pity on the town of Orleans, and has refused to suffer the enemy to have both the body of the lord of Orleans and his city.[14]

The context in which these rather acerbic exchanges took place was determined partly by topography, but also partly by the prevailing weather. Dunois and the other captains within Orleans had decided that the relieving force was probably not strong enough to force a passage into the city should the English attack it, encumbered as it would be by the carts and pack-animals. They had therefore concluded that the best way to get the victuals into the town was by floating them down the Loire, from a point opposite the English *bastille* of Saint-Loup, which was about a mile-and-a-half upstream from the city itself.

Unfortunately, the barges needed were at Orleans itself, the water was low in the river,[15] and the wind was contrary. Dunois had arranged for a skirmish before the *bastille* of Saint-Loup, in order to keep the besiegers busy, and this was carried through with great determination – the French even managed to capture an English standard.[16] But this effort would have been in vain if the weather had remained unfavourable. Suddenly, as Joan was berating Dunois, the wind changed direction, and the water rose in the Loire. This sudden change in the wind was afterwards said to have been miraculous. The boats were able to come into the bank on the French side,[17] were loaded with what the relieving army had brought, and returned downstream to Orleans, where the supplies were taken in without difficulty,[18] under cover of the diversion which had been arranged.

Dunois, meanwhile, wanted Joan to cross the river with him, to the village of Chécy on the opposite bank, leaving the main body of troops behind. Joan was most reluctant to do this, and the captains who had brought her were unwilling to let her go. Another argument took place. Dunois says:

I begged her to agree to cross the Loire and to enter the city of Orleans, where they were most eager for her. But here she made difficulties, saying that she was unwilling to send her soldiers away since they were all well confessed and repentant, and of good will, and therefore she was unwilling to come. I went to find the captains who were in charge of the soldiers, and begged and commanded them, for the king's sake, to agree to Joan's entering the city of Orleans while they, the captains, with their companies, went back to Blois.[19]

The reason for sending back the main force was that there was a second convoy of food to be fetched, and that, until this arrived, there would not be enough in Orleans to sustain so large a body of troops.[20]

Joan was afraid, not only that 'her' soldiers would lapse back into the evil ways from which she had converted them so short a time before, but that they would not return at all.[21] There seems to have been some justification for these fears, as when the force got back to Blois there was apparently an inclination amongst some of those who formed part of it to disperse and leave Orleans to its fate.[22]

Joan was at last persuaded that the course of action Dunois proposed was necessary, and she embarked with him to cross the river. With her went Jean d'Aulon,[23] and her page Louis de Coutes,[24] also her two brothers. Her confessor Pasquerel was, however, sent back to Blois with the main body, taking with him the priest's banner which Joan had had made.[25] His task was to make sure that there was no backsliding in Joan's absence.

Once she had crossed the river, at about 4 p.m., Joan waited. The pressure of expectation among the people was now so great that it was feared that there would be a riot if she came into the city during the hours of daylight.[26] Her entry was therefore delayed until eight at night.[27] The weather was still bad and stormy. As she rode through the city, mounted upon a white horse and armed at all points,[28] there was 'a great rain and thunder', an English chronicler tells us.[29] Her standard was borne before her, and Dunois rode on her left hand, richly armed and mounted, while a number of other captains followed in her wake.[30] She was bringing about two hundred lances with her into the town,[31] enough to make a considerable procession.

On the other hand came to receive her the other men of war, burgesses and matrons of Orleans, carrying numerous torches and making as much rejoicing as if they had seen God descend in their midst; and not without cause, for they had many cares, travails and difficulties and, worse than this, great fear lest they lose all, body and goods. But they now felt themselves already comforted and as if no longer besieged, by the divine virtue which they were told was in this simple maid, whom they all looked upon most affectionately – men, women and little children.[32]

In the excitement, one of the torchbearers pressed so close to Joan that her pennon, which she was carrying herself, caught alight. Joan acted quickly, showing her instinctive horsemanship: 'she stuck spurs in her horse, and turned him thus gently towards the pennon, and extinguished the fire as if she had long served in the wars'.[33]

When she entered Orleans, Joan's first act was to go to the cathedral, to give thanks for her safe arrival.[34] From there she was escorted to the house where she was to lodge, that of Jacques Boucher, the treasurer of the Duke of Orleans.[35] This was near the Porte Regnart, and from it she would have a panoramic view of the siege.[36] She had herself disarmed, and took the Eucharist.[37] She then attended an entertainment which had been prepared in her honour. Her hosts were struck by the moderation with which she ate and drank, though she had taken nothing throughout the day: 'She merely put wine in a silver cup, and the same quantity of water, and five or six sops [bits of toasted bread] within it, which she ate'.[38] After this frugal repast, she went to the room which had been allotted to her, and composed herself for sleep.

12

Having at last arrived in Orleans, Joan's instinct was to attack at once, without even waiting for the troops to return from Blois. She went to see Dunois, to press this upon him and returned to her lodgings very angry because he refused her.[1] The furthest Dunois would go was to order a skirmish, in which La Hire, Florent d'Illiers and other experienced captains took part. Joan did not participate in this, and, like most of the other skirmishes mounted from Orleans in the weary course of the siege, it was vigorous but unsuccessful.[2]

Dunois's preoccupation, at this moment, was with the troops who should now be getting ready to return to Orleans.[3] Joan, on the other hand, busied herself with exhorting the people, as she had exhorted the troops of the relieving force.[4] She was also worried about the fate of one of the two heralds whom she had sent to bear her letter of summons to the English. These had duly made their way to the English headquarters at Saint-Laurent, but the English refused to treat them according to the commonly accepted laws of war. They kept back the one called Guyenne, and sent the other with a message for Joan:

Ambleville reported that the English kept Guyenne in order to burn him. Then Joan replied to Ambleville, assuring him that in God's name they would do his companion no harm, and bidding him to go boldly back to the English, for no harm would befall him either, and he would bring back his companion safe and sound.[5]

Her second message was bold indeed, considering that she had been told by Ambleville that the English said that if they caught her they would burn her too. 'Say to Talbot,' Joan replied, 'that if he arms himself, I will arm myself also, so let him come before the city; and if he takes me, let him burn me, and if I discomfit him, then let them raise the siege and go back to their own country'.[6]

Even at this very early stage, the English were possessed with the idea that Joan was a witch. Their threat to Guyenne was not an idle one. They were quite prepared to execute him as a surrogate for Joan, and even sent to the University of Paris for an opinion, while they prepared the stake within their camp.[7] They were for the time being dissuaded from carrying out what they intended by Dunois's counter-measure. He seized the English heralds who were then in Orleans to treat for prisoners, and threatened to kill these, and the English captives also, if either Guyenne or Ambleville were to be harmed.[8] But even this, apparently, was not enough to secure Guyenne's release, though several sources allege that it took place. When the English retreated from the siege, the unfortunate herald was discovered in their camp, safe, but still in irons.[9]

In the evening, still dissatisfied because the English refused to take her summons seriously, she decided that she would cite them herself. For this purpose, she went out on to the bridge. The French had built a bulwark near the end of the broken span, at a place where a cross was erected. Called the Belle-Croix bulwark, it was as near as the besieged could get to their opponents, while still remaining within the safety of their own fortifications. Louis de Coutes probably accompanied her, and it is he who gives the vividest account of what happened:

She addressed the English opposite, requesting them in God's name to retire, otherwise she would drive them away. And one called the Bastard of Granville answered Joan most abusively, asking whether she expected them to surrender to a woman, and calling the French who were with Joan 'unbelieving pimps'.[10]

Other sources say that the English commander in the Tourelles, Sir William Glasdale, joined in the chorus of abuse. The English garrison called Joan a cow-girl, and repeated the threat that they would have her burned.[11] Joan's hot temper rose at this, and Glasdale seems to have enraged her in particular. She retorted that he was a liar and would die without being shriven.[12]

Afterwards, in order to compose herself, she went to the church of Sainte-Croix, where she found a priest who reassured her that those within the city believed in her mission, even if those without it abused her.[13] Indeed, Dunois himself remarks on the rapid rise in morale after her arrival. 'I swear,' he says, 'that the English, two hundred of whom had previously been sufficient to rout eight hundred or a thousand of the royal army, from that moment became so powerless that four or five hundred soldiers and men-at-arms could fight against what seemed to be the whole force of England.'[14]

The next day, Sunday, 1 May, a conference was held, to which Joan was invited. It was decided that Dunois and a number of the other captains should go towards Blois to escort the returning army. Jean d'Aulon was to be one of the men who accompanied Dunois, but Joan would remain behind in Orleans.[15] There was great eagerness amongst the people to see her – we are told that 'they almost broke down the door of the mansion in which she was lodged', and also that she had great difficulty in passing through the streets:

For people could not weary of seeing her, and it seemed to all a great marvel that she could sit on her horse with such ease and grace. And in truth she bore herself as highly in all ways as a man-at-arms who had followed the wars from his youth.[16]

She also made another attempt to parley with the English, telling them that if they surrendered their lives would be safe, but those only, and saying that in the name of God they should return to England. This approach proved as ineffective as the previous one had been, and those whom she addressed spoke to her as roughly as the garrison of the Tourelles had done the night before.[17]

On the following Monday, Joan made a reconnaissance of the English positions. She was mounted, but the citizens of Orleans followed her on foot in great numbers. Despite the apparent vulnerability of this citizen-rabble, the besiegers did not attack either Joan or her followers, and she examined their positions at her leisure.[18] The inertia of her opponents indicated how far the psychological balance had shifted, even though no serious combat had yet been fought. On the Tuesday, garrisons from a number of other towns came to join the forces in Orleans.[19] It was an indication that Charles VII was at last willing to stake everything on a single throw. The convoy from Blois, escorted by Dunois, did not make its appearance until the morning of 4 May. Joan, accompanied by La Hire, Florent d'Illiers and a number of other captains, plus about five hundred men, sallied out into the fields to meet it,[20] and to act as a flank guard.[21] On this occasion the leaders had decided to risk coming towards Orleans on the northern, or Beauce, side of the Loire, despite the fact that they were now encumbered with a great number of beasts – cattle, pigs and sheep.[22] Indeed the quantity of live-stock may have made transportation by water impracticable. They were also burdened, at least from the military point of view, with the company of priests and their banner. Among the priests was Pasquerel, and it is he who describes how they all came into Orleans:

> The astonishing thing is that the English, with all their great de-ployment of forces, armed and ready for battle, saw the king's men, so small a company compared with them; they saw them, they heard the priests singing – I was in the middle of them carrying the banner – and nevertheless not an Englishman stirred, and they made no attack on the soldiers and the priests.[23]

Soon after he arrived, Joan had another conference with Dunois. He came to her lodging, and gave her news that the English, too, were sending reinforcements and fresh supplies, under the leadership of Fastolf, the victor of the Battle of the Herrings. According to his information, they had already reached Janville in the Beauce. Joan was excited by this in-formation, but her reaction shows that her strategic ideas were still hazy, and that she had little notion of what the development implied. 'Bastard, Bastard,' she said to Dunois, 'in the name of God I command you to let me know as soon as you hear of Fastolf's coming. For if he gets through without my knowing it, I swear to you that I will have your head cut off.' Dunois replied drily that he did not doubt it, and they parted. Joan and Aulon, who was with her, composed themselves for a siesta[24] in separate chambers of Jacques Boucher's house.

Simultaneously, the inhabitants of Orleans, now worked up to fever pitch by the excitement of Joan's presence and by the events of the last few days, had gone to the town hall to demand equipment, such as culverins and scaling ladders.[25] As soon as they got them, they sallied out against the isolated *bastille* of Saint-Loup, convinced that they were invulnerable.[26]

Joan was aroused by the first sounds of combat. She sprang out of bed, and began to shout for Aulon and for Louis de Coutes. Fogged with sleep, she was at first uncertain what the situation was. She imagined for a moment that Fastolf had already arrived. Her quick temper fell on the page. 'Oh, bloody boy!' she cried, 'Why did you not tell me that French blood is being shed?' And she packed him off to fetch her horse. Meanwhile, she was having herself armed by her hostess and her hostess's daughter,[27] who were helped by Jean d'Aulon. As they fumbled with the buckles and straps, they heard loud voices through the window, as people in the street said that the French were getting the worst of it.[28] Aulon began to hurry to put on his own armour. Joan rushed downstairs, and here she found Louis de Coutes astride her horse, which he had harnessed. Immediately she made him dismount, and sent him up to fetch her standard from her room. He handed it to her out of the window,[29] and she galloped off towards the Burgundy gate, her horse striking sparks from the cobbles.[30] Aulon mounted and followed her, and Louis de Coutes ran after them.

Aulon caught up with Joan as she reached the gate itself, and here they found the first casualties coming in. Joan saw one severely wounded man who was being carried by his comrades, and asked who he was. She was told that he was a Frenchman. She had a movement of horror. 'I can never see French blood,' she said, 'without my hair standing on end.'[31] Then she and her party pressed on towards where the fighting was taking place. Joan was not the only person who had been aroused by the tumult. Dunois and other captains, followed by their companies, were also armed and riding towards Saint-Loup. The English near by also tried to sally forth to help their comrades, but this movement was observed from Orleans, and, as a warning bell sounded, a second company of Frenchmen issued out of the town, to head off these would-be rescuers.[32]

Saint-Loup did not have a large garrison – perhaps just over 150 men in all – but nevertheless it put up a fierce resistance, and the combat lasted for about three hours.[33] English morale might have sunk, but it had not yet reached its nadir. The little garrison's will to fight was stiffened by the fact that, when Joan arrived and planted her standard on the edge of the ditch, they asked to be received for ransom, and she refused, saying that she would take them in spite of themselves.[34] The *bastille* was built around an abandoned church, and it was into the belfry of this that the survivors retreated, when they had to fall back from their outer defences under the weight of French numbers – Aulon says that when he and Joan first emerged from the Burgundy gate he thought that he had never seen so many men-at-arms of his party as he saw then.[35]

At last, despairing of making any further defence, the remaining English, who by this time numbered about forty, put on the church vestments which had been left in the building when the monks abandoned it, and came out to sue for their lives.[36] This seems to have caused a flicker of astonishment, though the French cannot really have believed that there were any clergy left in the *bastille*. For a moment, however, they may have thought that their eyes were deceiving them.[37] Heated as they were by battle, the victors' immediate impulse was to massacre these masqueraders, but Joan stopped them from doing so, saying ironically that one should not question the bona fides of the men of the Church[38] – perhaps, at this moment of triumph, her mind was straying back to the way she had been examined in Poitiers, and the answers she had made then? At her orders, the prisoners were taken to Orleans.

When she herself got back to the city, the emotional reaction to this first experience of battle set in. It was the Vigil of the Ascension, a particularly solemn feast, and Joan was troubled by the thought of the English who had died unshriven. She wept bitterly when she told Pasquerel of this, and afterwards made her own confession to him. She also told him to urge all the soldiers on her own side to confess their sins and give thanks to God. He was to tell them that if they did not do so, Joan would stay with them no longer. Yet, despite this momentary depression, she remained full of optimism about the outcome of the siege, and predicted to Pasquerel that within five days it would be completely lifted, and that there would be no Englishmen left in front of Orleans.[39]

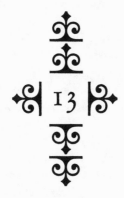

✠ 13 ✠

Thursday, 5 May was Ascension Day, and, because of the solemnity of the feast, it was decided by the French that they would not fight – a decision which Joan accepted, and which her confessor says she initiated.[1] In any case, Dunois and the other captains probably felt that they needed a breathing space in which to plan what they were going to do.

A council was held in the house of the treasurer of Orleans,[2] perhaps in the room which had a wall-painting showing the figures of Justice, Peace and Union in the guise of three women.[3] All the leading captains were present, as well as some of the chief citizens of the town.[4] It was decided that siege apparatus should be prepared, and that a powerful feint attack should be mounted on the Beauce side, against the principal English positions.[5] The true objective, however, was across the Loire – the Tourelles and the earthwork protecting it.[6]

Despite the fact that she was present under the same roof, Joan was not invited to take part in this deliberation. The exclusion, though perhaps consciously attributed by those present to lack of trust in Joan's discretion, at a preconscious level seems to reflect the unease she inspired even in the ranks of her supporters, at least among the men. On this occasion, when a plan had been decided, it was thought that she ought at least to be told about it. Some of those present protested that it was unnecessary to inform her where the main attack was to fall, and it was agreed to tell her of the diversion and to say it would be the main thrust. One of the most experienced captains, Ambroise de Loré, was then sent to fetch her.[7]

When she arrived, Joan was not deceived by the limited explanation which was offered to her. She said: 'Say what you have decided and appointed. I would keep secret much greater things than that.' Without even seating herself, she left the room in a huff. Dunois had to go running after her to bring her back. 'Joan, do not be angry,' he said. 'We cannot tell you everything at once.' He then told her what the true plan was, and Joan was gracious enough to say that she was content with it, although, as the chronicler who tells us this points out, it was never in fact put into effect.[8] Joan's relationships with the professional soldiers who were defending Orleans were never as smooth as her relationship with the mass of the civilian population. Dunois tells us that he 'began to have good hope' of Joan immediately after their first meeting, and the abrupt change of wind that followed it.[9] But other captains resented, not only her sex, but the fact that she was of low origin. One knight, Jean de Gamaches, brought this resentment into the open when he protested that it was wrong to take the advice 'of a girl of no quality, rather than that of a knight such as I am', and saying that he preferred to have a nobleman for master than a woman who was no one knew what.[10] Joan did not make matters any easier because she was full of the spirit of contradiction:

And very often did [Dunois] and the other captains come together to decide what to do; and whatever conclusion they came to, when Joan the Maid arrived, she concluded the contrary.[11]

The fact that her enterprises were so often successful did nothing to sweeten the situation.

Later historians have sometimes tried to make out that Joan was a champion of the people, the representative of the spirit of her class, especially as it opposed itself to other classes in the social structure. And indeed we often find, in her fierce retorts, a reflection of what 'everyone' was thinking. On a somewhat higher plane, her idealization of the monarchy, as a semi-divine institution, did correspond to something which lay deep in the hearts of the peasantry from which she sprang. Her real inpulse, however, was to identify herself with the chivalric and

1. Domrémy – Joan's birthplace

2. The castle of Mehun-sur-Yèvre where Charles VII was proclaimed king

3. Ste Cathérine-de-Fierbois – the chapel

4. Ste Cathérine-de-Fierbois – the Aumônerie de Bouccicaut where Joan lodged

5. The castle and town of Chinon

6. The Tour du Coudrai, Chinon

7. Ruins of the great hall of the Royal Lodging at Chinon

8. The keep at Beaugency with the abbey on the left

9. The battlefield of Patay with the remains of the hedges

10. The Royal Lodging, Loches

11.   The street in Selles where Joan lodged, with the west front of Saint-Eusice

12. Medieval street in the 'new town', Troyes

13. Rheims Cathedral, with the modern statue of Joan of Arc

14. The castle of Montépilloy

15. The church of Saint-Pierre-le-Moûtier

16. Statue of St Michael, Saint-Pierre-le-Moûtier

17. La Charité from across the Loire

18. Sully – the castle of Georges de La Trémoille

19. Crépy-en-Valois – the monastery ruins on the bluff

20. Beaulieu-les-Fontaines. According to tradition, Joan was imprisoned in the tower on the right

21. All that remains of the castle of Beaurevoir

22. The donjon of Rouen castle

23.   The churchyard of Saint-Ouen

martial world. She would much rather have had the good opinion of an Alençon, or even of a La Hire, than that of the citizens of Orleans who idolized her. This was one reason why the refusal of the English to treat her summons seriously, and their mistreatment of her heralds, wounded her so deeply. The major issue was, of course, their refusal to recognize the divine origin of her mission; but the minor one was the fact that, in her case, they felt free to flout chivalric custom, thus denying her a place in the part of society with which she now identified herself.

The matter of the heralds nagged at her like an aching tooth. On 5 May she made one last effort to obtain Guyenne's freedom, which was at the same time an effort to get her basic message across. She wrote a third letter of summons (the second had been entrusted to Ambleville when he went to demand Guyenne's release), and had it attached to an arrow, which an archer fired into the English positions, while Joan cried: 'Read, here is news!' In a postscript to her missive she said:

I would have sent you my letter in due form, but you detain my heralds, and continue to hold my herald Guyenne. Be good enough to send him back to me, and I will send you some of the men captured in the *bastille* of Saint-Loup, for not all of them were killed.[12]

The English received this approach with the same derision as they had all her others. As soon as they read what she had to say they began to shout with the full power of their lungs: 'Here's news from the Armagnac whore!' Joan burst into tears, but was soon comforted by a message from her voices. It prompted her to order Jean Pasquerel, who is our authority for this episode, to get her up especially early the following day, so that she could make her confession to him before she went into battle.[13]

In spite of what had been previously agreed at the council of war, the French made no sortie on the Beauce side on 6 May. Nor did they move directly against the Tourelles. Instead they sallied out at a relatively late hour – 9 a.m.[14] – crossed the Loire at a point just upstream from the city, and attacked the *bastille* called Saint-Jean-Le-Blanc. The crossing had to be made in two stages – first to an island which lay close against the southern bank, and thence by a bridge made of two boats,[15] which brought

111

the attackers almost directly to their objective. The French attack was made in considerable force. Joan was accompanied by Dunois, La Hire, Gilles de Rais, Florent d'Illiers and several other captains, plus, we are told, 'about 4,000 men'.[16] As usual, this figure is probably an exaggeration. Nevertheless, the French were sufficiently numerous for there to be some difficulty in getting them all across. A large part of the force was still piled up on the island when Joan and the advance-guard were already on the south bank. She, with her usual impatience, did not wait for the rest, but marched directly towards the goal.[17]

The French were using a sledge-hammer to crack a nut. Saint-Jean-Le-Blanc was a mere observation post. It had been finished only around 20 April, and seems to have been insufficiently garrisoned because of the withdrawal of the Burgundians from the siege. Warned by the fate which had befallen Saint-Loup, the English withdrew from it, and retreated into the much stronger Bastille des Augustins, which stood further downstream, just at the foot of the bridge. When Joan arrived, accompanied by the few who had been able to keep up with her, and planted her standard on the rampart, she found the *bastille* completely deserted.[18] The French now hesitated for a moment, thinking that the Augustins was too strong for them to attack, at least while their forces were still divided.[19] But the English, seeing this division, sallied out from the Augustins itself, and also probably from Saint-Privé, the *bastille* still further downstream.[20] The men with Joan had a moment of panic as they heard the loud cries of their assailants, who had advanced to a distance of 'two crossbow shots'[21] from the Augustins – that is to say, nearly as far as Saint-Jean-Le-Blanc itself. Much against her will, Joan was forced to join the retreat. The moment of failure rankled, even after it had been redeemed by much greater successes. When, at Rouen, she was asked: 'What *bastille* were you at when you told your men to retire?' she refused to remember its name.[22]

Joan and La Hire, who had regained the island where the rest of the French were stationed, now managed, by launching a boat from the side which faced towards Orleans, to get a couple of horses across to the south bank. They swiftly mounted, couched their lances, and attacked the advancing enemy[23] as Joan cried to those who surrounded her: 'Go forward boldly in the name of God!'[24] Taken aback by this sudden spurt of aggression on the part of an enemy they believed demoralized, the English, who had been shouting every insult they could think of at Joan, lost heart and turned back towards safety. Not content to leave matters thus, she and her companions pressed hard on their heels. Joan, who was accompanied by Gilles de Rais, came right up to the Bastille des Augustins, and planted her standard in the ditch.[25] It may have been while she was doing so that she was wounded by a caltrop in the foot.[26] Caltrops were spiked balls so designed that, however they rested on the ground, one spike was always pointing upwards. They were commonly scattered in the ditches in front of a fortification, in order to discourage would-be attackers.

The French on the island had a grandstand view of these proceedings. It is Jean d'Aulon who tells us what happened next. Essentially it was an affair of chivalric rivalry. He, Gaucourt and another captain had been put in charge of the rearguard, and with them was a Spanish mercenary called Alfonso de Pastada. One of the members of the company, 'a handsome man, tall and well-armed', moved as if to go forward and join the fighting. Aulon asked him to stay, and met with a blunt refusal. Pastada then joined the argument, saying to the man who wanted to leave that 'he could remain behind just as well as the others, as there were men just as brave as he in the rearguard'. The dispute grew heated, and haughty words were exchanged. The upshot was that they agreed to go against the enemy together 'to prove which of them was the braver and which performed his duty best'.[27] Pastada and his rival, who rushed towards the enemy at top speed 'hand in hand', were immediately followed by the rest of the rearguard who, by now too impatient to bother with the pontoon bridge, plunged into the Loire up to the armpits in order to get across.[28] Aulon moved towards the Augustins with the rest. When he got there, he saw that Pastada and his companion were in trouble:

I saw inside the palisade of the [Bastille des Augustins] a big, strong and powerful Englishman, well equipped and armed, who was putting up such a resistance that they could not break through the fence.[29]

Fortunately Aulon happened to have with him Jean de Lorraine, a famous culverineer who had already wrought prodigies in the defence of Orleans before Joan's arrival. He pointed to this conspicuous defender, and asked the marksman to pick him off. Jean de Lorraine obliged, and the two rival men-at-arms at once made their entry into the fortress, followed by the rest of the French. The Augustins was stormed, most of its defenders were killed, others were captured and the remainder made their escape to the Tourelles.[30]

The French found great numbers of prisoners within the Augustins,[31] and they also found much food and other stuff, which they set about plundering. Joan was worried when she saw the lack of discipline amongst the looters – the Tourelles, still full of English troops, was after all exceedingly close by – and, in order to put a stop to what was going on, she ordered the *bastille* to be set on fire.[32] By this time it was evening. Many of the combatants thought it would be best to camp for the night beside the captured fortress, so as to keep a watch on the still unconquered Tourelles and the activity within it. The other captains, seeing that Joan was exhausted, and knowing that she had been wounded, decided that she ought to go back within the walls. Joan protested at this, saying: 'Shall we leave our men?'[33] On this occasion she was overruled, and she crossed the river once more, leaving others to keep the watch.[34]

She was so tired when she got to Jacques Boucher's house that she was prevailed upon to break her fast, although it was a Friday.[35] While she dined, another council of war was being held. When it was over, one of the participants came to tell her what had been decided. He said that they were keenly aware that they were still inferior in numbers to the English, and that 'they knew it had been by God's especial grace that they had won the successes they had had' – a polite way of informing her that her impetuous conduct had created situations which might easily have ended in disaster rather than in triumph. He continued: 'Seeing that the town is well stocked with provisions, we shall be very likely to hold it until the king sends aid; and the council therefore do not think it necessary for the soldiers to go forth tomorrow.' Joan flared up at this, as she was bound to do. 'You have been to your council, and I to mine,' she said. 'And believe me, the counsel of my Lord will be put into effect, while your counsel will perish.' Then, turning to Pasquerel, who

114

was beside her, she said: 'Get up early tomorrow, even earlier than you did today, and do your very best. Keep close to me at all times. For tomorrow the blood will spurt from my body above the breast.'[36] She did not yet know that it had even been decided to guard the gates, in order to prevent the soldiers from going out to join the citizens in an assault upon the Tourelles.[37]

Quite how the council of war expected to enforce their wishes is not certain. Orleans was in a ferment after the events of the day. The town crier went round the streets, to ask the citizens to bring food for those who were encamped outside the town, laying siege to the Tourelles, and saying, too, that 'everyone should look after the pages and horses of the men-at-arms who were outside'.[38] There was, in fact, a constant bustle throughout the night as the Orléannais brought food and wine to refresh their fellow-citizens and the soldiers who had remained with them.[39] Those who watched beside the ruined Augustins, and those, too, who watched from the walls, must have been greatly encouraged to see the *bastille* of Saint-Privé suddenly burst into flames, though no attack had been made on it. Warned by the fate of Saint-Loup and Saint-Jean-Le-Blanc, which were similarly isolated outposts, the English had decided to abandon it, and had set it alight as they left.[40] Since the Tourelles was now blockaded, the garrison of Saint-Privé had to cross the Loire, to the main English camp at Saint-Laurent, in order to find safety. In their haste to be gone they were clumsy, and one at least of the boats they were using overturned, drowning a number of men who were pulled down by the weight of their armour. The Orléannais seem to have been unaware of this accident until some considerable time later, when they found in the river the harness of those who had died.[41]

14

The next morning, Pasquerel got up very early and sang mass as Joan had requested.[1] She then made ready to leave the house. As she did so, a delegation of citizens arrived, to tell her that the men of Orleans were opposed to the captains' decision not to fight that day. They formally requested her to 'accomplish the task given by God and also by the king'.[2] Joan answered as she was mounting her horse: 'In God's name, I will do it, and he who loves me will follow me.'[3] Someone presented her with a freshly caught fish, an *alose* or shad. 'Keep it till tonight,' said Joan, 'for I will bring you a *godon* this evening, and come back over the bridge.'[4] (*Godon* was the nickname which the French had long ago coined for the English soldiers. It was a corruption of 'God damn me!', the favourite English oath.)

When Joan left, she went to the Burgundy gate, meaning to cross the river and join those who were already blockading the Tourelles.[5] She had been anxious all night about the fate of those who had remained outside the walls,[6] and was in haste to discover what had become of them. She arrived at the gate, and found that orders had been given that the soldiers were not to pass. Gaucourt was there to see that these were enforced. Joan flew into a towering rage, perhaps the most impressive display she had yet given of the force of her will and the violence of her temper. She told Gaucourt forthrightly that he was 'a bad man', and added: 'Whether you wish it or not, the fighting men will come, and will obtain what they have elsewhere obtained'.[7]

As she passed through the streets, she had evidently accumulated a large retinue – though it was scarcely dawn, the whole city was astir, and had been so all night. Gaucourt found himself in some danger of being torn to pieces, and was forced to give way.[8] In any case, the effort to break the siege had now acquired a momentum of its own. Not only had arrangements been made to supply food and wine to those encamped outside the Tourelles, but cannons and culverins belonging to the town were being brought across the Loire to batter the fortress on the side away from Orleans.[9] On the bridge itself preparations were being made for an assault from that direction, and materials assembled to enable the attackers to cross the broken arches[10] – after the men of Orleans broke one of these down at the start of the siege, the English had destroyed another two.

Joan arrived outside the Tourelles with her followers sometime around 6 a.m.,[11] when it was just getting light.[12] She immediately convened a council of war (the first time, incidentally, that such a gathering seems to have been called on her own initiative), and they discussed what should be done. The correct tactics were in fact obvious. Before they could take the Tourelles, they must storm the earthwork on the south bank that protected it.[13] Though this had been destroyed at the beginning of the siege, when the French evacuated it, it had since been rebuilt by the English. At seven, the trumpets sounded for a general assault, and Joan went to plant her standard on the edge of the ditch.[14] The English put up a fierce resistance. 'It seemed,' says one of the chronicles, 'as if they thought they were immortal.'[15] As soon as scaling-ladders were in place, they tumbled their assailants down, firing on them with cannon and other firearms, attacking them with axes, lances, guisarmes, lead slingshots, and even with their bare hands.[16] Another source tells us that so much 'artificial fire' was used that the air seemed all aflame.[17] It seems as if several assaults must have been tried in the course of the morning, and all failed. Immediately after the midday meal, the French attacked again, and it was on this occasion that Joan was wounded.[18] She was raising a scaling-ladder against the earthwork, in the forefront of the attack, and she was hit by a crossbow bolt in the neck.[19] It was a nasty, but not a disabling wound, The bolt went into her neck just above the breast, and pierced her shoulder.[20]

Before she came to Orleans, Joan had predicted that she would be wounded in this way. She told her judges, when they inquired about it, that she had had it revealed to her by St Catherine and St Margaret, and that she had 'told her king about it'.[21] Evidently, he was not the only one she told, as the prophecy is recorded in a letter written from Lyons on 22 April 1429 – that is to say, before Joan had even arrived at the siege, and more than a fortnight before the attack on the Tourelles.[22] It is perhaps the best attested example of Joan's prophetic gifts; and it is not something for which we can provide a rational explanation. Though she was expecting the wound, the reality came as a shock. Pasquerel tells us that 'she was afraid and wept, and then was consoled, as she said'.[23] The consolation may have been the fact that her prediction had been so exactly fulfilled. One chronicle actually asserts that she was 'more joyful than troubled', and that, after removing the bolt herself, she remarked: 'Now the English have no further power; this wound is the sign of their confusion and misfortune, a sign God has revealed to me, and that I have not made known till now.'[24] But this sounds like an edifying improvement on what happened, made at some distance from the event.

Pasquerel also says that some soldiers who were near by came to her, when they saw that she was hurt, and offered to put a charm upon the wound. Joan would have nothing to do with such superstitions.

She refused it, saying: 'I would rather die than do what I know to be a sin, or to be against God's law.' She said that she knew that she must die one day, but did not know when, where, nor at what hour; but that if a salve could be put on her wound without sin, she would willingly be cured. And they put olive oil and pig's grease on it, and afterwards she confessed to me, with tears and lamentations.[25]

After being treated, the wound was bound up with cotton, to staunch the blood.[26]

The French continued to attack until it was nearly evening, but still without making any headway. It seemed to Dunois, by this time, that 'there was hardly any hope of victory that day'. He continues:

Therefore I was going to break off, and intended the army to retire into the city. Then the Maid came up to me and requested me to wait a little longer. Thereupon she mounted her horse and went off alone into a vineyard at some distance from the crowd of men, and in that vineyard she remained at prayer for the space of eight minutes.[27]

Aulon tells us that, notwithstanding Joan's request for a delay, the trumpet was now actually sounding the retreat. Her standard was in the hands of a standard-bearer, who had taken charge of it after she was wounded. This standard-bearer, being weary, handed it over to a Basque soldier whom Aulon knew:

And since I knew this Basque to be a brave man, and because I was certain that nothing but harm could come from the retreat, and that the *bastille* and the earthwork would remain in enemy hands, it occurred to me that if the standard was taken forward, the soldiers' courage being as great as I knew it to be, those who were with us might still take the earthwork that night. Then I asked the Basque whether, if I were to turn and run towards the earthwork, he would follow me, and he promised to do so. So I leapt into the ditch, and came under the wall of the earthwork, covering myself with my shield for fear of stones, and leaving my companion on the other side in the certainty that he would follow me. But when the Maid saw her standard in the hands of the Basque, she was afraid that she had lost it. For he was by now in the ditch. She then seized her standard by the pole so firmly that he could not hold it, crying: 'Ha, my standard! my standard!' And she shook the standard so vigorously that I imagined others might suppose she was making a sign to them. So I shouted: 'Ha, Basque, is this what you promised me?' Then the Basque tugged at the standard so hard that he tore it from the Maid's hands, and came on towards me. Whereupon all the Maid's army rushed together and immediately rallied.[28]

Aulon's persistence and quick wits served him better than perhaps he was aware. Joan had made some of those present a promise that 'when they saw the wind blowing her standard in the direction of the fortress, then they would capture it'.[29] Louis de Coutes heard her say so. As she shook the pole, having seized it from the grasp of the Basque, it must have seemed that the moment had come. The wind that blew was a sudden gust of enthusiasm which was to carry them over the wall.

When it was seen from the city that the assault on the earthwork had been renewed, it was decided to try an attack across the bridge.[30] Eventually a long wooden gutter was found, just three feet short of the length which was needed, and a carpenter added another piece of wood, pegging it to the gutter, and then going beneath, as it was pushed into position, to put on a stay. Over this precarious catwalk the attackers passed 'which many people said afterwards was our Lord's greatest miracle, seeing that the gutter was marvellously long and narrow, and high in the air, without having any support'.[31]

In addition to attacking the Tourelles from the town side, the citizens of Orleans were attempting to cut it off from the earth-work the main force was still trying to storm. As Joan, on the verge of triumph, shouted: 'Glasdale! Glasdale! Yield! Yield to the King of Heaven! You have called me whore, but I have great pity on your soul and your men's souls!',[32] a large boat 'full of faggots, horse-bones, shoes, sulphur, and all the most stinking things one could find' was being run under the wooden bridge which joined the Tourelles to the bank. Once in position, it was set on fire.[33] The crackle of the flames as they licked the bridge was perhaps the thing that tipped the scales. The English, having resisted magnificently throughout the day, suddenly broke. The French swarmed in. 'Never,' says a chronicler, 'was seen a flock of birds lighting upon a hedgerow as thick as were these climbing up the said earthwork.'[34]

Glasdale and about thirty of his best men formed a rearguard as the force within the earthwork made for the limited safety of the Tourelles.[35] By the time they tried to cross the drawbridge themselves the fire had taken hold, and it collapsed beneath them. Glasdale was drowned, thus fulfilling Joan's prophecy that he would die unshriven, and so were a number of others with him.[36] 'This,' comments the *Journal of the Siege*, 'was a great blow to English morale, and a great pity for the valiant French, who could have got much money from their ransoms.'[37] In fact, the mortality amongst the leaders seems to have been particularly heavy, though about two hundred prisoners were taken.[38] The English garrison, at most, had numbered six hundred men – a figure which includes those who had made their escape from the Augustins the day before. French casualties were light. Joan later estimated that 'a hundred and more were wounded'.[39] In the last assault, says another source, 'not more than sixteen to twenty people died'.[40]

Curiously enough, there is some disagreement among the

sources as to what happened when the fight was over. Some tell us that Joan, instead of crossing over the bridge as she had promised, remained on the Sologne side of the river that night, not only 'because the bridges were broken',[41] but partly to guard the Tourelles thus valiantly conquered, partly to discover if the English from Saint-Laurent would come out.[42] Dunois, who ought to know, tells us the contrary. He says:

I returned, together with the Maid and the rest of the French, to the city of Orleans, where we were received with great transports of joy and thanksgiving. And Joan was taken to her lodging so that her wound could be dressed. Once the surgeon had done his work, she had her supper, eating four or five toasts soaked in wine heavily watered, and she had taken no other food or drink all that day.[43]

Evidently the shad she had been given in the morning was eaten by somebody else.

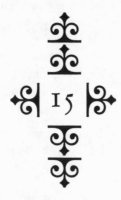

The main body of the English army on the north bank of the Loire played what may seem to be a surprisingly passive part during the events of 6 and 7 May. Whatever the reasons, Glasdale's little garrison was allowed to fight unaided until it was overwhelmed.

That night, as the bells rang in Orleans, the English held a council of war.[1] The next morning, which was Sunday, they emerged from the main camp and from the other *bastilles* before sunrise,[2] and ranged themselves for battle.[3] With them they brought everything they could carry, and a certain number of prisoners (the more valuable ones, who would be worth substantial ransoms). But other prisoners were left behind in their camp, and so were cannon, powder, siege-equipment, carts and food.[4] The English also abandoned a number of their own sick,[5] for their army was for the most part on foot.[6]

When Joan was told what was happening, she rose from her bed, and put on a *jessaran*, or light coat of mail.[7] Because of her wound, she could not wear her heavy armour, though she was able to sit a horse. She came out of the city accompanied by a number of the most notable captains and their men-at-arms. The French, however, could not marshal all their forces on this occasion, as quite a number were still encamped on the other side of the Loire, around the captured Tourelles.[8] Though the broken bridge had been mended with remarkable rapidity, so as to allow small numbers to pass over it,[9] obviously it would not have been possible to transfer a substantial body of fighting men at great speed from one side of the river to the other. So on this occasion the English forces may even have slightly outnumbered the French who came to confront them. One source estimates that the English army, on the day of its departure, and after the losses which it had recently suffered through the recall of the Burgundians, through desertions, and through the fall of various *bastilles*, still numbered about 4,000 men.[10] This was inadequate for besieging a city the size of Orleans, but was still a formidable force. For almost an hour there was a tense confrontation between the two armies.[11] The English may genuinely have been hoping that the French would move against them, and that a decisive battle would take place.[12] Since they fought dismounted, relying on their longbowmen to decimate an advancing enemy, they preferred to challenge an attacker by taking up a fixed position, rather than to attack an army which awaited their onslaught. Agincourt had been a textbook example of this particular tactic.

Excited by their successes on the previous day, the French on this occasion might easily have accepted the challenge, probably with disastrous consequences. Their leaders had some difficulty in holding them back.[13] Joan, though hot-headed, did not lack common sense, and on this occasion she was in favour of restraint. Her reasons were religious as well as practical. She did not want to fight on a Sunday, unless the English themselves were the first to make an assault.[14] Her method of ensuring that her commands were obeyed shows what a shrewd instinctive psychologist she could be. She commanded some of the clergymen of Orleans to put on their vestments and come into the fields with the troops, and here they 'sang with great solemnity hymns, responses and devout orisons, giving praise and thanks to God'.[15] A portable altar was brought, and two masses were said. Once this had been done, Joan asked: 'Now, look and see if they have their faces towards you, or their backs?' She was told that the enemy were retreating, and said: 'Let them go. It is not Messire's [God's] pleasure that they should be fought today. You will have them another time.'[16]

The fact that Joan had prohibited the troops from fighting a set battle did not prevent La Hire and others, to the number of about 100 to 120 lances, from harrying the rear of the English column, as it marched away downriver towards Meung-sur-Loire, with banners flying.[17] This force of skirmishers followed the English for about three leagues, before giving up the pursuit.[18] They succeeded in capturing most of the cannon and siege engines which their opponents had tried to take with them.[19] Meanwhile the common people of Orleans came out of the city, to plunder what the English had left in the *bastilles* they had abandoned. At the command of the captains, the *bastilles* themselves were destroyed.[20]

As La Hire continued to harry the departing English, Joan and the rest of the garrison re-entered Orleans in triumph. There was a solemn procession and sermon, and people began to think of what was to happen next.[21] Some of the captains were already keenly anxious to get away. Florent d'Illiers, for example, left that afternoon, to take the garrison back to Châteaudun, which had been left unprotected while the siege was being broken at Orleans.[22] The bulk of the garrison did not leave until about two days later. To their surprise, the population of Orleans discovered that they were almost sorry to see them go. Normally, cities such as Orleans were most reluctant to admit troops, whether or not these were supposed to be friendly. Orleans had only accepted the presence of Charles's soldiers – they included Gascons, Spaniards and Scotsmen – as a matter of dire necessity. But the experiences of the siege had forged a spirit of comradeship. The citizens, so the *Journal of the Siege* informs us, 'lodged [the soldiers] among themselves, in their houses, and nourished them with such goods as God had given them, as familiarly as if they had been their own children'.[23]

The news of what had happened made a tremendous stir in the outside world. Charles VII took good care to inform his 'good towns' of what had been taking place. The news was soon received in Germany and Brittany, where the relief of Orleans was immediately recognized as a decisive event. And if Charles VII was delighted with the outcome, the Duke of Burgundy too was not wholly unhappy to see Bedford and the English taught a lesson. A contemporary letter-writer reports him as being 'not less pleased than the rest' with the lifting of the siege.[24]

The Burgundians, however, were disinclined to give Joan too much credit for what had happened. Monstrelet, who is the principal Burgundian chronicler of the period, says rather coolly:

And despite the fact that in these assaults the said Maid was given in the common report as leader, nevertheless all the captains were there, or the greater part of them, who during the said siege had been in the city of Orleans.[25]

The Orléannais themselves were quite certain that Joan had been the decisive factor in achieving their deliverance. They immediately turned her into a heroine, and never afterwards wavered in their devotion to her, even after she had been condemned as a heretic and burned. Joan returned their affection. There is even evidence that she planned to go and live there – a document shows that she leased a house from the chapter of Orleans cathedral. On 27 February 1432, that is to say rather less than a year after Joan's death, the lease had forty-three years to run.[26] After Joan's death, the city behaved with great liberality to her family. Her mother Isabelle Romée went to live there, and became a municipal pensioner until she died at Orleans in November 1458.[27] Joan's brothers Jean and Pierre were also the recipients of various kinds of municipal bounty.[28] Even while Joan's reputation was still under a cloud, the city marked the anniversary of her death. From 1432 to 1439 we find a record in the accounts of payments being made for candles to be burnt for her soul. In 1435, eight monks of the four mendicant orders were paid to sing eight masses for the dead on her behalf.[29]

The main celebration, however, took place annually upon 8 May, the anniversary of the lifting of the siege. This continued until the time of the French Revolution – the continuity was not broken until 1793,[30] and the ceremony was revived under the Empire, in 1803.[31] Joan's nephew, Jean du Lys, son of her brother Pierre, used to come to Orleans every year to take part in the procession. It was customary to carry a large lighted candle before him, with Joan's image painted upon it. This fact was attested in 1550, forty-eight years after Jean du Lys's death, by the old man who had been his servant.[32]

16

Joan was not received by Charles VII until a fortnight had passed. We do not know if the delay was caused by the king's renewed hesitations or by the time her wound took to heal. The meeting was at Tours, where Joan's entry preceded that of the king by a few hours. Knowing that he was on the road, she took her banner and went out on horseback to meet him. At their encounter, she showed the graceful good manners which had impressed the court at Chinon, bowing low in the saddle until Charles told her to raise herself up. 'You would have thought,' says the chronicler who tells us of this, 'that he would have embraced her, he was so joyful.'[1]

From Tours, the court, now accompanied by Joan, moved to Loches,[2] and here the debates on policy were renewed. Joan grew increasingly impatient with these, as to her the course was obvious. The second part of her mission must now be accomplished, and she must take the king to Rheims to be crowned. Eventually, she could bear it no longer. It is Dunois who tells us what happened:

The king was in his private room – what we call in French his 'retreat' – and with him were my lord Christophe de Harcourt, and the Bishop of Castres [Gérard Machet], then the king's confessor, and my lord of Trèves, who had formerly been Chancellor of France. Before entering this room, the Maid knocked on the door, and the moment she was inside fell on her knees and embraced the king's feet, pronouncing these words or others like them: 'Noble dauphin, do not take such long and copious counsel, but come as quickly as you can to receive a worthy coronation.' Then my lord Christophe de Harcourt engaged her in conversation, and asked her whether it was her Counsellor who said that. She answered yes, and that she was receiving urgent promptings upon this subject. Then Christophe said to Joan: 'Will you not tell us, here before the king, what your Counsellor does when he speaks to you?' She answered with a blush: 'I understand well enough what you want to know, and will gladly tell you.' Then the king said to her: 'Joan, please tell him what he asks, in the presence of all of us here.' And she answered the king that she would, and said these words or others like them: that when something was not going well because they would not leave it to her to follow the counsel that was sent her from God, she would retire apart and pray to God, complaining to Him that the men to whom she spoke would not readily believe in her. And when she had prayed to God, she heard a voice which said to her: 'Go, child of God, go, go! Go, and I will help you.' And when she heard this voice she felt a great joy, and wanted to be in that state always. And, what is more, when she thus repeated the words of her voices, she was seized with a marvellous rapture, and raised her eyes to heaven.[3]

This scene must have taken place in the retiring room behind the great hall in the Royal Lodging at Loches. Loches, unlike Chinon, is not a ruin, and though the Royal Lodging, which resembles that at Chinon by being a separate building within the confines of a vast castle with a number of different *enceintes*, has been altered and extended since Charles VII's time, the room in which the confrontation took place, like the great hall itself, is still substantially intact. Standing there today, in that gaunt chamber which must always have been more a place where business was transacted than one for comfortable conversation, it is possible to imagine the confrontation precisely. How did Joan's rapturous, mystical, and slightly overweening outburst sound to the four men who surrounded her? Despite Dunois's favourable recollection, many years after the event, it must surely have jarred a little. Joan's embarrassment in telling some part of her secret was surely echoed by the embarrassment of hearing it.

Eventually it was decided that the king would go to Rheims as Joan requested, but that before this could be done, it was necessary to take some of the places which the English still possessed along the line of the Loire. Chief among these were Jargeau, Meung and Beaugency, the bases which the English had established for themselves before attempting the siege of Orleans. Alençon was appointed Lieutenant-General, and put in charge of the army, which may eventually have numbered as many as 8,000 men. Joan was to go with Alençon, and he was expressly commanded 'that he should use and do entirely according to her counsel. And he did so, like one who took great pleasure at seeing her in his company.'[4]

The point of concentration for the royal army was Romorantin, south of the Loire, and, in order to be near what was going on, Joan separated from the king. By 4 June, she was at Selles-en-Berri.[5] We have a vivid description of Joan at this point in her life from the pen of the young nobleman Gui de Laval. His letter breathes high-spirited enthusiasm for Joan and her enterprises.

Laval first went to the king at Saint-Aignan, and Charles gave him a welcome which showed all his usual graciousness on these occasions. In the king's company, Laval went on to Selles, and Joan was sent for in order that he might see her. She arrived in complete armour, except for her helmet, and holding a lance in her hand, and there was an exchange of courtesies. Later that day, which was a Sunday, Laval went to visit Joan in her lodging: 'She sent for wine, and told me she would soon have me drinking in Paris.' A noble young admirer such as this was bound to bring out her strain of boastful graciousness, just as Alençon did.[6]

The next day, Monday, 6 June, Laval saw her setting out for Romorantin and the coming campaign.

I saw her mount her horse, all in plain armour but unhelmeted, holding a little battle-axe in her hand. She had a big black charger which, at the door of her lodgings, cavorted wildly and would not let her mount. Then she said: 'Take him to the cross' – this was in front of the near-by church, beside the road. And there she mounted, while the horse never moved, but stood as if he were tied. And she turned towards the door of the church which was quite near and said, in a womanly enough voice: 'You, the priests and churchmen, make procession and prayers to God.' Then she turned once more upon her way, saying: 'Forward, forward,' with her standard furled and carried by a gracious page, and with her little battle-axe in her hand.

And one of her brothers, who came eight days ago, departed with her, also in a full suit of plain armour.[7]

Anyone who knows the sleepy little town of Selles as it is today will find it easy to visualize the scene. The church, a handsome Romanesque building dedicated to St Eusice, has some particularly fine carvings. The cross where Joan mounted has disappeared, but undoubtedly stood by the main, or west door. The west façade faces a small square, and there is a street which leads into this, on the opposite side from the church itself. If Joan lodged in this westward-leading street, as seems entirely probable from the description, then when she came out to mount at vespers, her horse, facing towards the church, would have seen his own shadow stretching before him in the light of a fine June evening. Excellent horsewoman that she was, Joan immediately grasped the reason why he was baulking and shying, and had him led down to the square, and turned around so that he could no longer see what was frightening him. Meanwhile, the clergy attached to the church came crowding to the door to watch her go.

Alençon's army, like that which had been brought together for the relief of Orleans, had been gathered in the face of some difficulty. Laval says in his letter that there is no money at court, and that 'things are so tight, that for the present time I hope for no recourse or sustenance'. He tells his mother, who has his seal, not to hesitate to sell or mortgage his lands in order to raise troops. The feeling is that those around him are in the same mood.[8] So in the most concrete way Joan's success had begun to bring new strength to the king's cause. The spirit in which the war was pursued was no longer, at least for the moment, the mercenary one which had prevailed heretofore.

Having concentrated at Romorantin, the army set out for Orleans, where it arrived on 9 June. Here they were 'received with great joy by the citizens, and above all the Maid, whom they could never see enough of'.[9] The first objective was to be the town of Jargeau. A previous, but rather half-hearted, attempt had been made to take this in the days immediately following the raising of the siege. The attack had soon been given up because the level of the river was high, and the ditches which defended the town were therefore full of water. The one thing the attackers did achieve on this occasion was the death of the English captain of the town, Sir Henry Bisset, who was killed in the course of a skirmish.[10]

It seems as if Jargeau had already been put under some kind of investment before Alençon's troops set out, which apparently happened on 10 June. The advance-guard, which consisted of some 600 lances, led by Alençon himself, 'slept in a wood', and was joined upon the following day by a force of approximately equal size under Florent d'Illiers.[11] The men Alençon found waiting for him in front of the town were already discouraged, as they had again had word that Fastolf was coming with English reinforcements. But when Joan arrived, late on 11 June, the mood changed at once.

The common people, by this time convinced that nothing could stand against them in her presence, made an improvised assault without even waiting for her to join them, and without the support of the men-at-arms, and were thoroughly routed.[12] It may have been at this point that some of the captains who were with Alençon began to advise that the attempt to take the town should be given up, because of the strength of the English garrison, which was now commanded by Suffolk.[13] Joan, as one might expect, vigorously opposed this pessimistic view:

She told them to fear no numbers and assured them that they would have no difficulty in attacking the English, for God was conducting their campaign. She said that if she were not sure that God was conducting their campaign, she would rather keep sheep than expose herself to dangers such as these.[14]

This speech seems to show a wry acceptance of her own growing legend. Nevertheless it served its purpose in encouraging the French forces, and they made an assault on the suburbs of Jargeau, hoping to take them and spend the night in shelter. But the English garrison came out of the walls and at first drove the troops back. Joan then picked up her standard and led the French forward, and at the second attempt the suburbs were taken.[15] While this was going on the guns were brought into position, and began to fire at the walls. Almost immediately, the French artillery scored a notable success, when one of the great bombards of Orleans brought down the biggest tower of the fortifications with its first three shots.[16] At the same time, the English nearly scored a comparable triumph, when Alençon narrowly escaped death from one of their cannon.[17] It was Joan who saved his life by pointing out to him that he was directly in the line of fire[18] – yet another example of the quickness of her eye and of her reflexes.

Throughout the night the French artillery continued to bombard the town,[19] which means that no one can have had much sleep. The besieging forces seem to have been possessed not only by euphoria, but by an accompanying carelessness. Alençon afterwards shuddered to remember that no proper guards had been posted, and that the French could easily have been the victims of a night attack.[20] During the night, as she had done at Orleans, Joan attempted to summon the defenders of the town, shouting up to them: 'Surrender the place to the King of Heaven and the gentle King Charles, and you can go off, but otherwise we will massacre you.'[21] To this the defenders made no reply, but the notion of composition may have struck a responsive chord. When, the next morning, the French leaders held an early council to decide what they should do, news was brought to them that La Hire was parleying with Suffolk.[22] Suffolk offered to surrender the town if not relieved within fifteen days.[23] Annoyed by the fact that La Hire had acted without consulting them, the other captains would have none of this.[24] The best they would offer was that the garrison could go, and take their horses, but within the hour. Joan herself would have been yet more stringent – she was willing to see the English go, safe and sound, but taking nothing with them except the clothes they stood up in.[25]

It was now Sunday, 12 June, and at about 9 a.m. the trumpets sounded, while the heralds cried: 'To the attack'. Joan took her standard, and began to move forward to the assault, but Alençon still hesitated.[26] Joan said: 'Forward, gentle duke, to the attack!'

And as it seemed to me premature to start the attack so quickly, Joan said to me: 'Do not have doubts – when God pleases, the hour is ripe,' and that we must act when God wills it. 'Act, and God will act.' And a little later she said to me: 'Oh, gentle duke, are you afraid? Do you not know that I have promised your wife to bring you back safe and sound?'[27]

131

The assault endured for three or four hours,[28] and was marked by at least two notable incidents. The hero of the first of these was Jean de Lorraine, the culverineer. Just as the attack on the Augustins had been held up until Aulon asked this marksman to pick off a particularly energetic defender, so now the English defence had at its heart a man 'who was very large and broad, armed at all points, and wearing on his head a bassinet'. He threw down great stones upon the attackers and overturned the ladders loaded with men until Alençon asked that he should be picked off. Jean de Lorraine caught him full in the chest, and he tumbled back dead into the town.[29]

His death may have knocked much of the stuffing out of the defence, and, just as the French were on the point of breaking in, Suffolk had his herald call to Alençon that he again wished to parley, but the offer was not heard amid the confusion of the battle.[30] It seems to have been at this moment that Joan, who was now on a scaling ladder with her standard still in her hand, was knocked sprawling into the ditch by a stone which tore the stuff of the flag and shattered on Joan's steel cap. Fortunately for her, she was on this occasion wearing a *chapeline*, which was a kind of tin hat especially used by the men at the heads of storming columns. The phrase *homme de chapeline* came to signify someone particularly courageous.[31] Joan was not hurt, nor even stunned, and as she picked herself up she cried to the soldiers: 'Up, friends, up! Our Lord has doomed the English. At this very moment they are ours. Be of good cheer!' With this encouragement, the French broke into the town.[32]

Suffolk, and those surrounding him, including his two brothers and several other captains, retreated hastily through Jargeau towards the fortified bridge that crossed the Loire. So did most of the other members of the garrison. The French pressed hard on their heels and the pursuit turned into a massacre. Jargeau is on the south bank of the Loire, and what Suffolk had been hoping to do, in this moment of extremity, was to regain the north side, where he might find and rejoin Fastolf; or else he hoped to hold the fortified bridge till help arrived. He soon saw that both these enterprises were useless – the French were hot on his heels, and the bridge itself was too feeble to be defended now that he had lost at least half his force.[33] Foremost amongst his pursuers was an Auvergnat squire named Guillaume Regnault, hungry for the ransom which a great captain like Suffolk would bring. Suffolk found time to ask him if he was a gentleman. Regnault replied that he was. Suffolk then asked if he was a knight. Regnault answered that he was not. So the English earl knighted him on the spot, disdaining to be taken by a man of any lower rank, and then surrendered to him.[34] The pretty legend that he insisted on making his surrender to Joan[35] will not, unfortunately, bear examination, as it is completely at variance with everything we know about English attitudes towards her.

The sequel to the fall of Jargeau was sickening. Both the town and the church, which is in part one of the most ancient in the region with a tower dating from the tenth century, were thoroughly sacked.[36] The church stands near the Orleans gate, and was therefore right in the path of the attackers as they swept in. Though French casualties had been extremely light – perhaps as few as sixteen or twenty killed,[37] the prevailing atmosphere was so excited that it was decided that the most important prisoners should be sent to Orleans by river, and under the cover of night, as it was feared that their lives might otherwise be in danger.[38] This fear was only too well founded. Most of the other prisoners were massacred on the road, when a quarrel sprang up between 'the gentlemen' – that is to say, the professional soldiers – who had charge of them, and the common people of Orleans who had taken part in the attack on Jargeau,[39] and who perhaps still felt insufficiently rewarded by the considerable plunder they had taken. As a result of the storming of Jargeau, and of this subsequent massacre, only about fifty prisoners survived[40] from what may originally have been a force of about 700.[41] This caused less stir than it might have done, since the most notable men were kept safe. But we catch an echo of resentment in the questions asked at Joan's trial. Here was another incident to prove that she could be treated as an exception to the laws of war, since she did not respect them herself.

17

On the morning of 13 June,[1] Joan and Alençon returned to
Orleans. From thence news of the fall of Jargeau was sent to the
king. More captains and more troops had arrived at Orleans –
among them were Gui de Laval and his brother André – and the
army was now considerably larger than the one which set out
two days before.[2] So large was it, indeed, that it could not all be
accommodated within Orleans itself, and many of the men
camped in the villages around.[3] Here they remained for Monday
and Tuesday. Tuesday was for the most part a day of celebration, but in the evening Joan went to see Alençon and told him
that next day it would be time to set out. 'Tomorrow after
dinner', she said, 'I want to go and see those who are at Meung.
Have the company ready to leave at that hour.'[4]

On 15 June, therefore, the French army set out, accompanied
by a considerable siege-train. Despite this encumbrance they
seem to have made reasonably good speed. Some of their
heavier guns must have gone by water. Their first halt was at
Meung-sur-Loire,[5] just down river from Orleans. Here there was
a fortified bridge, garrisoned by the English, which was separated from the town of Meung, also in English hands. The French
took the bridge with little trouble, and garrisoned it,[6] but
decided to by-pass the town and go on to Beaugency, further
on along the Loire. That night Alençon bivouacked in a church
near Meung. He says, mysteriously, that on this occasion he
'ran into great danger'.[7] Perhaps, once again, he had forgotten

to provide proper outposts. On the following day, he arrived before Beaugency, where he found other contingents of the French army encamped in the fields round about. The main body of the French force did not arrive at their objective until midday, and the afternoon passed in skirmishing. The English, who had only about 500 men,[8] felt that they were not strong enough to try to hold the town, so they dismantled as much of the defences as they could, and retired into the castle and the bridge, leaving behind ambushes in some of the houses, and in some cisterns near the bridgehead.[9] These managed to give the French a nasty surprise just as they were settling in.[10] In the evening, the French positioned their artillery, and started to bombard the castle[11] – the attack was being made from the Beauce side, since Beaugency lay on the north bank of the Loire.

Though matters seemed to be going reasonably well from the military point of view, Alençon was worried. That evening he found himself faced with a first-class political crisis, and one of a particularly difficult nature. News arrived that the constable, Artur de Richemont, was arriving upon the scene with the intention of taking part in the siege, and bringing with him a considerable force which he had raised himself. Alençon was so disconcerted by this piece of information that he actually considered moving the army from Beaugency because of it.[12]

The reasons for his reaction are complex, and need to be explained. Richemont had been forbidden the French court ever since he had fallen out with La Trémoille, who had once been his protégé. In 1428, he had been in open rebellion against the king. Charles knew of his intention to meddle in the Loire campaign, and had already sent him a warning. The royal emissary had found Richemont at Loudun, and had drawn him aside 'and told him that he should not be so bold as to advance any further, and that if he passed beyond [the place where he now was], the king would fight him'. With typical pigheadedness, Richemont refused to pay any heed. He said that 'what he did was for the good of the kingdom of the king, and he would see who tried to fight him'.[13] He pressed onwards in defiance of Charles's command. When he got near Beaugency he sent two of the nobles who were with him to ask that quarters be assigned to him by those who were keeping the siege. Alençon's riposte was to say that, if Richemont came, he would go.[14] He had been given specific orders not to receive the constable. Joan, perhaps, was prepared to go even further than this. When a group of the captains at Beaugency came to ask her what she intended to do, she is said to have answered that it was necessary to fight Richemont:

And they told her that if she went to do that, she would find plenty of people to talk to, and that there were those in the company who were more for him than for her, and that they loved him and his company more than all the Maids in France.[15]

Alençon, at any rate, must have seen that this largely volunteer army could never be prevailed upon to fight the first action of a new civil war in the very presence of the hereditary enemy. La Trémoille might control the king, but there was no way in which he could impose himself upon the present situation. No doubt this was precisely what Richemont had already calculated. As it happened neither Joan's nor Alençon's resolution was put to the test, since the next morning a new factor was added to the situation. News came that the English relieving army was approaching, under the leadership of Fastolf, and that of Talbot, who had escaped from Beaugency shortly before the siege began.[16] This changed Joan's mind for her, and she immediately set to work to change Alençon's, saying to him, as the soldiers shouted 'To arms!', that the two factions had to help one another. What Alençon seems to have done was to leave a small force, and his artillery, behind him at Beaugency, and to take the rest of his troops toward Richemont in order to make a junction with him. Joan's ultimate reaction to Richemont's arrival is likely to be preserved for us in a remark that Alençon reports. 'Ah, noble constable,' she said to the newcomer, 'you have not come through any act of mine, but since you have come, you shall be welcome.'[17] For some reason Alençon places this encounter upon the following day, when the English in Beaugency had already surrendered. Perhaps, in the first instance at least, it was considered better to keep two such combustible natures apart.

After the conjunction with Richemont's force had taken place, the French army was put into battle-array, upon a little hill.[18] When it was ranged and ready, Alençon and others publicly asked Joan what should be done.

She answered loudly with the words: 'See that you all have good spurs.' When those present heard this they asked her: 'What did you say? Are we to turn our backs on them?' – 'No,' said Joan, 'it will be the English who will put up no defence. They will be beaten, and you will have to have good spurs to pursue them.'[19]

The English army meanwhile had come in sight of the French. When they saw it already ranged for battle they thought the combat must be imminent, and followed their usual tactics. The horsemen dismounted, the archers advanced and planted their pikes in front of them, and they awaited the French onslaught.[20] But this did not come. The French had learned their lesson from the defeats they had suffered in the past. Growing impatient, the English sent forward two heralds. These delivered the usual chivalric challenge. Their message was that there were three knights ready to fight, if the French would come down from their hill and join issue with them. The hope, presumably, was that these individual combats would develop into a general mêlée, with the French at a disadvantage. The reply to the heralds' message was lazily contemptuous: 'Go to your quarters for today, for it is rather late. But tomorrow, if it please God and Our Lady, we shall take a closer look at you.'[21]

It is likely that, with Richemont's arrival, the French army looked even more formidable than the English had feared at first. The disparity in numbers must certainly have been marked, if it overawed even the impetuous Talbot. The presence of the constable's banner in the host may also have made the English commanders think that Richemont had composed his differences with the king – something which boded no good for the English cause as a whole.[22] At any rate, when their challenge was refused, the English remounted, turned tail, and rode for Meung, where the town was still in their hands.[23] Knowing that once they got there they would immediately attack the French who were holding the bridge, Richemont detached a small force consisting of twenty lances and some archers to help the garrison.[24] The rest of the French army, now swollen by Richemont's troops, flowed back towards the siege. They arrived to find that the men they had left behind had succeeded in containing the enemy. As the French made arrangements for the night, the provisional nature of the reconciliation between Richemont and the royal forces serving under Alençon was stressed in subtle ways. For example, though he had requested 'lodgings' at the siege, Richemont had none officially assigned to him.[25] Rather than joining the rest of the besieging force on the north bank of the Loire, it was arranged that he and his men should station themselves on the south, or Sologne side, divided from the rest of the army by the breadth of the river.[26]

The position of the English garrison was unenviable. They saw that they were surrounded on all sides, and that the large army which had arrived the day before had now grown in numbers. Watching the withdrawal of the French troops, and then their return, they must have understood that an attempt had been made to break the siege from outside, and that this had failed. In any case, the French lost no time in letting them know that the English army of relief was now retreating towards Paris.[27] The besieged, in the course of a sally, had actually succeeded in getting a messenger out to Talbot. To his entreaties, Talbot had replied rather vaguely that the English in Beaugency 'should be of good cheer and do their duty as they would shortly have good news of him'.[28] It is uncertain whether or not this answer reached its destination, but if it did, it had been belied by events.

Beaugency itself was much less easily defensible than biographers of Joan of Arc have tended to suppose. The situation explains itself more easily if one has actually seen the town, the main features of which are little altered since Joan's day. The castle, though without roof or floors, still stands on a low hill near the river. It is a massive, square, Norman-style keep, dating from the eleventh century. Unlike many castles of this date, it does not have, in addition to the donjon, an elaborate series of outer defences built at some later epoch. In front of the castle, and somewhat to the left as one faces the Loire, is the large Romanesque church of Notre-Dame, which is the principal remnant of an important abbey. The abbey buildings occupied the entire slope down to the river, to the point where the bridge begins its crossing. An old-fashioned, slab-sided donjon of this type was particularly vulnerable to artillery fire, and we know that the French had brought a great many guns with them. The tangle of abbey buildings would have given plenty of cover to anyone who wanted to attack the castle, unless the English themselves kept them manned. Keeping them manned would also have been the only way of maintaining communication with the bridge itself. We are told that there was a good deal of skirmishing in the course of 17 June,[29] and we may imagine that in the circumstances, it was mostly for possession of the abbey. No experienced military man of the fifteenth century could have imagined that Beaugency would be defensible for long, once the town walls themselves had been abandoned.

When night came, the nerves of the English garrison were additionally frayed by the activities of Richemont's troops. The constable, in order to emphasize that his force was now a corps of the whole army rather than a separate entity, insisted that his men should keep the watch on the night of the seventeenth, on the grounds that this was the traditional duty of newcomers. 'And they kept watch that night before the castle, and it was the finest watch that had been kept in France for a long time.'[30] These factors would in themselves have been enough to enforce a rapid surrender, but there was, too, Joan's reputation to put in the scale. The Burgundian chronicler Monstrelet, who denies Joan a preponderating part in the success of the operations at Orleans, says that the garrison at Beaugency felt that, thanks to her, 'fortune was completely turned against them'.[31]

The upshot was that about midnight on the night of this day, it was agreed that the English would surrender the bridge and castle, and could leave on the morrow, taking their horses and harness and some of their goods, a silver mark's worth to each man; and they would also have to swear not to bear arms again until ten days had passed, and upon these conditions they departed on the morrow, which was the eighteenth day of June, and went to Meung, and the French entered the castle, and reinforced it with men to guard it.[32]

The English troops were convoyed on their way by Ambroise de Loré,[33] but their principal captains, Richard Guethin and Mathew Gough (quaintly called 'Mathago' by the French), were kept as sureties for the terms being carried out.[34]

Some sources tell us that the English surrender was made to Joan and the Duke of Alençon.[35] Alençon himself says merely that they 'surrendered the castle on terms, and retired with a safe-conduct which I granted them, being at that time the king's lieutenant in the army'.[36] This is a way of saying that Richemont was not permitted to exercise the constable's traditional right to command.

While the English garrison was evacuating the castle, which happened around dawn on 18 June, misleading information was received from La Hire's scouts that the English army was again on the march towards Beaugency, and that the French would soon be face to face with them. They claimed to have seen a body of a thousand men.[37] Despite the fact that the French had outfaced the English on the previous day, there was a moment of panic, and Joan immediately turned her energies to encouraging the waverers, who were saying that it would be a good thing to send for the horses. 'In God's name,' she cried, 'we must fight them. If they were hanging in the clouds we should get them, for God has sent them to us to punish them.'[38] It may, however, have been Richemont, rather than Joan, who supplied the impulse which put the French army in motion. If the panic was momentary, there also seems to have been a feeling amongst the French that it would be a good thing to hang on to the gains they had already made, and some turned for the town. One of Richemont's lieutenants, the sire de Rostrenen (a good Breton name), came to him, and said: 'If you make your standard go forward, everyone will follow you.' Richemont immediately gave the order, 'and the Maid and all the others came after', as Gruel complacently tells us.[39] It may well have been at this moment that Joan at last bestowed upon the constable the accolade of her approval, somewhat grudging though it was. At any rate we may be certain that she was vehemently in favour of pursuing the English.[40] The decision to go in pursuit of Fastolf and Talbot marks a turning point in the war. For the first time for a number of years, Charles's forces had taken the offensive, not merely against some limited objective, but against the whole English power in France.

18

Bedford's army of reinforcement, about 3,000 strong when it left Paris, had reached Étampes on 13 June. Here it received news of the fall of Jargeau. On 16 June, Fastolf, who was in charge of the force, summoned a council to discuss what should be done; and, while it was deliberating, Talbot entered Janville with a small force of forty lances and 200 archers. He had slipped out of Beaugency just as the siege began, and he must have brought news of the French attack on the bridge at Meung.[1] It was immediately apparent that the hot-tempered Talbot and the cautious Fastolf were at loggerheads. Fastolf's advice was to leave the garrison at Beaugency to its fate. He was in no hurry to fight until he had a clearer view of the situation. Talbot threatened to take the initiative himself, with his own small force, and he carried the subordinate commanders with him. In the morning, when the army was already assembled and ready to march, Fastolf made a despairing final effort to get his colleagues to see reason. He pointed out that they were now outnumbered by the French, and that, if they were defeated, 'all that the late King Henry had won in France, with great labour and over a long period, would be upon the road to perdition'.[2] But his words were in vain. It was nevertheless an extremely divided and indecisive group of English commanders who confronted the French host between Beaugency and Meung on the afternoon of 17 June. Their decision to turn about, and make for Meung, when the French refused to accept their challenge, reflected not only a sensible assessment of the odds against victory, but the decline in the aggressive spirit of English arms. The English bombarded the fortified bridge at Meung all night long, and next morning preparations were just being made to storm the shaken bridge defences when news arrived that Beaugency had surrendered.[3] This immediately made the enterprise pointless, as the whole object had been to relieve the besieged town by crossing to the south side of the Loire. The attack was called off, and the English army was led out of Meung and put into line of march. This, though not of the quality of the armies that Henry V had put in the field, was still a well-disciplined force. The advance-guard was led by a knight who carried a white standard, and immediately behind them came the artillery and the supply-train, followed by the main body, led by Fastolf and Talbot, and then by a rearguard made up of picked English troops.[4] The decision was to return to base at Janville.

The pursuing French had also arranged themselves in three divisions. The first, which consisted of the men who were the best mounted,[5] was led by La Hire[6] and some of the fieriest of the other captains, including Poton de Xantrailles. About sixty or eighty of the most expert were delegated to serve as scouts and skirmishers.[7] Their job was to harass the English, and to try, as far as possible, to hold them back until the main body could come up.[8] In the main battle were Alençon, Richemont and Dunois, as well as the king's cousin, the Count of Vendôme – the very one who had taken Joan by the hand and led her into the great hall at Chinon with its blazing torches and its throng of richly dressed courtiers.[9] Joan, much to her rage, was relegated to the rearguard.[10] The decision to place her there tells us much about her still ambiguous status. The French leaders, even Dunois and Alençon, who by now must have known a lot about her personality, reverted to the idea that she must be treated as a kind of talisman now that a major battle was imminent, and not as someone who could be trusted to act upon her own responsibility. Joan nevertheless was full of enthusiasm. She was confident that the French would have an easy victory, saying to the captains: 'Strike them boldly, they will take to flight', and promising that there would be few casualties.[11] When the French lost contact with Fastolf's army after nearly catching it outside Meung, she was again consulted:

She replied that she was certain and knew in truth that the English, their enemies, were waiting to fight them; and she said in addition that, in the name of God, people should ride against them, and that they would be beaten. Some then asked where the English were to be found; to which she answered: 'Ride boldly on, and you will have a good guide.'[12]

In fact, the two forces were converging on Patay by slightly different routes, and were concealed from one another by thick woods. Looking at the broad agricultural lands of the Beauce today, it is difficult to believe that they were ever as thickly forested as the descriptions of the battle imply. What we must remember is the fact that a great deal of land, here as in more northerly areas, had fallen out of cultivation as a result of the war.

The English leaders decided that the French were now so hot on their tail that it was necessary to try and make a stand before they even reached the town of Patay itself, and it is likely that they were just dismounting when a random incident gave away their position to the French. 'By chance,' says the chronicler Wavrin, who was present at the battle, 'the front rank saw a stag spring out of the woods, and this made towards Patay, and went in among the English army, which raised a loud shout, not knowing that their enemies were so close.'[13] This alerted the French scouts, who burst out of cover to find the English very close to them, and in a state of some disarray.

Patay was not a 'set' battle of the classical kind beloved by military historians. Events moved so fast, and the crisis was over so quickly, that naturally there has been a good deal of confusion over what took place. The sequence of events seems to have been as follows. Marching in haste, as they were, through flat and rather featureless country, the English found difficulty in selecting a suitable position for the kind of defensive battle which they liked to fight. At last two strong hedges were found, one at the bottom of a dip, one somewhat above it, which seemed to offer strategic possibilities. It is probable that the upper hedge is that which still survives today, in the fields near Patay. It is mostly planted with hawthorn.

Since the commanders were riding with the third of the four divisions, the English advance-guard, and the supply-train also, had actually gone beyond the place chosen before it was decided to use it, and they were ordered to return with the guns, and also with the carts, which could be placed along the line of the hedges to strengthen the barrier. Fastolf was thus thinking in terms of his successful defence against Clermont, in similarly flat country, at the Battle of the Herrings.[14] Talbot offered to dismount, with a force of 500 élite archers, and man the hedges until the rest of the force could come into position.[15] Fastolf started to move off towards what was now the rear.

The French caught sight of the English force just at the moment of confusion, when Talbot was dismounting, before the archers had planted their stakes, and when the cumbersome supply train was being turned in its tracks.[16] La Hire and his handful of men saw their opportunity, and instead of waiting for their main body to come up, charged Talbot and his force and completely routed them. Instead of attacking the hedges from the front, they rode in from the flanks, so that the position became a narrow corridor in which the English were trapped.[17] Talbot was captured by Poton de Xantrailles's archers.[18] When taken, he was on horseback, but without spurs – that is, he had hastily remounted, and was preparing to flee.[19]

Seeing what was taking place, Fastolf galloped towards the advance-guard, hoping to rally them and make a counter-attack. When he came on in such desperate haste, the advance-guard concluded that all was lost, and that Fastolf and those who accompanied him were in flight. So they, still led by the knight with the white standard, promptly took to their heels and left the rest of the army to its fate.[20] Fastolf was now in a state of rage and despair. Those with him suggested that he too would be wise to make off while he still could, 'but he at any price wanted to re-enter the battle, and there meet what chance Our Lord might wish to send him, saying he would rather be slain or taken than flee shamefully and thus leave his men'.[21] At that very moment, however, Talbot's force was being cut down and Talbot himself was being made prisoner. The English had lost all chance of taking the initiative.[22] Fastolf therefore allowed himself to be led from the battlefield. The chronicler, Wavrin, who describes Fastolf's reactions at first hand, accompanied him, and thus escaped the massacre which was to follow.[23]

The second phase of the battle of Patay consisted of the slaughter of the English foot, deprived of their leaders through flight or capture. The dead, as Monstrelet contemptuously tells us, were mostly of 'small and middling estate, and so made as they were accustomed to bring from their country to die in France'.[24] The French killed them because they were not worth taking for their ransoms. Those who escaped did so by taking to the woods, or by hiding in a village near by.[25] Probably just over 2,000 English were killed and 200 taken prisoner.[26] French casualties were remarkably light – Perceval de Boulainvilliers asserts that only three Frenchmen were killed.[27]

Joan came onto the battlefield while the slaughter was still going on. Her page, Louis de Coutes, describes how she saw a Frenchman bringing in a group of English prisoners, and how the captor suddenly knocked one of these on the head and left him for dead. Joan was shocked by this, as she often was when she encountered the realities of war. She dismounted and received the dying Englishman's confession, 'raising his head and comforting him as much as she could'.[28]

The remnants of the English army were pursued as far as Janville, suffering further casualties on the way. When they reached the town, they found the gates shut, and the townspeople manning the walls against them. An English squire, with a tiny garrison, was in charge of the castle. He, hearing of the defeat of the English army, immediately entered into negotiations with the inhabitants, with a view to surrendering to them. He clinched the deal by taking an oath to behave henceforth as a 'good and loyal Frenchman'. The tower was a rich prize, since it contained the artillery, war-equipment and foodstuffs which the English had left behind them when they set out.[29] Some of the citizens also profited from Fastolf's war-chest, which had been placed for safekeeping in their hands.[30]

Fastolf himself went first to Étampes, and next day to Corbeil.[31] Bedford, enraged by the defeat, deprived him of his Order of the Garter, but later restored it when he realized that Fastolf's advice during the campaign had been consistently sound. Talbot, however, continued to regard Fastolf with smouldering resentment, and, after he had paid his ransom and been released, had a violent quarrel with his former colleague.[32]

As for the French army, the bulk of it remained on the battlefield, where the troops spent the night.[33] Joan, Alençon and Richemont entered the town, though Richemont at least seems to have left again in order to spend the night with his men.[34] When they were in Patay, the captured Talbot was brought before Alençon and Richemont. Joan was also present at the interview. Alençon behaved with less than perfect tact: 'I told Talbot I had not believed in the morning that things would turn out so.' The Englishman contained himself, and answered gruffly that it was the fortune of war.[35]

Joan and Alençon remained at Patay until midday on 19 June.[36] The problem which had now begun to occupy everybody was what was to be done about Richemont. Alençon told the constable that, despite the victory they had just achieved, he did not dare bring him to the court, but he seems to have agreed to act as mediator.[37] Joan and the other captains may also have agreed to take part in the negotiations.[38] Richemont went to Beaugency, to wait for an answer,[39] while the rest went back to Orleans, which they found in a mood of celebration.[40] The expectation was that the king himself would come to the city to join in the rejoicings of his loyal subjects, and the streets were decorated ready for his coming. Charles, however, remained stubbornly at Sully,[41] in the company of Georges de La Trémoille, who now enjoyed a greater ascendancy over him than ever.[42] La Trémoille had no intention of permitting Richemont's return, as he knew what the consequences would be for his own influence. Richemont was told that he must go back to his estates at Parthenay and was forced to obey, even though he sent further emissaries of his own to try and make peace, not only with the king but with the favourite.[43]

Joan was actively pressing the king to make the journey to his coronation at Rheims. She went to Sully to see him, and in addition they had a meeting at Saint-Benoît-sur-Loire. Here Charles rather wearily implored Joan to calm herself and not take so much trouble on his behalf. She wept and said: 'Have no doubt, you will gain your whole kingdom and will soon be crowned.'[44] If doubts were stirring in Charles's mind, they were not precisely of this order, but concerned Joan herself and her hold on the public imagination. The taking of Jargeau and Beaugency, and the brilliant victory of Patay, had consolidated the renown she had won at Orleans, and this despite the fact that she had played little practical part at Beaugency and none at Patay. Her presence had been enough to fire men's hearts. Now recruits came flocking from all parts of the kingdom, eager to serve Charles at their own expense.[45] One can see why La Trémoille and some of the other men who surrounded the king should mistrust this outburst of popular enthusiasm, as indeed they did.[46] It threatened the situation they had made for themselves, and that was something which may now have focused their hostility upon Joan in a more specific way than previously. And here, in turn, was something which quite a number of people understood: 'People said that La Trémoille and others of the king's council were very angry that so many came, for fear of their own persons.'[47] What Charles himself felt we have no means of knowing, but he may well have feared that Joan was creating a monster which would in due course turn upon the monarch.

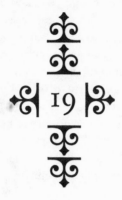

The decision to go to Rheims was not taken without much heart-searching. On 22 June a council of war was held at Châteauneuf-sur-Loire, in the king's presence. It is not certain if Joan attended, though she is said to have inspired the meeting in the first place.[1] On 23 June she was once more in Orleans, and here she made an attempt to set matters in motion by acting on her own account. She told Alençon to have the trumpets sounded and to mount his horse, saying: 'It is time to go to the gentle King Charles to put him on his road to his coronation at Rheims.'[2] The malleable Alençon did as she commanded.

The king was now at Gien, the logical stepping-off point if he really meant to go towards Champagne, but he was still hesitant. Some of his councillors advised him that it would be unwise to set out without first cleaning up the military situation on the Loire. This meant that the remaining enemy strong-points, such as Cosne and La Charité, should be besieged before any further move was made.[3] At one point the queen was brought to Gien, with the idea that she would go to Rheims with her husband. Then the king changed his mind, and sent her back again to the safety of Bourges.[4] Joan was much put out by the continuing delay, and eventually she left her quarters at Gien, and went to sulk in the fields outside the town.[5] On 25 June, the day after she arrived at Gien from Orleans, she had written a letter to the citizens of Tournai. This gives us an interesting glimpse of her state of mind, and of the powers she now saw fit to arrogate to herself. In the letter, she took complete credit for the military successes which had just been achieved, saying that 'in eight days she had thrust the English out from all the places they held on the Loire, by assault or otherwise'. She then continued:

And I pray and require you to be ready to come to the anointing of the gentle King Charles at Rheims where we shall be soon, and to come into our presence when you know that we approach.[6]

Meanwhile, men continued to flock to her standard, making it plain that it was for her sake that they came.[7] The spell she exercised was so strong that it even broke down the rigid hierarchical barriers of the military caste. A number of those who were technically gentlemen, but who did not have the means to arm and mount themselves as their rank required, joined the army as archers and simple soldiers, mounted upon ponies rather than upon the expensive warhorses which befitted the knight or the squire. 'For everyone had great hopes that by means of this Joan much good would befall the kingdom of France, and wished and desired to serve her, and know her deeds, as a thing sent by God.'[8] The army eventually swelled to about 12,000 combatants.[9] This figure, which appears in a good source, has often been doubted, but seems not unreasonable in view of the enthusiasm which we know that Joan had aroused. For Charles, the army was too large for comfort, as his finances were still in an extremely parlous state. The most he could manage, when he at last resigned himself to setting out, was a token payment of two or three francs per man.[10] Subsequent events were to prove that the army was very inadequately supplied. Indeed, it seems to have had almost no provisions at all.

On Wednesday, 29 June, Charles was at last prepared to move on.[11] The first success scored by his forces was inconsiderable. The little town of Saint-Fargeau, later to be a place of exile for Louis XIV's turbulent cousin, La Grande Mademoiselle, opened its gates to the king.[12] Joan was now acting as the marshal of the host, and we possess a vivid description of the way in which she comported herself:

And she rode always armed in habiliments of war, and the other people of her company were also thus, and she spoke as prudently of war as any captain could. And when it happened that there was in the host any cry or affray, she came whether on horseback or on foot, as valiantly as a captain of the company would have known how to do, giving courage and hardiness to all the others, and admonishing them to keep good watch and guard in the army, as reasonably one ought to do.[13]

One suspects that some of these summer days on the way to Rheims were the happiest she ever spent.

At Auxerre, the expedition received its first check, for the city closed its gates against the king.[14] The most they would do was to say that they would give the king 'a like obedience to that which would be given to him by those of the cities of Troyes, Châlons and Rheims',[15] all of which lay further along the route. Their reluctance to submit was not surprising, for two reasons, first that the city was part of the Duke of Burgundy's apanage, and had long been Burgundian in sympathy; and second, that the citizens were mortally afraid of the depredations which a large and hungry army might commit. The Auxerrois looked for a way to get themselves out of their difficulty, and came up with the idea of giving La Trémoille a bribe, in order 'to have a truce for this occasion'.[16] La Trémoille accepted the honorarium of 2,000 *écus*[17] which was offered him, and kept his side of the bargain by preventing an assault. This made Joan and some of the other captains very angry, as they considered it would have been easy to take the city.[18] There was much grumbling about the conduct of the favourite. The royal army lingered for three days, trading for victuals, which were already scarce. After this, it took the road for Troyes. When the royal army arrived there, it was to find the gates firmly shut. The only greeting they received was two or three cannon shots from the garrison, which fortunately did no damage. The inhabitants crowded the walls to see the king and those who followed him, but made no particular show of defiance.[19] However, the garrison, which numbered about 500 or 600 Anglo–Burgundian troops, not content with a few cannon shots, came out and conducted a token skirmish. Inevitably, in view of the vast disparity of forces, this was rapidly turned back.[20]

There now followed a period of waiting and negotiation. The Bishop of Troyes, Jean Laiguisé, came out to see the king, and blamed the failure of the inhabitants to open the gates upon the bailli and the garrison. He begged Charles to have patience until he had discussed matters with the inhabitants of the town.[21] Laiguisé was, from Charles's point of view, a piece of luck. Unlike many holders of important sees, he had actually been born in the place where he now held ecclesiastical office. In his youth, he had been educated at the College of Navarre – the most notoriously Armagnac component of the University of Paris. Gérard Machet, the king's confessor, had been a fellow student there. Bedford had always considered Laiguisé suspect, and when he was elected bishop in 1426, the temporalities of the chapter and their personal possessions were seized as a result. Altogether, Charles had good reason to regard him as the right man in the right place.

If Charles received a visit from the bishop, Joan was also visited by an envoy. This was the famous, or notorious, Brother Richard who, after a meteoric career in Paris, had quartered himself in Troyes. To her judges in Rouen, Joan gave a curtly amusing account of their first meeting:

'Did you ever know Brother Richard?'
'I never saw him, before I came to Troyes.'
'What greeting did Brother Richard make you?'
'It seemed to me that the people of Troyes, fearing that this was something that did not come from God, sent him to me. And when he came to me, approaching, he made the sign of the cross, and threw holy water, and I said to him: 'Approach boldly – I will not fly away.'[22]

This unpromising start was to lead to a close association which did Joan harm, though initially her cause benefited from it. It is therefore worth giving a brief description of Brother Richard's career.

He was a Franciscan. We first hear of him preaching in the dioceses of Troyes and Châlons in Advent 1428. He arrived in Paris around 11 April 1429,[23] and on 16 April preached the first in a series of sensational sermons, which drew crowds of 5,000 or 6,000 people a time despite the fact that he often went on for five or six hours.[24] His theme was the coming of Antichrist. He claimed to have come from Jerusalem, and said that, while he was in the East, he had met bands of Jews making their way to Babylon, where Antichrist had just been born.[25] He also claimed, and perhaps more plausibly, to be a disciple of St Vincent

Ferrer – who also thought that Antichrist had already been born – and he was, too, an admirer of St Bernardino of Siena.[26] Like the latter, he preached devotion to the monogram of Jesus.[27] His specific mention of St Bernardino makes it probable that he had spent some part of his life beyond the Alps, if not actually across the Mediterranean. Like Savonarola after him, Brother Richard denounced the vanities of this world. At his behest the Parisians burned their chess and backgammon sets, their dice and packs of cards. The women immolated their tall headgear, and shortened their trains.[28] His activities did not take long to attract the attention of the authorities, who viewed them with no very favourable eye. Having preached the last of his planned series of sermons on 26 April, Brother Richard was persuaded to begin all over again. The first oration of the new series was announced for Sunday, 1 May, and a huge crowd of Parisians went to Montmartre, where the sermon was scheduled to take place, in order to secure good positions. But the preacher did not turn up.[29] It is evident that he had been warned to make himself scarce. It was not only that the Faculty of Theology was beginning to take an interest in his activities, and perhaps wished to prosecute him,[30] but his sermons had begun to take on a political tinge. Just before he left Paris, for example, he predicted that the coming year 'would see the greatest wonders that ever happened'.[31] The implication was that some kind of great political change would take place. Monstrelet says roundly that he was turned out of Paris 'because he showed himself too plainly favourable to the French party'.[32] Brother Richard prudently returned to the no-man's-land of Champagne, where he had previously known success.

Since he was agog for wonders of all kinds, it was natural that Joan should impress him. She, on the other hand, found in him another representative of the emotional, popular religion which she had got from her mother. His devotion to the name of Jesus was also a point they had in common. When Joan arrived at Troyes, Brother Richard seems to have decided, almost on the instant, that she was the colleague he was looking for. He knelt to her, she knelt to him, and when their interview was over, he went back into the city and started to preach, telling the people to accept the king.[33] He made claims that Joan would not have made herself, saying that

[She] had as much power to know God's secrets as any saint in paradise with St John the Evangelist, and that she could, if she wanted, make the King's army enter over the walls in any way she wanted.[34]

Joan's act, in kneeling to Brother Richard as soon as he knelt to her, was meant to indicate that she laid no claim to the honours paid to God or the saints. Nevertheless, for a while, they became close friends – that is, insofar as Joan's mission allowed her to be capable of friendship. Brother Richard accompanied her the rest of the way to Rheims;[35] and, during the long coronation service, he seems to have been allowed to hold her standard when she grew weary of the burden.[36] He was one of her confessors, and there is an eye-witness account of her taking communion from his hands, in the company of Clermont and Alençon, 'before Senlis', during the tense days in August 1429 when the French were face to face with Bedford's army.[37] The trouble was that Brother Richard, though a useful propagandist for Joan's cause, also encouraged her in her tendency towards religious excess. The Bourgeois of Paris makes a spiteful allegation that, on one occasion, she took communion from him no less than three times in one day.[38] If this is true, her conduct, as well as his, was definitely heterodox.

Joan's alliance with the friar was destined to be troubled. Not satisfied with one holy woman, he went on to become a kind of collector of female visionaries. At Jargeau, at Christmas 1429, he had no less than three others in his company, in addition to Joan herself.[39] One of these was Catherine de la Rochelle, over whom he and Joan had quarrelled. Brother Richard had a high opinion of Catherine, and wanted Charles VII to make use of her. Joan opposed him, and her opposition seems to have caused considerable ill-feeling.[40] The tone which Joan adopted, when speaking of Brother Richard at her trial, suggests that the breach was never fully healed, or else that they had had a fresh reason to fall out with one another. There were elements of rivalry as well as of attraction in their relationship. Her link with this reckless and emotional personage did her no good at all in the eyes of her enemies. We find, for example, that Bedford linked Joan and Brother Richard together in the denunciatory letter which he sent to Charles VII shortly after the latter's coronation.[41] Brother Richard's reputation as a sorcerer[42] may well have helped to confirm the idea that Joan was a witch, though it was probably no better founded. At Troyes, however, he knew how to make himself useful.

Despite the good will of both the friar and the bishop, and the efforts which they were making within the walls upon the king's behalf, the royal army was subjected to a long wait outside Troyes. So long was it, indeed, that it nearly proved disastrous to the whole enterprise which Joan had persuaded Charles to undertake. The troops were ill-supplied with provisions when they set out, and they seem to have arrived at Troyes when they were already in a starving condition. We are told that, while the siege of Troyes lasted for five days, 'there were 5,000 or 6,000 who were nearly eight days without eating bread'.[43] What saved them was the fact that the people of Troyes had taken one of Brother Richard's apocalyptic sermons very much to heart. What he had said was: 'Sow, good people, sow plenty of beans, for he who should come will come very soon.'[44] People afterwards saw these words as a prophecy of the arrival of Charles VII, but it seems more likely that Brother Richard, anticipating the coming of Antichrist, was exhorting his listeners to prepare for the calamities that would soon take place by planting the quickest growing of all crops. The beans fed the army, together with what they could rub from the ears of wheat which were just ripening in the fields.[45]

As the time stretched out, and the city seemed no nearer to opening its gates, Charles held anxious meetings of his council. At what was meant to be the last of these, before an ignominious retreat, the king's chancellor, Regnault de Chartres, Archbishop of Rheims, summed up the sense of the discussion, which was pessimistic. The majority of those present were for a return to base, thinking that if they had failed at Auxerre they had not got much chance at Troyes, which was more strongly garrisoned and fortified.[46] It was decided, however, that Joan should be given a chance to put her case. Sent for, she 'knocked loudly on the door of the room'.[47] She knelt to the king, and Regnault de Chartres explained why she had been summoned and what the general opinion of the council was. Joan began her answer by turning to Charles, and asking if he was prepared to believe what she would now say. Cornered, Charles replied somewhat uncomfortably that 'if she said something profitable, she would willingly be believed'.[48] It is Dunois who preserved what is probably the most accurate version of Joan's response to this:

'Noble dauphin, command your people to come and besiege the city of Troyes, and drag out your debates no longer. For in God's name, within three days I will lead you into the city of Troyes, by love, force or courage, and that false Burgundy will be quite thunderstruck.'[49]

The chancellor then said: 'Joan, if it were certain that we would have [the city] in six days, we would of course wait.'[50] Joan needed no further permission. She left the council, and returned at once to the siege. Here she put everyone to work – even the knights and squires – on bringing up the materials needed for an assault. She also began to place such artillery as they had.[51] 'The positions she took up were so admirable,' says Dunois, 'that the most famous and experienced captains would not have made so good a plan of battle.'[52] Joan had evidently been a good student at Jargeau and at Beaugency.

The crucial council evidently took place in the afternoon of 9 July, and the same evening Joan began her preparations for a determined attack.[53] When the citizens of Troyes saw what was happening, a panic began, and many people took refuge in the churches.[54] The next morning Joan had the assault sounded,[55] whereupon the bishop and the principal citizens of the town came out to treat with the king. The terms were not onerous. The garrison were to go with their possessions, while the town would submit to the king, and all the citizens would receive a general pardon. The churchmen who had received benefices from the government of Henry VI were to keep them, but must take their titles again from Charles VII.[56] The one point of dispute turned out to be the fate of the prisoners who were in the keeping of the soldiers of the garrison. These maintained that, under the terms of the treaty of composition, they were allowed to take prisoners away, and when they began to evacuate, they had their captives with them. Joan refused to allow this, and posted herself at the gate 'declaring that, in God's name, they should not carry them off'.[57] In order to settle the matter, Charles, short of money as he was, had to pay the prisoners' ransoms. Not all the garrison left under the terms that were offered. A number decided to change sides, and take service with the victors.[58]

Early next morning Joan entered Troyes in order to make arrangements for the king's ceremonial entry. She placed archers to line the streets,[59] and then re-emerged to take part in the procession. As the king made his entry, she rode beside him, with her standard in her hand.[60] They were followed by most of the principal captains, richly apparelled, but Ambroise de Loré remained outside with the bulk of the army.[61] Brother Richard also took part in the ceremonial entry and seems to have been careful to make himself conspicuous. Perhaps he again offered to Joan the honours due only to the saints, though Joan stoutly denied that she had seen him doing so. She also denied that she had heard the sermon he preached that day, which we may imagine to have been a notably extravagant one.[62] In fact, one thing she found time to do, in addition to taking part in the procession, was to act as godmother to some child which had got itself born at the right moment.[63] The office of godmother was one that she was to be called upon to perform increasingly often.

The next day, the whole army was allowed to enter the city, to view what it had conquered,[64] and also perhaps to trade for food. The town the troops saw is still, in many of its aspects, the same today, and one can understand how the atmosphere was generated which allowed the dauphinists to gain entry despite the Anglo–Burgundian garrison. Troyes is really two cities in one – the old town that surrounds the cathedral, and a newer town, dating from the late middle ages, which is almost a separate entity. It is this new town which contains most of the principal churches. The narrow streets are still largely lined with houses dating from Joan's day or even earlier. In some places, as in the famous Rue des Chats, the dwellings lean so close that the corbel beams of the projecting upper stories link together. It was in this prosperous, somewhat claustrophobic merchant quarter that the wave of emotion rose which led to the surrender. The very plan of the place would have made it difficult for a small garrison to control. In any case, the leaders of the garrison seem to have seriously underrated the bishop, Brother Richard, and Joan in particular. At one stage in the negotiations Joan was face to face with the Anglo–Burgundian captains. An eye-witness reported that 'she was the simplest thing he ever saw, and in what she did there was neither rhyme nor reason, any more than in the stupidest thing he ever saw'. He thought that she was not to be compared with Madame d'Or, the female jester of the Duke of Burgundy who was famous for her long blond hair.[65] There were always a few who took this view of Joan, mistaking her simplicity of speech for stupidity. Contrariwise, there were always those who wanted to add an adventitious element of the miraculous to her actions. At Troyes, there were even some who claimed that they had seen an infinity of white butterflies fluttering around her standard.[66] When the royal army took the road for Châlons, the citizens of Troyes again crowded the walls to see them depart. The king went first, and after him went a large company of men-at-arms, all in armour, with lances tipped with white pennons upright in their hands. They caught up with the king just as he and they were almost out of sight, and the townspeople had the illusion that the horsemen disappeared in a twinkling as they dipped their lances in salute.[67]

Châlons, which duly surrendered, was the nearest that Joan had come to her birthplace since she had gone to seek the king at Chinon, and a number of the villagers made the trip to see her. One was Joan's godfather, Jean Morel. To him she made a present of the red dress she had worn when she made her way to Vaucouleurs to seek Robert de Baudricourt.[1] She must have known that it would be treated as a relic. Another visitor was Gérardin d'Épinal, whom she had once, half-jestingly, condemned as a Burgundian. To him she now said: 'I fear only one thing – treason!'[2]

Why should Joan make such an outburst, just when her fortunes seemed to have reached their height? The immediate reason may have been the strain imposed on her by Charles's perpetual hesitations. Even at Châlons she was forced to reassure him about the reception which awaited him at Rheims. 'Have no fear,' she said, 'the bourgeois of Rheims will come before you.'[3] Charles's fears were now based upon his lack of siege-machines and artillery.[4] Then, too, Joan was experiencing the intrigues of the court at close quarters, for on this occasion nearly all Charles's principal advisers travelled with the army. She may have wondered whether La Trémoille might not find some means, once Rheims was in sight, of repeating the trick he had pulled off at Auxerre. But finally, we must remember the nature of her voices. If they were a projection of her wishes and desires, they were also a projection of her anxieties, and these anxieties must have seemed doubly menacing when they came to her in such apparently objective form. Her obsession demanded of her that she establish complete control over the situation in which she found herself, so that events would follow the patterns it prescribed. She now had that control, but she must have sensed how precarious it was. Her voices were expressing her lingering self-doubts as to her destiny, and her fears that her apparently confident judgements might after all be ill founded.

From Châlons the army went towards the castle of the archbishops of Rheims at Sepsaulx, an enormous frowning pile with a twelfth-century donjon at its core. This was about four leagues from the city itself, and would be a convenient place for Charles to receive any embassy the citizens might care to send him. The struggle for the minds and hearts of the Rémois had already been going on for some time. As soon as the royal army left Gien, Philip the Good of Burgundy was expressing fears that Charles must have made arrangements with some of the leading citizens, so as to make sure the gates would be opened to him.[5] And on 4 July, Charles wrote officially to the Rémois, inviting them to send him an embassy.

Though the general feeling in Rheims was for submission to the king, there was also an attempt to put matters off – presumably in order to see what the Duke of Burgundy had to offer. When Charles first sent emissaries, the Rémois asked for time to consult. Joan opposed delay, and succeeded in making the king go forward without waiting for a further reply. At last the Rémois held a public meeting, and it was decided by acclamation that they should cast in their lot with Charles VII.[6] On 16 July a delegation came out to meet the king at Sepsaulx, and brought him the keys of the city.[7] The day was a Saturday, and it was traditional for the coronations of the kings of France to be held on a Sunday. This meant that matters must now be conducted with great rapidity. It was also prudent to crown Charles as soon as possible because Rheims occupied a position which was extremely exposed from the military point of view. Only five leagues away lay Épernay, which the English occupied until October 1435, and eight leagues away was the Burgundian county of Rethel. The delegation of citizens arrived in the morning. Almost immediately, Regnault de Chartres set off to make his ceremonial entry as archbishop[8] – he had never yet set foot in Rheims. As he went in at one gate, the remaining Anglo–Burgundian troops went out at another.[9] In the evening, Charles VII made his own entry into the city where he was to be crowned, accompanied by Joan and the whole army.[10] Naturally both the king and the Maid excited enormous curiosity amongst the crowds who had gathered to see them come in, but it was Joan, even more than Charles, who was the true focus of attention.[11]

As Charles came to Rheims, a new contingent of reinforcements arrived. Some were troops led by his brother-in-law, René of Anjou, who was Duke of Bar as well as titular king of Sicily; others were a force under Robert de Saarbruck, damoiseau de Commercy, the mercenary captain who had once levied tribute from Domrémy.

Due to the fact that the ceremony was being held at such short notice, there was frantic haste to get things ready in time. Not all could be done in the traditional manner, as much of the royal regalia were kept at Saint-Denis, near Paris, the burial place of the kings of France, which was still in English hands. Yet somehow everything necessary was either found in store, or in the king's baggage, or else improvised.[12] At 3 a.m. Charles entered the cathedral to keep the traditional vigil before he was knighted, and at nine the doors of the church were opened, and the ritual began.[13]

First, the *Veni Creator* was sung, and the office of tierce was said. During this time four 'hostages' went to fetch the holy ampulla from the church of Saint-Rémy. One of these was Gilles de Rais. They were all in full armour, and on horseback, and each of the four carried his banner in his hand.[14] Arrived at Saint-Rémy they took the traditional oath to take what was put in their charge safely to the cathedral and bring it safely back.[15] The ampulla itself was a little glass flask, dating from about the twelfth century, though legend made it out to be much earlier. It contained the holy oil which was used to consecrate the kings of France, and, in the religious sense, this consecration meant far more than the actual crowning. It was Joan's belief in the virtues of the anointing which made her insist that Charles should come to Rheims. In her eyes, and those of many other simple people, he was no true king until this had been done. Conscious of the importance of the holy ampulla, the Anglo–Burgundian garrison had, at one point, thought of trying to take it away with them,[16] but this would certainly have aroused such fury among the townspeople that they wisely refrained from making the attempt. Now, on the morning of 17 July, the ampulla was carried by the abbot of Saint-Rémy.[17] The glass flask was enclosed in the belly of a golden dove, which had claws and feet of coral. The bird was, in turn, fitted into a kind of plate or plaque made of silver-gilt, studded with precious stones. The plaque hung by a chain from the abbot's neck. He was mounted on a horse, paid for by the king. Above him was borne a canopy of cloth of gold.[18] He and his escort rode right into the cathedral, as far as the choir.[19] Here they dismounted, and the Archbishop of Rheims, attended by the canons, took the ampulla and placed it upon the high altar.[20] Charles took the usual coronation oath,[21] in which he promised three things – to keep the peace of the Church and preserve its privileges; to protect the people from exaction and injustice; and to govern with justice and mercy. He was then knighted by Alençon.[22]

Regnault de Chartres now blessed the royal ornaments and proceeded to the anointing. At this point in the ceremony the king was on his knees before the seated prelate, who held in his hands the paten of the chalice of Saint-Rémy (the chalice can still be seen in the cathedral museum), on which was the holy unction. The crowning itself followed. 'And, at the hour when the king was anointed, and also when the crown was put on his head, everyone cried *Noël*! and trumpets sounded in such a manner, that it seemed that the vaults of the church would split.'[23]

Though every care was taken to make the service as orthodox as possible, there were certain features of it which departed from the established pattern. For example, when the twelve peers of France, six of them lay and six ecclesiastical, were 'evoked and summoned before the high altar of the said church by the king of arms of France, in the way in which he is accustomed to do',[24] twelve men duly stood forward, but most of them were substitutes. Of the six lay peerages, five had fallen in to the crown, and the sixth belonged to the absent Duke of Burgundy. Three of the ecclesiastical peers were present – the Archbishop of Rheims, the Bishop-Duke of Laon, and the Bishop-Count of Châlons – and substitutes were again found for the absentees. Among the three who were missing was Pierre Cauchon, Bishop of Beauvais, one of the fiercest French supporters of the English cause. In place of the disgraced and absent Richemont, the constable's sword was held by Charles d'Albret, the half-brother of Georges de La Trémoille.[25] The most striking departure from precedent, however, was the presence of Joan herself, the cynosure of all eyes. 'And during the said mystery, the Maid stood always beside the king, holding her standard in her hand. And it was a fine thing to see the way in which the king and the Maid conducted themselves.'[26] Joan's judges at Rouen later asked her about the presence of her standard in the cathedral, when those of the other captains were excluded. To this she made what is perhaps the most sublime of all her answers. 'It had borne the burden,' she said, 'and it was right that it should have the honour.'[27]

When the two main parts of the rite were at last accomplished, Joan was overwhelmed with emotion.

And when the Maid saw that the king was consecrated and crowned, she knelt before him in the presence of all the lords, and said to him, embracing him by the knees and weeping hot tears: 'Gentle king, now is fulfilled the pleasure of God, who wished that the siege of Orleans should be lifted, and that you should be brought into this city of Rheims to receive your holy consecration, thus showing that you are true king, and he to whom the kingdom of France should belong.' And those who watched this were much moved.[28]

Joan saw in the ceremony at Rheims the justification of her mission, if not its full accomplishment. She, no less than others, found an element of the miraculous in what she had achieved. Her confessor Pasquerel tells us:

Several times I heard Joan say there was a mystery about her achievement, and when men said to her: 'Never have such things been seen as have been seen in your actions. Such actions are not to be read of in any book,' she would reply: 'My Lord has a book in which no clerk has ever read, so perfect is its instruction.'[29]

Evidently, even now, she was still smarting from the scepticism she had encountered among some of the board of assessors at Poitiers.

The coronation ceremony lasted until two in the afternoon,[30] and afterwards the coronation banquet was held in the archbishop's palace near by. According to etiquette, the king was served by Alençon, Clermont, and the other principal lords who were present.[31] For the rest of the day, Charles, wearing his crown, rode round the city to show himself to the people.[32] Joan accompanied him, and the crowds, particularly the women, thronged close about her. These fancied there was some special virtue in the ring she so frequently looked at, and tried to take her hands and to press their own rings to hers.[33]

Among those present in the city was Joan's father – a fact we know from entries in the official accounts. He stayed at an inn called L'Âne Rayé, or Striped Donkey, in the Parvis de Nôtre-Dame, directly opposite the cathedral. Even after the junketings were over, he was in no particular hurry to depart.[34] He lingered in Rheims until after 5 September, enjoying what must have been the only real holiday of his life. Joan's first convert, her 'uncle' Laxart, was also there to see the coronation and her part in it.[35] The throngs who had come to see the king crowned were immense, despite the short notice of his arrival. So many people crowded towards Rheims that the vines planted in the fields surrounding the city were trampled down by their horses.

Even if the ceremonies and the processions had not been enough to fill the day, Joan was busied with great affairs and small ones. Some were trivial indeed. At the coronation a distribution of gloves took place – these were often given as presents at feasts, when knights were made, and on other solemn occasions. One of those who got a pair of gloves promptly lost them, and applied to Joan for help. The idea that she was no more than a vulgar sorceress died hard, even amongst some of Charles VII's enthusiastic supporters. The incident of the lost gloves was for some reason remembered against Joan, and it was brought up when she stood her trial at Rouen. Now the story was that she had stolen the gloves which the king wore during part of the ceremony, and which therefore bore traces of the holy unction, in order to use them for some devilish purpose.[36]

And on 17 July, that day of days, she also found time to dictate a letter to the Duke of Burgundy. It was scarcely more conciliatory in tone than her original letter of summons to Bedford. Joan demanded in God's name that Philip the Good should now make a lasting peace with the king. 'If you want to go to war,' she said, 'go against the Saracens.' She went on to warn him:

You will not win a battle against the loyal Frenchmen, and all those who make war against the holy realm of France, make war against King Jesus, king of heaven and all the world, my rightful and sovereign Lord.[37]

When this letter was written, Joan thought she was stating the obvious. Philip's duty, as a good vassal, was to reconcile himself to his suzerain. Charles VII's mind, on the other hand, was of a more practical cast. Like Joan, he felt that reconciliation with Burgundy was the only foundation upon which peace could be built. He recognized that his coronation, by affirming his position as legitimate king, had enormously strengthened his hand, quite apart from the amount of territory he had gained on the way to it. But he knew, too, that Philip the Good would drive a hard bargain, and he was interested in finding out the terms. For Joan, such terms as the king was likely to get would mean a curtailment of the mission God had imposed on her. The king and his saviour were soon to be in direct conflict with one another.

21

According to custom, Charles VII should, immediately after
his coronation, have gone directly to the priory of Saint-
Marcoul, at Corbigny, there to be invested with the royal power
to touch for scrofula.[1] He delayed because of negotiations with
the Duke of Burgundy. Though Philip the Good would not himself attend the ceremony, his ambassadors were in Rheims upon
the day.[2] The negotiations continued as Charles made his tri-
umphal progress towards Paris, with new towns submitting
every day. At one of these, Château-Thierry, Joan asked the
king for one of the few material favours she ever requested.
Prompted by her, he signed an *ordonnance* exempting the inhabitants of Domrémy and Greux from taxes.

As the army marched onward, there was constant news of
Bedford, but no actual encounter. When a decisive battle failed
to materialize, Charles began to think of abandoning the attempt
on Paris. Indeed, he made an abortive attempt at retreat. He
had been promised passage for his army at Bray-sur-Seine, but
when his advance-guard arrived there at daybreak, it was to
find that the town had been reinforced by the English in the
course of the previous night, and his troops were sharply re-
pulsed.

It seems likely that the advance-guard went to Bray-sur-
Seine without Joan's knowledge, much less her consent. At any
rate, it was at this moment that she chose to address an extraordinary letter to the inhabitants of Rheims. It is written 'from

quarters on the road to Paris' and dated 5 August 1429. She says in part:

And it is true that the king has made a truce with the Duke of Burgundy to last for fifteen days, by which the duke must surrender the city to him peaceably at the end of the fifteenth day. However, do not be surprised if I do not enter Paris as soon as this, since I am not content with the truce which has been thus made and do not know if I will keep it. But if I do keep it, it will be only for the sake of the king's honour. Yet they will not abuse the blood royal, for I will hold and keep together the king's army, so as to be ready at the end of the fifteenth of the said days, if they do not make peace.[3]

Philip the Good's ambassadors had again been with Charles since 27 July, and this brief truce was evidently the upshot of their preliminary conversations.[4] Joan's letter upon the subject perfectly exemplifies the breach which was now developing between herself and the king; and, despite the arrogance of its tone, it shows her pathetic helplessness to do anything about it. If she had very clearly been in charge during the march from Gien to Rheims, she was now, less than three weeks after the coronation, deposed from that position.

On 11 August, Charles arrived at Crépy-en-Valois, and here he received a letter which Bedford had written to him some days previously, from Montereau. Addressing his opponent as 'you, who used to call yourself dauphin of Viennois, and who now, without cause, say you are king', Bedford claimed that he had 'pursued and continued to pursue' Charles from place to place, and now summoned him to stand fast and be ready to give battle 'either in the land of Brie, where both of us now are, or in the Île-de-France, which is close enough to both of us'. In fact, Bedford had no intention of risking a pitched battle with his inferior force, except on terms as favourable as possible to himself. He proceeded to indulge in a long series of marches and counter marches designed to draw the royal army away from Paris. At the end of these, a confrontation was seen to be inevitable, and the opponents came into closer and closer contact with one another in the district near Senlis. On 14 August, Charles decided to direct his troops towards Montépilloy, a castle on a hill which conveniently overlooked the whole of the potential battlefield.[5] By early evening, Joan, Alençon and others were encamped in the fields below the castle.[6] At the same time, Bedford was taking up a position just in front of Senlis. He decided to put his army across a little river called the Nonette, which he would use to guard his rear, while his front would be protected in the usual manner by stakes, ditches and the baggage-carts.[7] His position was based upon the abbey of La Victoire, and its surrounding village.[8] One possible weakness in his plan was the fact that the ford across the Nonette was so narrow that the English could only bring one or two horses across at a time. When Loré and Xantrailles reported this fact, it was decided to try and catch the English at the ford, but the French arrived to find that the enemy were for the most part safely across.[9] Nevertheless, skirmishing continued until nearly sunset. The next day the French were sure that a decisive battle was at hand. They confessed, heard mass, and mounted, then moved forward to come to grips with their opponents.[10] Charles VII, who had remained the night at Crépy, came to join his army which was awaiting him close to the enemy position.[11] The French battle-array was quite complex, and reflected the size of the forces at their disposal, which may have amounted to about 7,000 men[12] – a figure which would allow for natural wastage from desertions and sickness during the coronation campaign, and also for the garrisons Charles's army had left behind in some of the places which had surrendered to him. There was a main battle, commanded by Alençon and Vendôme, flanked by two wings. An *avant-garde* of skirmishers included La Hire, Dunois, d'Albret and Joan herself, who thus got her wish to be in the thick of things. In addition to these groups, there was a separate force of archers and the king's own personal guard. With the king were Clermont and La Trémoille.[13]

Bedford's force was much smaller in numbers,[14] and was drawn up in a far less intricate pattern. They stood dismounted, in one main body, except for a small force of mounted Burgundian skirmishers[15] – the Burgundians amounted to about 600 to 800 men altogether, and the rest were English, Picards and other Frenchmen from the English territories. Over the host flew two banners – that of England and that of France. A third banner, with the red cross of St George, had been entrusted to the famous Burgundian captain, Villiers de l'Isle Adam.[16] During the night, the English position had been strengthened with strong thorn barriers, and, with battle imminent, the archers had planted their stakes in the accustomed fashion.[17] The French saw that their opponents, despite the disparity in the size of the armies, were formidably strong. La Hire's experienced eye, for example, was quick to appreciate the good sense of Bedford's dispositions.[18] Nevertheless, after the king had ridden out in front of his army, accompanied by Bourbon and La Trémoille,[19] it was decided to make a practical test of the enemy's determination, though Charles had been advised by his council not to attempt an all-out attack.[20] Bedford's victory at Verneuil in 1424 must in any case have been vividly present in the king's mind, and still more so in that of Alençon, who had so nearly lost his life there. At Verneuil Bedford had stood his ground from early morning until four in the afternoon, before making a move. A series of skirmishes began when Joan took her banner in her hand, and rode up to the front line of the enemy to challenge them in her usual fashion.[21] It was the signal for a day of bitter but inconclusive fighting, during which neither side could gain the advantage. At one moment, the French managed to set up two cannon on the flank of the English position, and these had just begun to do a certain amount of damage when the mounted Burgundians sallied out of the English stockade, drove off La Hire, who was keeping guard with a small company of men-at-arms, and captured the guns.[22]

Seeing that his men were making no progress, Alençon tried the time-honoured device of sending a challenge to his opponents. He told the English that, if they wished to give battle, the French would retire for a sufficient distance to allow them to range themselves in battle-order. Bedford refused to budge.[23] He knew he had too much at stake. During the day, Joan was in a state of considerable distress of mind. The pressure of her obsession drove her forward. Her newly developed military instinct, on the other hand, told her that an all-out frontal attack would certainly be disastrous. Monstrelet reports that 'she all the time had contradictory opinions, sometimes wishing to fight the enemy, sometimes not'.[24] One irritant factor was the dust. It was an extremely hot day, and the dust rose from the parched fields to envelop the combatants.[25] Tempers grew short, and few prisoners were taken, even when their ransoms would have been worth something.[26] The last skirmish of the day was also the most determined and the most prolonged. It lasted for an hour and a half, and in the course of it the Picards who formed the right wing of Bedford's army were for a moment hard pressed.[27] The French brought up most of their archers, supported by a company of horsemen, and Bedford had to send reinforcements.[28] The combat churned up so much dust 'that one could not tell Frenchman from Englishman'.[29] It was in this skirmish that La Trémoille was nearly killed or captured. He rode up to the enemy, then dug his spurs into his horse to make it threaten the front rank with its steelshod hooves. Rearing sharply, the beast slipped and fell on the much trampled ground, and La Trémoille with it. Since he was such a heavy man, there was great difficulty in getting him remounted.[30]

By this time it was sunset, and the French army had had enough. They disengaged, and the king rode off to spend the night at Crépy, while Joan and Alençon returned to their encampment below Montépilloy, where they waited until noon of the next day, to see what Bedford's intentions were.[31] Bedford was, in fact, advised by some of his captains to pursue the French, but he considered that, in view of the disparity of forces, the risk was too great. He renewed his victuals from Senlis, from which he had been receiving supplies throughout the day,[32] and in the morning retreated towards Paris.[33] One consequence of this was that Pierre Cauchon, Bishop of Beauvais, lost control over his episcopal seat.

While Charles was prepared to fight Bedford if he had to, he preferred to negotiate with Philip the Good. The reasons were very simple. Bedford laid claim to the crown on behalf of the infant Henry VI. He had reaffirmed the claim in his letter of defiance written on 7 August, and had rubbed salt in old wounds, not only by sending it from Montereau, but by actually alluding to the crime which had taken place there.[34] The Duke of Burgundy, on the other hand, made no claim to the crown of France, though he considered himself deeply injured by the man who at present wore it. The traditional view of diplomatic relations at this period between Charles VII and Philip the Good is that Charles was perpetually the dupe. This needs to be taken with a pinch of salt. In fact, we can best understand the relationship between the two powers by looking at it, not from

Charles's point of view, but from that of the Burgundian ruler. Philip the Good was a man of very different temperament from his father, John the Fearless, and his policies developed in an entirely different way. Whereas John had been mesmerized by what took place in France, and obsessed by his own attempt to get control, not only of the royal revenues, but of the machinery of government, his son was far more interested in what was happening in the Low Countries. The factors which kept him in the English camp were largely personal. He considered Charles VII to be his own father's murderer; and Bedford was married to his sister Anne, for whom he had a particular fondness. Charles of course knew this, and was prepared to bid high for Burgundy's friendship. The suggestions he made to yet another Burgundian embassy, when it came to him at Compiègne, which had opened its gates on 18 August, were comprehensive in the extreme. One of the most interesting things about them is that they were also prophetic, being almost exactly the same as those which Philip finally accepted by the Treaty of Arras in 1435, which marked a decisive stage in the recovery of the French monarchy – at least as decisive at the coronation at Rheims. If the terms offered at Compiègne were unnecessarily humiliating, as almost all Joan's admirers have claimed, then at any rate we know how much store the king set by them. The Treaty of Arras was pushed through with immense energy when the opportunity came, and Charles was so anxious to get it signed on that occasion that he indulged in wholesale bribery of the duke's most trusted counsellors. The ideas and considerations which motivated Charles VII's diplomacy were both subtle and reasonable, and, in the upshot, he, not Philip the Good, benefited from the peace treaty. But of course all this was hidden from the popular mind, which saw nothing but shameful weakness; and it was hidden, too, from Joan. When she wrote to Philip the Good from Rheims, on 17 July, exhorting him to make 'a good firm peace, which will last for a long time',[35] we may be certain that what she was thinking of was very different from the set of conditions which Charles put forward in mid August.

While the king talked to the Duke of Burgundy's ambassadors at Compiègne, Joan also received an embassy, but of a much more curious and unexpected nature. A letter arrived from Jean IV, Count of Armagnac, asking her advice about the papal schism.[36] Armagnac had persisted in supporting the Avignon popes at a time when practically everybody else had recognized Martin V. On 4 March 1429, the latter had declared him schismatic, heretic and relapsed. It seems likely that he was now looking for a way out of his dilemma, and hoped that Joan's authority would provide him with an excuse to reconcile himself to the Roman papacy.[37] Joan's reply, as preserved in the letter which forms part of the trial document, was both ambiguous and unwise. Her answer was:

Upon this [question] I cannot well tell you rightly at the present moment, until I am in repose at Paris or elsewhere; for I am now too much occupied in making war. But when you know me to be in Paris, send me a messenger and I will let you know in all truth in which [pope] you should believe and what I will then have learned through the counsel of my rightful and sovereign Lord, the King of the whole world, and what you ought to do about it, according to all my power.[38]

When this letter was read back to her in Rouen, Joan was plainly both confused and alarmed by its content. She said first that she was just mounting her horse when the messenger came to her, and secondly that she thought the answer was only partly hers. After some further questions on the subject, she added that

She had said to the count's messenger something else which was not contained in this copy of the letters, and that if the said messenger had not gone off at once, he would have been thrown into the water, and not, certainly, by Joan herself.[39]

But she did admit that she had indeed told the Count of Armagnac that she did not know which pope God wanted him to obey.[40] It has sometimes been suspected that Joan's letter of reply, in the form in which it was read out, was nothing much better than a forgery concocted to trap her. But in fact the incident, considered as a whole, does not have precisely this flavour. We can imagine Joan caught just in the act of mounting, and, while surrounded by her usual mob of jostling admirers, being waylaid by this courier who had travelled all the way from Languedoc to find her. We can imagine, too, that the pious people of Compiègne, when they heard what the courier's mission was, were not well disposed towards him. Joan, therefore, threw a few hasty words over her shoulder as she got on her horse, and instructed some member of her entourage to reply. We may think we detect the indiscreet enthusiasm of Brother Richard. Nevertheless, what we have already learned of Joan's character may easily allow us to think that she was indeed prepared to act as a self- (or as she would have had it, God-) appointed judge on the question of the schism. Her arrogance was fully equal to such a reply, and the reference to Paris, as well as her own subsequent admissions, makes it seem certain that in substance, if not in detail, the letter produced at Rouen is a true reflection of what she said. As the king, in his Burgundian negotiations, took the first steps towards abandoning Joan, so, too, the directness of her own original inspiration began to falter.

22

Joan was still anxious to mount the promised assault upon Paris, even though enthusiasm for the enterprise had visibly cooled elsewhere. While the king conferred with Jean de Luxembourg and his colleagues, she nursed her impatience. But, eventually, as was so often the case with her, she could endure the delay no longer. She went to Alençon and said: 'My good duke, get ready your men and the other captains.' Then she added: 'By my staff, I want to go and see Paris nearer than I have seen it hitherto.'[1] She was referring to the distant glimpse which she had already had of it from the heights of Dammartin, as the two armies manoeuvred and counter-manoeuvred in the boiling August heat. Leaving the king, she and Alençon went to Senlis. A force had been sent against this before Charles left Crépy-en-Valois, and, frightened by the success of the royal army and discouraged by Bedford's withdrawal, the city had surrendered.[2] A junction was now made with the troops who had remained there, instead of going to Compiègne.[3]

It was at Senlis that there occurred the curious case of the Bishop of Senlis' horse. The accusation that Joan stole this is generally dismissed as one of the pettiest that was levelled against her in the whole course of her trial. Yet the episode is interesting as an illustration of her high-handedness. Joan admitted, implicitly at least, that she had taken the animal without permission. The horse, she said, was valued at 200 *saluts*, and the bishop was given an assignation for this.[4] Later, having discovered that the beast was not strong enough for her purposes, she wrote to its former owner to say that 'he could have it back, if he liked', and it was then given to La Trémoille to be returned to him.[5] She did not wish to keep it because she heard that the bishop was annoyed that the horse had been taken, and the horse was no good for men-at-arms. But she never learned if the prelate was paid, or if he had his horse returned to him, though she thought not.[6] The certainty is that Joan wantonly offended an important churchman who was also a key political figure. Jean Fouquerel had been Bishop of Senlis since 1423, and he had until 1429 been a supporter of the Anglo–Burgundian cause. He took a large sum of money into Paris for safety when Charles approached. Joan's quarrel with him – for that is what it amounted to – must have been a bitter one if it was sufficiently keenly remembered to form part of the trial proceedings. Then, too, the episode makes a curious contrast with Joan's known hatred of plunderers. One witness at the Trial of Rehabilitation tells us how angry she was when a Scottish soldier told her that she had been eating plundered food. She wanted to have him hanged on the spot.[7] What happened at Senlis supplies yet another instance of Joan's feeling that she was not subject to the rules that applied to ordinary people.

Having collected more troops, Joan and Alençon made for the town of Saint-Denis, just outside Paris. Their *avant-garde* arrived on 25 August,[8] to find that part of the walls had been thrown down, and the moat filled up,[9] while the more important citizens had taken to their heels and fled to Paris.[10] When Joan and the duke arrived the next day,[11] they found the town 'as if abandoned'.[12] A vigorous series of skirmishes immediately began, at different points outside the walls of the capital. Many were at a windmill between the Porte Saint-Denis and La Chapelle, a little village which lay halfway between the town which the royal army had just occupied and Paris itself. Joan took the opportunity to survey the situation, and decided that La Chapelle would make the best base if a serious assault was to be tried.[13] The result of their activities was an immediate rise in prices within the city, as the inhabitants were cut off from the little plots which many of them cultivated outside its limits.[14]

Paris at this time had about 100,000 inhabitants,[15] and, though depopulated by the misfortunes it had recently suffered, was still the largest city in Christendom. To guard it, Louis de Luxembourg had only 3,000 men, commanded by sixteen Burgundian captains and sixteen English ones – a division of responsibility which was meant to symbolize the fact that Bedford, as regent, and Philip the Good, as governor, were both equally concerned with its fate.[16] Given the immense size of the place, and the comparatively small number of men available, the struggle for Paris was bound to be as much a struggle for the minds and hearts of the inhabitants as a struggle for physical possession. Pro-dauphinist conspiracies were by no means uncommon – there were no less than eight between 1422 and 1433 – and Louis de Luxembourg had every reason to be worried.

On 26 August, when the main body of the besiegers arrived, he held a ceremony in the *Parlement* of Paris. The three chambers swore, as they had sworn several times previously, 'to live in peace and union in this town, under the obedience of the King of France and England, according to the peace treaty'.[17] By 'peace treaty' was meant, of course, the Treaty of Troyes.

Things were not less busy elsewhere. Charles had continued to negotiate with the Burgundian envoys, and, since he was unable to conclude a peace treaty with them, on 28 August he settled for a general armistice. This included all the territory on the right bank of the Seine, from Nogent-sur-Seine to Harfleur, but expressly excluded Paris. For the moment both the fact of the armistice, and its terms, were kept secret, and were therefore unknown to those at Saint-Denis. They continued to prepare for the attack on Paris, attacking and taking a number of English strongpoints near the city. Despite these successes, Alençon was increasingly anxious about the king's attitude, and on 1 September went to see him. He was told that the king would leave Senlis, where he then was, upon the following day, but nothing happened.[18] The besiegers could see that the Parisians were steadily strengthening their fortifications. During the first week of September, the *quarterniers* – those responsible for the different quarters of the city – each began to organize the defence of their own particular section. Guns were brought up, and placed on the ramparts, and barrels full of stones were made ready, and also placed upon the walls. The moats were repaired, and barricades were raised to divide one quarter from another, in case of an insurrection.[19] The stone-cutters were kept particularly busy making cannon balls. One Hilaire Caillet made no less than 1,176 balls, for which he asked four *livres* per hundred.[20]

Alençon sent a letter to the Provost of Paris and to the provost of the merchants and the aldermen. Its conciliatory tone was meant to arouse sympathy for the royal cause.[21] And on the fifth, he, Joan, Clermont, Vendôme, Charles d'Albret, Gilles de Rais, Gui de Laval and others set up an advance headquarters at the village of La Chapelle.[22] On the same day, he again went to see the king, probably to tell him that the attack would go forward with his presence or without it. He made such a fuss that Charles was finally forced to move, and finally arrived at Saint-Denis upon the morning of 7 September. At this point spirits rose, and everyone was again confident that Paris would be taken.[23]

It may have been upon this day, however, that Joan had a mishap which greatly upset the superstitious king. It concerned her sword – the supposedly magic sword which she had got from Sainte-Cathérine-de-Fierbois. According to Alençon, who saw what happened, Joan was chasing one of the prostitutes who persisted in following the army, and struck her with the flat of the blade, which promptly shattered.[24] It was not the first time that Joan had thus pursued one of the camp-followers – Louis de Coutes saw her doing so with drawn sword when the army was near Château-Thierry, but on that occasion she moderated her temper and admonished the woman without striking her.[25] Charles was much upset when the sword broke, and told Joan that she 'should have taken a good stick for the purpose, and should not thus have lost a sword which she claimed had come to her from God'.[26] It was a bad omen for the enterprise she was just about to take part in, and the accident was duly noted, not merely by the king, but by all those who now followed Joan's progress with such excited attention. The rumour among the common people was that the royal armourers, try as they might, were unable to mend the broken blade, and that once it was shattered, Joan ceased to 'prosper in arms, to the king's benefit or otherwise'.[27] We need not doubt that this apparently trivial accident delivered a telling blow to Joan's own self-confidence, as well as to her prestige.

On 8 September the long-anticipated assault on Paris was finally begun. Since it ended in failure rather than in success, Joan's judges at Rouen naturally questioned her closely about it. There were several issues that interested them. One was the fact that the attack had been made upon a major feast of the church – the Nativity of the Virgin.[28] Another was whether or not it had been undertaken 'by the revelation of her voices'.[29] Joan's answers to their questions were uneasy. About the motivation for the events of this day in particular, she would only reply that she went to Paris 'at the request of the gentlemen who wished to make a skirmish or feat of arms, and she indeed had the intention of going beyond, and passing the fortifications of Paris'.[30] This makes it look as if counsels were still divided at the crucial moment. The attack began quite late, at about eleven or twelve in the morning,[31] and, despite all doubts and divisions, the royal army deployed a large number of men. The excited Bourgeois of Paris, who was an eye-witness, estimated that there were 'a good 12,000 or more men'.[32] Here we must assume that his eyes deceived him, as Charles's forces can hardly have increased so rapidly in number since the drawn fight at Montépilloy. Yet for a mere 'skirmish or feat of arms' this was an effort on a considerable scale.

As soon as they saw what was happening, the Anglo–Burgundian garrison paraded bravely on the walls, carrying several standards of different colours, among them an enormous cross of St George.[33] Nevertheless, at the first assault the besiegers scored a considerable success, taking and burning the outwork which guarded the Porte Saint-Honoré.[34] The French commanders now anticipated that a sally would be made against them from the neighbouring Porte Saint-Denis, and therefore held back their main force behind the shelter of a hillock.[35] There was heavy artillery fire from the ramparts, but the Parisians were apparently short of powder, as their shots seemed to have little force. A number of soldiers were knocked to the ground by them, but were not otherwise injured.[36] The assailants had brought with them large quantities of huge, trebly-roped faggots with which to try and fill up the moats.[37] Joan now decided that it was time to test the true strength of the fortifications. She dismounted, and accompanied by several of the captains, among them Gilles de Rais, went down into the first ditch, which was dry.[38] She then mounted the ridge between the two ditches, and moved towards the second, which was full of water.[39] It was the signal for a general rush forward. The French surged to attack the whole stretch of wall between the Porte Saint-Honoré and the Porte Saint-Denis, shouting abuse at the defenders.[40] The fire of the assailants was so hot that their opponents were forced to duck down behind the ramparts,[41] and for a moment it seemed that all the oncoming troops had to do was to plant their ladders to be up and over the wall.[42] As they struggled with the job a cry rose within Paris that all was lost, and the populace came pouring out of the churches, where they had been attending services to celebrate the feast-day, hurried home, and locked their doors. But the internal uprising which some of Charles's councillors had hoped for failed to materialize.[43]

Joan had been probing the water in the moat with her lance, to see how deep it was, and whether it would be possible to fill up the ditch with the fascines which had been brought.[44] At the same time she was calling out to the defenders to give up the fight. The Bourgeois of Paris reports her words, though perhaps inaccurately. Of all our witnesses, he is one of the most violently prejudiced against her. 'Surrender to us quickly, in Jesus' name', she is supposed to have said. 'If you don't surrender before nightfall we shall come in by force and you will all be killed.'[45] Joan was later to deny to her judges that she had said: 'Surrender the town to Jesus.' What she had shouted was: 'Surrender to the King of France.'[46]

While she was uttering her threat that all the defenders would be killed if the city was stormed, a crossbowman was taking aim. 'Shall we, you bloody tart?' he yelled, and put his bolt through the fleshy part of her thigh. As she turned away, her standard-bearer was shot in the foot, and then, as the unfortunate man lifted his visor to examine the wound, another bolt caught him full between the eyes and killed him.[47] Joan dragged herself to shelter behind the ridge that divided the two ditches, and here for some time she remained, trying to direct the bringing up and positioning of the fascines, so that the ladders could be planted. But the water in the moat was so deep that it made the work very difficult, and there were now not enough men for the job, despite the considerable force that had begun the attack.[48]

Joan is said to have been very angry that she was at this time so little backed up, 'but the captains did not agree among themselves about the attack on the city, [and] several of the king's councillors withdrew their troops'.[49] Most of the French casualties – from 500 to 700 dead[50] – were sustained during this general assault and its aftermath.

The defenders took fresh heart when they saw that Joan had been wounded, and made an even more energetic resistance than they had done previously. Shortly after 4 p.m. the besiegers started to withdraw. The Bourgeois of Paris gives a dramatic description of the manner of their going. He tells us that a large barn just outside the walls was set on fire, and that the Parisians thought they saw their enemies piling their own dead on the flames, as if a Roman funeral. What they must in fact have been doing was to burn the siege material they had brought up before it could fall into enemy hands. This, however, was a plain enough sign of their discouragement and reluctance to return to the attack the next day.[51] Some of the royal troops were disillusioned with Joan herself, as they had come to expect that everything would be easy in her presence:

They cursed the Maid bitterly, for she had promised them that Paris would certainly fall to their assault, that she would sleep there that night and so would they all, that they would all be made rich by the city's wealth, and anyone who resisted would be cut down or burned in his house. . .[52]

Some of these promises certainly have an authentic ring to them – Joan had made similar prophecies at Orleans. The more bloodthirsty ones we may discount, considering the nature of the source. Though the assault had plainly failed, Joan was still reluctant to give up the attempt, and ignored a series of messages asking her to leave her position.[53] Eventually Raoul de Gaucourt and others had to come and fetch her. As they carried her away, she cried: 'By my staff, the place would have been taken!' so reluctant was she to face the reality of this first major failure. Those who were with her put her on a horse and took her back to La Chapelle.[54]

The next day, despite the effects of her wound, she rose early and went to Alençon, to ask him to have the trumpets sounded for a renewed assault. Alençon was ready to agree, but some of the other captains were discouraged, and unwilling to try again. As they were arguing, René of Anjou and the Count of Clermont came from the king's headquarters at Saint-Denis, with orders for Joan, and also for Alençon and the rest. Charles commanded that they were not to make a fresh attempt, but were to come instead to him. Reluctantly, these orders were obeyed. Joan, and those who thought as she did, now had the idea that it might be possible to make an attack upon the other side of Paris, by taking the troops across the Seine by means of a bridge which Alençon had already had constructed near Saint-Denis.[55] The troops left behind at La Chapelle could do nothing on the day that followed the assault save to send to the city under a flag of truce to ask permission to bury their dead. It was thus that the Parisians learned how heavy the casualties amongst their assailants had actually been.[56]

In conformity with his usual practice, Charles held not one but several sessions of the council, during which the current position was discussed. In fact the basic decision was made early. Charles distrusted both Joan's and Alençon's intentions, and feared they might defy his wishes. Throughout the night of 9 September, men under his orders were dismantling the bridge that Alençon had had constructed, in order to make quite certain that no unauthorized move was made.[57] The reasons that weighed with the king, and also with his habitual advisers, when they decided that retreat was the best course, seem to have been at least fourfold. First, there were the hopes Charles now entertained about the possible upshot of his negotiations with Burgundy. Secondly there was the fact that the hoped-for revolt within the city had not taken place, and showed no signs of doing so.[58] Thirdly, there was the fear – forcibly expressed by La Trémoille and supported by the events of 1418 – that a terrible massacre would ensue if Paris was taken by force.[59] And lastly, there was the king's usual lack of money to pay his troops.[60] As she listened to the arguments which were being put forward in favour of the decision to go, Joan can have been little soothed by the praise which was at the same time lavished upon her courage during the unsuccessful assault.[61]

On 13 September, Charles took his departure from Saint-Denis,[62] and Joan was compelled to follow him, despite the fact that her voices told her to remain. She was later to excuse this disobedience by saying that the lords of her party took her away against her will, and that 'had she not been wounded she would not have gone'.[63] Yet this wound, which was considerably less serious than the one she received at Orleans, since it healed in five days, can have made little real difference to the situation. Unhurt, Joan would still have had no choice, and this fact was acknowledged by her at some deep level, and was reflected in the processes of her unconscious mind. When she went, she admitted, she 'had permission to go'.[64] Before she left, she dedicated a suit of armour and a sword in the abbey church of Saint-Denis.[65] In doing so, she was once again identifying herself with the noble and knightly caste. Why, she was asked, did she offer these arms?

Out of devotion, as is the custom of men-at-arms when they have been wounded; and because she had been wounded before Paris, she offered them to St Denis, because this is the battle-cry of France.[66]

The sword she left behind her was not, however, the one from Sainte-Cathérine-de-Fierbois which she had just broken, but another weapon altogether.[67]

As soon as the retreat began, matters began to lapse into their habitual condition of disorder. The march of the retreating army, for example, was so precipitous that often no kind of order was kept as they went pell-mell towards the Loire.[68] And though Charles had made arrangements for the government of the territories which had newly returned to his obedience, these turned out to be both ramshackle and ineffective. If those who had returned to Charles's obedience suffered, those who had not suffered perhaps still more. The Bourgeois of Paris tells us that, despite the extension of the truce, all the villages round Paris were forced to pay protection money to the king's garrisons, and that 'not a man dared set foot outside the suburbs – he would be lost, killed, held to a ransom higher than all he possessed and dared take no revenge.'[69]

The retreat from Paris marks a distinct break in Joan's career. From the time she arrived at Chinon she had known nothing but triumph. Now she was to know almost nothing but disaster. The interesting thing is that her popular reputation survived the misfortunes that befell her, and continued to flourish not only at Orleans but elsewhere. It was the king's confidence which was fatally shaken. We have already seen the immense effect which Joan had upon the people of Orleans as soon as she arrived. From that moment on, she caught the popular imagination. At Loches, when she was there to plead with the king in late May, the common people threw themselves at the legs of her horse, and kissed her hands and feet, just as they were to do later, when she rode around Rheims on the day of the king's coronation. On this earlier occasion she was in the company of Pierre de Versailles who had been a member of the tribunal of assessors at Poitiers:

Pierre said to Joan: 'You do ill to allow these things. This is not due to you. Defend yourself from them or you will lead men into idolatry.' Joan said: 'In truth, I do not know how to guard myself from it, if God does not guard me.'[1]

Her judges at Rouen were also to make plain their disapproval of her attitudes towards her humble admirers:

Asked if she knew what was in the minds of those who belonged to her party, when they kissed her feet, her hands and her clothing?

She replied that many wanted to see her, and kissed her hands, but as little as she could manage. The poor came willingly to her because she brought them no evil, but helped them to bear misfortune.[2]

Everywhere she went on her campaigns, she tended to raise up a rabble of country people, who enlisted under her banner, and who considered themselves to be Joan's soldiers rather than the king's.[3] These simple folk nicknamed her *l'Angélique* – the Angelic one – and she became the subject of popular songs.[4] This information comes to us from a Burgundian source, and it is another Burgundian, namely Chastellain, who tells us that 'the French made her their idol'.[5] He also remarks that

The name of the Maid was so great already and so famous that everyone recognized her as something which could not be judged either for good or for ill.[6]

In the articles of accusation put forward at her trial, we find the allegation that Joan was adored as a saint, and that masses and collects were said in her honour:

And furthermore they called her greater than all the saints of God, after the Blessed Virgin; they put up images and representations of her in the basilicas of the saints and also carried upon their persons representations in lead and other metals, as it is customary to do for the memory and representation of saints canonized by the Church, and they preach publicly that she is a messenger of God and an angel rather than a woman.[7]

This description of her cult is confirmed by one or two bits of outside evidence. A Parisian clerk, hostile to Joan, describes how children offered lighted candles to her on their knees:

[This] happened in several notable towns in the obedience of our adversaries, and she accepted these candles as a kind of offering. . . In many places people have raised up already and venerate portraits of this Maid, as if she were already beatified. . .[8]

We have a record of a sermon being preached at Périgueux, at a solemn sung mass on 13 December 1429, whose subject was 'the great miracles accomplished in France by the intervention of the Maid, who came to find the King our Lord, upon God's behalf'.[9] And two lead medallions connected with Joan still exist. One shows, upon one side, the Eternal Father on his throne; and upon the other the arms which are considered to have been Joan's,[10] though she denied at her trial that she had borne them.[11] It is thought that these medallions, which were found in the Seine, were prepared in readiness for a coup in Paris in September 1429. Much of the excitement generated by Joan was, however, irrelevant to her own view of her mission. Her voices might call her 'daughter of God', but they never seem to have promised her the sainthood which the populace conferred on her in her own lifetime.

Whatever the common opinion of Joan, Charles and his court were prepared to ignore it. Charles was interested in pursuing his negotiations with the Duke of Burgundy. These were not going as well as he had hoped. The stumbling-block was not the Maid, but the attitude of the town of Compiègne, which had so recently come into the king's hands. Despite its strategic importance, Charles was quite prepared to give it up if by so doing he could buy peace with Burgundy. But he had reckoned without the inhabitants. They firmly refused to be handed over to the duke. Charles therefore found that his negotiations with Burgundy had reached an impasse. Compiègne was what Philip the Good wanted, and if he could not have it, then he would strengthen his ties with Bedford. From all this busy diplomacy Joan was excluded It is unlikely, in any case, that she could have played a useful part, even had she been qualified to do so. When she arrived back at Gien, her real wish was to go campaigning again as soon as possible. Alençon was assembling troops to make war on the English in Normandy, and asked the king to allow Joan to go with him. But this was opposed by Regnault de Chartres, by La Trémoille and by Gaucourt, so Charles refused permission. Joan and Alençon were never allowed to campaign together again.[12]

This refusal demonstrates the extent to which Joan had, by this time, become identified with the faction of the princes of the blood, which was regarded with great suspicion not only by the ruling favourite, but by the king himself. For example, he was by no means at one with Joan on the subject of the release of Charles of Orleans. He found the duke's absence extremely convenient. When Orleans was at last freed in 1440, it was through the intervention of none other than Philip the Good, who thought he might make a useful ally. The King of France

184

was almost the only French prince to make no contribution to the enormous ransom of 240,000 crowns.[13]

Forbidden to go campaigning, Joan had to resign herself to some weeks of idleness. From Gien, where he crossed the Loire, Charles made his way towards Bourges, his administrative capital, where he had left the queen. Queen Marie rode out to meet him at Selles, accompanied by the woman who was now to be Joan's hostess for a brief period. She was called Margaret La Touroulde, and her deposition at the Trial of Rehabilitation gives us some intimate glimpses of Joan at this period of her life. She was married to Regnier de Boullengy, royal councillor in charge of finances, and her husband had served not only Charles VII but Charles VI. Margaret formed part of the queen's suite at Selles, and this was the first time she had seen the personage whom everyone was talking about. Naturally, she was extremely curious about her. This curiosity was to be to some extent satisfied when she was asked to provide lodgings for Joan at her house in Bourges. Significantly enough, the request was made by Charles d'Albret, La Trémoille's half-brother. Margaret's reminiscences run in part as follows:

She was in my house for a period of three weeks, sleeping, drinking and eating, and almost every day I slept with Joan and I neither saw nor perceived anything wrong, but she behaved as an honest and Catholic woman, for she went very often to confession, willingly heard mass and often asked me to go to matins. And at her insistence I went, and took her with me several times.

Sometimes we talked together and someone said to Joan that doubtless she was not afraid to go into battle because she was certain that she would not be killed. She replied that she was no safer than any other combatant. . .

I remember that several times women came to the house while Joan was staying there, and brought rosaries and other objects of piety so that she might touch them, which made her laugh and say to me: 'Touch them yourself, they will be as good from your touch as they will from mine.' She was open-handed in almsgiving, and most willingly gave to the needy and to the poor, saying that she had been sent for the consolation of the poor and needy.

And several times I saw her at the bath and in the bath-houses, and so far as I was able to see she was a virgin. And from all that I know, she was all innocence, except in arms, for I saw her riding on horseback as the best of soldiers would have done, and at that the men-at-arms marvelled.[14]

This vivid description is completely consistent with everything we have heard before, and shows that the main outlines of Joan's character were firmly enough drawn for most people to recognize them – descriptions of her conduct, from her constant almsgiving to her skill in horsemanship, are in fact remarkably consistent throughout her career. But there are also some points that call for further commentary.

To share one's bed with another person of the same sex was a medieval custom, and we need draw no sinister inferences from it. At Orleans Joan slept with the young daughter of her host Jacques Boucher,[15] and we also hear that she shared a bed with his wife.[16] It was Gaucourt, who probably did not much like Joan, who tells us that 'she always had another woman sleeping with her at night',[17] when she was not actually on campaign, as a means of guarding her chastity. But we do nevertheless learn from another witness that 'Joan always slept in the company of young girls and did not like to lie with old women',[18] and from this we may perhaps deduce an element of homosexual attraction, though noting that it was certainly unconscious.

Women were always amongst Joan's most fervent admirers, one suspects because she represented some kind of ego-ideal, and it was they who usually made the demonstrations of enthusiasm which alarmed the men of the church. At the same time, her relationships with individuals of her own sex seem to have been easy and free from strain. It is a quality which emerges from Margaret La Touroulde's deposition, and also from what we know of Joan's encounters with such great ladies as the Duchess of Alençon and (after she was captured) the wife of Jean de Luxembourg. The bath-houses which La Touroulde mentions were a common feature of medieval towns – people seem to have washed more frequently in those days than we now give them credit for. If we want to know what the interior of one of these places looked like, we have only to consult Dürer's well-known drawing 'The Women's Bath', though this dates from 1496. Joan seems to have waxed confidential in the relaxed atmosphere. Though Margaret knew her so briefly, her description of Joan is one of the most convincing character-sketches we possess.

186

Why did the royal council, then in session at Mehun-sur-Yèvre,[1] think it desirable to launch an attack on Perrinet Gressart, when the matter was discussed in October 1429? Gressart's principal stronghold was the Loire town of La Charité. This was, in Joan's time, a river-port which had originally grown up around an important Cluniac abbey – so important that we find it described as the 'first daughter' of Cluny. The town was well sited for defence, lying, as it did, with two low hills upon either side and with the river in front. In the fifteenth century it was heavily fortified, and important remains of its walls can still be seen today.

Gressart was a man of humble birth, who became one of the most successful mercenary captains of the age. He started life as a mason, and in 1415 he first appears in the documents as a member of a band operating in the Nivernais. By 1420, he was at the head of a company paid by the Duke of Burgundy, and in 1423 he took La Charité from the partisans of the dauphin, and proclaimed himself captain, in the joint names of the Duke of Burgundy and of the 'King of France and England'. In December 1425, La Trémoille, who had been on a mission to the Duke of Burgundy, was seized by Gressart despite the duke's safe-conduct, and was forced to pay a ransom of 14,000 écus, plus presents to Gressart's wife and companions which amounted to another 6,000 écus.[2]

In mounting an attack on Gressart in the autumn of 1429,

Charles was reverting to an old plan, which had already been thoroughly discussed before the march to Rheims. He could see it as a means of getting back at the Duke of Burgundy for his acceptance of the lieutenant-generalcy of the kingdom from Bedford (13 October), but one which did not technically violate the truces. In addition, La Trémoille would be happy to take revenge for the insult and the financial loss which he had suffered in 1425. We do, indeed, have specific information that the campaign was in part at least due to La Trémoille's initiative,[3] and even if this was not the case Albret's involvement would make it certain. Joan seems to have been by no means unwilling to set out for the wars again. At her trial she said that 'she herself wanted to go into France, but the men-at-arms told her it would be better to go before La Charité'.[4] She denied, however, that she had gone there upon the instructions of her voices.[5]

The campaign began, not with a direct attack upon Gressart's main stronghold, but by an assault on the smaller and weaker fortress of Saint-Pierre-le-Moûtier, which was commanded by his lieutenant, Galarden de Soulat. This, too, was apparently La Trémoille's decision.[6] Saint-Pierre-le-Moûtier is a small place now, and must have been small then. It lies a little way back from the river Allier, at an important crossroads. Today the heavy traffic grinds through it all day long. It has no natural features to help the defence, since it lies on the flat. Though few medieval buildings are left, the street plan suggests that what Joan and Albret found when they arrived was a largish fortified village, huddled tightly around the church which still exists. This building does not, by its size, suggest that there was a big population.

The attacking force assembled at Bourges, and the assault was not delivered for some time after Saint-Pierre had first been invested. It is Aulon who gives us an account of what took place:

Because of the great number of soldiers in the town and its great strength, and also because of the resistance which the garrison put up, the French were forcibly compelled to retire. At that moment I came up. But I had already been so severely wounded in the heel by an arrow that I could neither stand nor walk without crutches. I saw that the Maid had been left with a very small company of her own men and others, and had no doubt that harm would ensue. So I mounted a horse and rushed towards her. I asked her what she was doing alone there like that, and why she did not retire with the rest. After taking her helmet from her head, she answered that she was not alone, that she still had 50,000 men in her company, and that she would not leave that spot until she had taken the town.

At that moment, whatever she might say, she had not more than four or five men with her, which I know for certain, as do several others who also saw her. Therefore I told her out of hand to go away and retire like the rest. She told me, however, to send for faggots and withies to make a bridge over the moat so that it might be possible to get near. And when she had said this she shouted: 'Faggots and withies, everybody, so that we can make a bridge!' And they were immediately brought and put in position. The whole thing utterly astonished me, for the town was immediately taken by assault, and at that time there was no great resistance.[7]

The importance of this description is what it tells us about Joan's mental condition. The taking of Saint-Pierre-le-Moûtier has since been sentimentalized as the *'Victoire-aux-Anges'*, though no mention of angels is made in the sources. But what Aulon seems to describe for us is a woman in a state of fugue, no longer in touch with the reality surrounding her. If this was the case, her disorientation did not last for long. The troops she and Albret had with them were mostly foreign mercenaries,[8] and they no sooner broke into the town than they rushed to the church and started to plunder it, taking the church treasures as well as the goods of the inhabitants which had been stored there for safety. Joan rounded on them and stopped the plundering.[9]

Today, when one visits Saint-Pierre, it is of course the church, with its fine Romanesque tympanum, which most vividly recalls Joan's presence. Within the building is one especially intriguing object – an early fifteenth-century stone statue of St Michael. But there is nothing to indicate that this representation of one of her tutelary saints is connected with Joan's victory.

The traditional date for the storming of Saint-Pierre-le-Moûtier is 2 November 1429. By 9 November Joan and Albret were at Moulins, preparing for the siege of La Charité.[10] She and Albret are found writing to the inhabitants of Riom, reporting that Saint-Pierre-le-Moûtier has been taken, and asking for help with the next stage of the campaign. Joan tells her correspondents that there has been a great expense of 'powder, arrows and other supplies of war',[11] and asks for materials. Albret writes at greater length, but in the same strain, and names Joan and another captain as joint-commanders with himself.[12] A similar letter had been sent to the town of Clermont two days earlier, and this responded not only by sending supplies, but by sending Joan herself a sword, two daggers and a suit of armour.[13] Another town which sent supplies for the purpose was Orleans, which not only had a great affection for Joan but stood to gain materially if navigation on the upper Loire was freed of Gressart's depredations. They sent not only supplies but men, and a payment was made for refurbishing the banner of the city, which indicates the presence at the siege of an official contingent.[14]

Despite the help given by these and other towns, the siege of La Charité was a failure. The French bombarded the town.[15] They also delivered at least one assault.[16] But after sitting in front of it for about a month,[17] they were compelled to withdraw. When they withdrew, they had to leave behind them most of their artillery,[18] perhaps because of the wintry weather which had also hampered siege operations.[19] We know that Perrinet Gressart succeeded in beating off his attackers without getting help from outside.[20] Contemporary opinion was inclined to lay the blame for the failure directly at the king's door. The chronicler Perceval de Cagny tells us that

When [Joan] had passed a space of time [at La Charité], because the king did not give money to provide victuals nor money to maintain her company, she had to raise her siege and depart in great displeasure.[21]

Another source, a letter dated simply 22 December, and written by the counts of Nevers and Rethel to their cousin the Duke of Burgundy, indicates that, even at this date, the siege was still going on, though La Trémoille was now trying to negotiate a withdrawal. It also tells us that the besieging troops were mostly mercenaries who had not been paid.[22] We may therefore suppose that a considerable gap existed between the taking of Saint-Pierre-le-Moûtier and the attempt to tackle the problem of La Charité itself, and that the siege continued from late November until nearly the end of December, with the

190

interval being used both to try and reorganize supplies, as the documents indicate, and to capture one or two other small places as well.[23] Joan left La Charité before Christmas, as we know that on Christmas Day she was at Jargeau, further down the Loire.[24] But she could have got there comparatively swiftly, by using the river for transport.

Gressart survived Joan's attempt to crush him by a number of years. Indeed, his is one of the major success stories of the latter part of the Hundred Years War. After the Treaty of Arras, he reconciled himself to Charles VII. He held on to La Charité, and was now named captain for the King of France. It did not revert to the French crown until 1440, by which time Gressart was dead.[25]

The period of the unsuccessful campaign on the Upper Loire also seems to have been the time when the tensions between Joan and Brother Richard rose to a climax, and it was certainly the period at which she quarrelled with her fellow-visionary Catherine de la Rochelle. This woman seems to have been a born trouble-maker. She was later to fall into the hands of the ecclesiastical authorities in Paris and to be the source of some of the accusations levelled against Joan at Rouen.[26] Joan cannot at first have been wholly cautious with her, as there is evidence that she told her about the Fairies' Tree at Domrémy.[27] Their first meeting took place before the siege of La Charité. We know that Catherine advised Joan not to go there, and said that it was too cold.[28] Catherine's alternative plan was to go on a mission to the Duke of Burgundy, in order to make peace.[29] What interested Joan about Catherine was the latter's claim that a white lady, clad in gold, came to her

Telling her that she should travel through the good towns, and that the king should give her heralds and trumpeters to have it cried that anyone having gold, silver or hidden treasure should bring it at once; and that those in possession of such things hidden away who did not bring them would soon be found out by her, Catherine, and she would thus pay Joan's men-at-arms.[30]

Joan was suspicious of this rigmarole from the very start, but nevertheless consulted her voices, who told her that it was 'but folly and all nothing', so she wrote and told the king not to employ Catherine. Brother Richard, however, was insistent, and at some later stage (one suspects, from the flow of Joan's narrative at her trial, that it was now after the failure of the siege), she decided that Catherine's claims must be investigated further. The opportunity seems to have occurred when they were both at Jargeau, at Christmas 1429:

[Joan] asked Catherine if this white lady who appeared to her came each night, saying that she wanted, for this reason, to lie with her in the same bed. And in fact Joan slept with her and watched until midnight and saw nothing. Afterwards she slept. And when morning came, she asked Catherine if this lady had come to her. Catherine said yes, while Joan slept, and that she had been unable to waken her. Then Joan asked if this lady would come the next night; and Catherine said yes, so Joan slept during the day so as to be able to watch the whole of the next night. And she went to bed that night with Catherine and watched all night and saw nothing, though she often asked Catherine whether the lady would come or not and Catherine said: 'Yes, soon.'[31]

The modern mind is not necessarily frivolous when it discovers an element of ironic comedy in this contest of visionaries. After all, Joan was asking Catherine for exactly the same kind of sign which she consistently refused to give herself. One recalls her crushing retort to poor Jean d'Aulon when he asked if, just once, she would let him see 'her counsel'. She replied: 'You are not sufficiently worthy and virtuous to see it.'[32]

Catherine was certainly filled with some of the same religious fervour that Joan possessed. She told the ecclesiastical Court in Paris when she was brought before it that 'when the precious body of Our Lord [was] consecrated, she used to see the great and secret wonders of Our Lord God'.[33] But, unlike her companion, Pieronne, a woman from 'Breton-speaking Brittany', who held out steadfastly, both for her own visions and in support of Joan, Catherine supplied what evidence she could, and escaped with her life. In August 1430 she was once more in Charles's dominions, and had been making trouble in Tours.[34] Pieronne was burned in Paris on 3 September 1430, but less for supporting Joan than for saying that 'God often appeared to her in human form and talked to her as one friend does to another', which was adjudged to be blasphemous.[35]

In December 1429, when Joan's military fortunes were at a low ebb, she and her whole family were ennobled by Charles VII. The document which confers this new rank confers it not only upon Joan, her father, mother and three brothers, but extends to their whole posterity, both male and female. Among the witnesses was Georges de La Trémoille.[1] It is difficult to know what to make of this act on the part of the king. If it was an attempt to regularize what was, in terms of the society of the time, a thoroughly irregular situation, then it went much further than it need have done. If it was an act of simple gratitude, then it was curiously timed. The difficulties are increased when we consider a subject intimately connected with Joan's claim to be noble, and with her position in the social and military hierarchy. It is that of Joan's arms. One of the most puzzling denials made by Joan at the time of her trial came when she was questioned about precisely this topic:

Asked if she had had a shield and arms, she replied that she had never had them; but her king gave her brothers arms, to wit an azure shield upon which were two golden lilies with a sword in the midst; and in this town [Rouen] she had described these arms to a painter who asked her what arms she bore. *Item*, she said that these arms had been given by her king to her brothers, without request made by her, Joan, and without revelation.[2]

Joan's denial is contradicted by the whole of the rest of the evidence, and indeed by the disputed arms themselves. These are accurately described in the schedule of seventy accusations drawn up against Joan at one point in the trial. They consisted of: 'Two lilies upon an azure field, and in the midst a silver sword with hilt and guard of gold, pointing upwards with, at the tip, a crown of gold.'[3] They were a heraldic representation of Joan's mission, wherein her sword, flanked by the *fleurs-de-lys*, was seen supporting the crown of France. Gilles de Rais, for his services during the campaign of 1429, was allowed to augment his arms with the royal lilies, and the allusion in Joan's case is even more pointed.

It is Louis de Coutes who tells us that Joan 'received her rank from the king'[4] while she was still at Tours, being outfitted for her part in the attempt to relieve Orleans. This means simply that it had been decided to treat her as being at least the equal of the other captains. But on 2 June 1429 – that is, just a few days before Joan set out for the campaign which was to culminate in the victory of Patay a fortnight later – Charles, who, was then at Chinon, gave Joan arms 'for her standard and to adorn herself.'[5] We may reasonably suppose that these arms were those which Joan later refused to acknowledge. The suspicion is confirmed by the description of a standard borne by members of Cardinal Beaufort's army, which entered Paris in late July. This had a white ground, in imitation of Joan's own standard, and upon it was a distaff from which hung a bobbin half-filled with thread, with other bobbins in the field and the inscription 'Let the beauty come!' The whole thing was an elaborate pun upon the two senses of the word *filer*, which can mean either 'to spin', or, more colloquially 'to take oneself off'.[6] But there was another element as well. The design on the standard was obviously intended as a parody of what was widely known to be Joan's heraldic device. To this we must add the fact that the disputed arms appear upon the lead medallions found in the Seine which have already been described. Given the popular and symbolic function of these objects, the use of the design is extremely significant.

Why then did Joan feel compelled to renounce her arms, even though she had already incautiously admitted that they were hers to the painter who came to ask about them? The reason can only be their close connection to the royal arms of France. This is confirmed by the letter sent, in Henry VI's name and after Joan's execution, to the prelates, nobles and cities of France. This specifically accuses her of having 'asked to have and carry the most noble and excellent arms of France, which she obtained in part; and she and her brothers, according to what is said, bore them in several combats and assaults'.[7] Throughout her trial Joan was anxious to protect Charles VII's reputation, even if it meant, as on this occasion, that she had to renounce the noble status she had so much coveted. One reason for Joan's ennoblement may have been that a different role was now envisaged for her, but, if this was the case, it did not immediately come to pass. Of her movements during this period we only know that she was at Orleans on 19 January 1431,[8] and that she may have been at Bourges immediately before.[9]

We pick up her trail again in the month of March, when she was with the court at Sully, the great castle by the Loire which belonged to Georges de La Trémoille, and which the king treated as if it was one of his own residences. What we have are copies of three letters, two of them addressed to the people of Rheims, and the third, which is in quite a different style, to the Hussites. The first letter to Rheims is dated 16 March. Joan has heard that the city is threatened with being besieged, and wants to assure its citizens that there will be no siege if she can first get at the enemy, 'but if I do not meet them and they come towards you, shut your gates, and I will be there and will make them put on their spurs in such haste that they won't know where to go'. In a postscript, she promises good news.[10] Her second letter refers to rumours of a Burgundian conspiracy within the city, which we also find referred to in letters written by Charles VII, which have reached us only in the form of abstracts.[11] Joan again promises good news of her own activities. The letter to the Hussites, like her letter to the Count of Armagnac, is a curious excrescence upon her career. It survives only in a German version, but it is plain that the original was written in Latin. Joan's fulminations against the Bohemian heretics have nothing to do with her usual epistolary manner, nor with her usual preoccupations, and it has been plausibly conjectured[12] that the letter was written by some cleric in her name, perhaps her confessor Pasquerel. Brother Richard would be another, and even more attractive, possibility.

What Joan seems to have meant, when she promised good

195

news to the people of Rheims, was her own imminent departure for the war. But she had difficulty in getting permission to go. At last, as so often previously, she took the law into her own hands. At the end of March, or at the beginning of April, when she was still kept in idleness at Sully, she pretended that she wanted to ride out for her own diversion. Instead of this, she made straight for Lagny-sur-Marne, where she knew that the garrison were actively harassing the Anglo–Burgundians.[13] She seems to have lured a small number of men into going with her.[14] From what took place subsequently, we may imagine that they included Aulon and her brother Pierre. Many of the details of Joan's last campaign are mysterious, and likely to remain so. But one or two background details can be filled in, and if we keep these in mind, we get a clearer picture of what may have taken place during the weeks of frantic activity which ended in her capture at Compiègne. First, if she left Sully without permission, she was soon reinstated. In mid May, we find her keeping company with Regnault de Chartres, the chancellor of the kingdom, and with Vendôme, who was now Charles's lieutenant-general in the region near Paris. Joan would hardly have been riding with those two if she was, at the same time, in bad odour with the king. An even more telling point can be culled from the record of Joan's trial. She was asked what money she had at the time when she was captured, and replied: '10,000 or 12,000 écus in ready money, which was not a great treasure with which to wage war: it is even very little. . . And she said that what she has comes from the king's own money.'[15] There is only one way of interpreting this. When she was captured, Joan had her own war-chest. And this means, in turn, that she was exercising an independent command. She had never enjoyed this kind of freedom before.

Joan's departure from Sully may have been prompted by news of a conspiracy brewing in Paris, discovered by the Anglo–Burgundians during the first week in April.[16] The plot was simple – Scottish troops were to serve as decoys, and, dressed as drovers, would take their cattle through one of the gates of the city. When this was opened, other troops lying in ambush nearby would rush the defences, and would be assisted with sympathizers within. When the conspiracy was revealed, more than 150 people were arrested.[17]

Paris, throughout this period, was in a state of economic decline. By 1432, when the misery of the inhabitants reached a climax, there were no less than 20,000 empty houses in the city, which were sometimes put to new use as stables and pig-pens.[18] In early 1430, the population was in an unstable and excitable condition, and the Bourgeois of Paris describes how those in charge of the city had great watchfires lit, because everyone was alarmed at the apparently unending successes scored by dauphinist freebooters.[19] The plot might well have succeeded, had it not become so widespread.

Not all the freebooters who harried the countryside fought on the French side. Soon after the conspiracy in Paris failed, Joan had an encounter with a captain who supported the opposite party. His name was Franquet d'Arras, and he had served long in the wars. He was in the service of the Duke of Burgundy (at that time John the Fearless) as early as 1416, when we find him associated with Perrinet Gressart.[20] Now, after a successful raid into French territory, he was returning to base.[21] He had about 300 men with him.[22] Joan heard of his activities when she was at Lagny, and immediately decided to deal with him.[23] Her force was slightly superior to his in numbers – it consisted of about 400 men-at-arms[24] – and she had with her several other captains. One was the Scotsman, Sir Hugh Kennedy, who had taken part in the relief of Orleans.[25] Another was a Piedmontese mercenary called Bartolommeo Barretta. Barretta seems to have been Joan's immediate subordinate – we certainly know that he was serving as her lieutenant some weeks later, at the time of her capture.[26] Seeing that he was about to be attacked, and unable to escape because of the booty he was carrying, Franquet followed standard tactics. He dismounted his men in the meadows bordering the Marne, and ranged them behind a hedge, deploying archers to protect them.[27] Joan made two assaults on his position, but could not at first make any impression.[28] But Franquet had had the bad luck to be caught very near to Lagny itself. Joan was able to send back to the town for the help of the garrison, which came up under its commanders Ambroise de Loré and Jean Foucault, and Franquet was overwhelmed.[29] It was a bloody little battle.[30] Joan's force probably suffered quite heavily in its two unsuccessful assaults; and though the third brought comparatively light casualties,[31] it was followed by a massacre of Franquet's troops.[32] Franquet himself survived, and was taken prisoner. Joan's treatment of Franquet d'Arras was to raise serious complaints against her, and not merely among her opponents.[33] At her trial she was questioned about her behaviour towards him. It was alleged that she had received him for ransom, but had later had him put to death.[34] She replied that her intention had been to exchange him for Jacquet Guillaume, the landlord of the Bear Inn near the Porte Baudoyer in Paris, who had been involved in the recent conspiracy, but she discovered that the latter had already been executed.[35] Her intention then was to arrange that Franquet should be freed in the usual way, but the bailli of Senlis had protested to her that this would be a 'great wrong'. So Joan had surrendered her prisoner to stand trial, saying: 'Because my man is dead whom I wished to save, do with him what you ought to do in justice.'[36]

Franquet's catalogue of crimes was so extensive that his trial lasted a full fifteen days, and at the end of it he was decapitated,[37] having confessed to being 'murderer, thief and traitor'.[38] But his admitted bad character did not excuse Joan, in the eyes of professional military men, from her breach of the accepted laws of war. What they remembered about Franquet was that he had been 'a valiant man and a good fighter'.[39] It has been said that Joan's handling of this case showed that she represented 'new anti-feudal and national codes of values, new social forces rising from the bottom of society'.[40] The truth of the matter seems to me to be rather different. What we see here is the conflict between two different systems of morality, with Joan caught between them. The bailli of Senlis was the spokesman of bourgeois values, as against chivalric ones, and he must have been a persuasive man indeed to get Joan to listen to his case on this occasion. Everything seems to show that the Joan who fought Franquet d'Arras near Lagny was a considerably different person from the naively enthusiastic visionary who had harangued the royal army on its way to the relief of Orleans. At Orleans itself she had not wanted to fight on a major feast of the church – Ascension Day – nor to attack the retreating English army on a Sunday. But Sunday was the day upon which Jargeau was stormed, and Paris was assailed on another major feast of the Church. One of the few occasions during her trial when Joan was almost at a loss for words was the time that they questioned her about this. To the query: 'Was it well done to go to attack Paris on the day of the Nativity of Our Lady?' she replied:

It is well done to keep the feasts of Our Lady and it seems to me in my conscience that it would be well done to keep the feasts of Our Lady from beginning to end.[41]

Perhaps more significant still is the change in her associates. We know that, from the beginning, she was attracted by the braggadocio of professional mercenary captains like La Hire. But now, during her last campaign, we find her associated almost exclusively with men of this stamp. We may judge that her victory over Franquet had considerable symbolic value for her from the fact that it was at Lagny that she at last ceased to carry the sword she had fetched from Sainte-Cathérine-de-Fierbois, and which she had broken at Saint-Denis. Henceforth she wore 'a sword taken from a Burgundian' – who can have been none other than Franquet himself – which was 'good for giving fine strokes and slashes'.[42] How good was something she had had the opportunity to observe at close quarters.

Yet, just at the moment when she identified herself most thoroughly with the professional soldiers by whom she was surrounded, she found herself being pulled back by her own legend into quite a different context. During her time at Lagny, an apparently stillborn child was produced by one of the women there. The girls of the town went to pray at the abbey church of Saint-Pierre before a miraculous statue of the virgin which had been venerated since the time of a plague three hundred years before. Joan was asked to join these prayers of intercession:

Then she went with the others and prayed and finally life appeared in the child which yawned three times and was afterwards baptized. Then it died and was buried in consecrated ground.[43]

The two main incidents connected with Joan's stay at Lagny illustrate very neatly the dilemma of her situation – a dilemma from which she could never escape.

Joan herself first had a premonition of imminent disaster at Melun. It was here 'during Easter week' that St Catherine and St Margaret began to warn her that she would be taken before midsummer, 'that it must be so, and that she must not be struck by stupor, but take it in good part and God would help her'.[1] Melun had been besieged by the forces of Charles VII, and seems to have capitulated almost at the moment when Joan states that she was there.

We pick up her trail again at Senlis. Her presence there is recorded by Perceval de Cagny,[2] and confirmed by a resolution of the town council dated 24 April 1430. Hearing that she was on her way to them, they decided to ask her not to enter the town with more than thirty or forty of the most notable of her company.[3] The citizens of Senlis, in the months since their submission, had had plenty of experience of the turbulence of the king's troops, and this, no doubt, was the reason for their reluctance to receive more than a small number more. But this reluctance may also have had its roots in a knowledge of the kind of company Joan was now keeping. And they may have recalled the episode of the bishop's horse.

By the beginning of May it was obvious that Compiègne was soon to be besieged by the Burgundians, and Joan decided to go there. On the evening of 13 May 1430,[4] she entered the town. Her mood was still disturbed and anxious. She lodged with a royal official, and shared a bed with his wife, who was called

Marie Boucher. Several times during the night she roused her companion, and made her go and warn her husband 'against several treasons of the Burgundians'.[5] The next morning, very early, she rose, heard mass at the church of Saint-Jacques, confessed and took communion as was her custom whenever she meant to fight that day. The townspeople had heard of her arrival, and crowded into the building to see her, particularly the children. Joan, standing near one of the pillars, suddenly gave vent to an extraordinary outburst:

My children and dear friends, I signify to you that I have been sold and betrayed, and that soon I shall be delivered to death. So I beg you to pray God for me, for I will no longer have any power to serve the king, or the kingdom of France.[6]

This story, written down long after the event, has often been doubted, but has great psychological plausibility. It is supported by Joan's similarly paranoid outburst at Châlons, on the way to the coronation.

A little after she had heard mass, the *attournés*, or elected representatives of the town, came to see Joan and offered her three pots of wine. It was the kind of gift that was usually only made to royalty, and people afterwards grumbled that the price paid for the wine was excessive.[7] The same day, with a considerable force – Monstrelet says she had 2,000 men and a number of well-known captains with her, among them Poton de Xantrailles – she went to attack the Duke of Burgundy's men at Pont l'Évêque, a bridge over the Oise near Noyon,[8] which was then the Burgundian headquarters. They arrived very early on 15 May, 'between dawn and sunrise',[9] and launched a surprise assault which for a moment carried them right into the place. The bridge was guarded by two English captains, who managed to defend themselves until Burgundian reinforcements could come up from Noyon.[10] There were about thirty casualties on each side,[11] but the honours of battle remained with the garrison. Joan was forced to return to Compiègne, to find that the important outpost of Choisy-au-Bac was about to surrender. It was immediately demolished by the Burgundians.[12] The very light casualties sustained by so large a force, during this attempt to cut the Duke of Burgundy's communications, may lead us to suppose that the attack was not pressed home with much vigour. This supposition is backed by what Joan said later.

Asked if she had some revelation to go to Pont l'Évêque, [she] replied that after she had had revelation before the fortifications of Melun that she would be taken, she most often put herself in the hands of the captains as to the conduct of the war, and she never told them it had been revealed to her she would be taken.[13]

This answer, though evasive, is also revealing. It points to Joan's feelings of inadequacy once she had achieved independent command – Monstrelet, describing this very skirmish, says that she was *comme chef de la guerre du roi* – 'like the king's commander'.[14] Did she need the opposition of those who were nominally superior to her in the military hierarchy to fuel her temper and trigger her need to establish control? And her reply confirms the impression we get from other, and less authentic, sources that she was at this time in a mood of deep depression. But she was still sufficiently herself to make another attempt at accomplishing what she had failed to do at Pont l'Évêque. On 18 May she went to Soissons, hoping to use the bridge there to take the enemy from behind. She was accompanied by Regnault de Chartres and by Vendôme. The journey was made in one stage, and they arrived at the town in the evening.[15] Here they had a rude shock, for the captain of the place refused to admit them.[16] The reluctance, on this occasion, was not due to Joan's tactlessness and the indiscipline of the king's troops. It sprang from a more sinister cause.

The captain of Soissons was called Guichard Bournel, and he was planning to sell the place to the Duke of Burgundy. He persuaded the townspeople that Joan, Regnault and Vendôme intended to make them accept a large garrison[17] – the very thing no town wanted. He may have found the job all the easier because Soissons was already treating with Philip the Good for a truce which would last till late June, during which period they would deliver food to his troops. That night the troops were forced to sleep in the fields, and only the three leaders, with a few attendants, were admitted to the town. The next day the decision was made that the force must be broken up, as there would not be enough provisions in Compiègne to feed it. Joan was left to her own devices.[18] Probably all the troops she now had with her were the 200 Italians of Barretta's company.[19] Her days as an army commander were therefore over almost as soon as they had begun. As soon as he saw the back of the royal army, Bournel clinched the deal which he was negotiating. He surrendered the town against a payment of 4,000 *saluts d'or*.[20] Joan flew into a tremendous range when she heard of the betrayal, and said that 'if she could get hold of the said captain she would cut him into four pieces'.[21] When reminded of this statement at Rouen she did not bother to deny it, but only denied that she had used an oath to accompany it.

It has been supposed that, after she left Soissons on 19 May, Joan returned to Compiègne. It is more likely that she went at once to Lagny,[22] thinking that this might be threatened by the loss of Soissons, and then on to Crépy-en-Valois.[23] Crépy is not far from Compiègne, but was separated from it, then as now, by thick forest. Joan's presence there is easy to explain when one has seen the place. Crépy stands high up – the highest part is a steep bluff crowned with a monastery (now in ruins) on the side towards Compiègne. It was a good place to keep watch over the surrounding countryside. Here, probably as late as the afternoon of 22 May, she got news that the siege of Compiègne had begun two days previously. Though she now had only 300 or 400 men with her, and though some of her companions thought the venture was too risky, she decided to return to the town immediately. To protests she replied curtly: 'By my staff, we are enough. I will go to see my good friends at Compiègne.'[24] Nevertheless, for greater security, the cavalcade did not set out till midnight. They arrived at their destination at the hour of the false dawn – about four or five a.m. – and entered the town without attracting the attention of the besiegers, who were gathered on the other side of it, beyond the Oise. The Burgundian army in front of Compiègne consisted of about 6,000 men, and was divided into three groups. The first, which consisted of Burgundians and Flemings, was at Clairoix, about four kilometres from the city, near the point where the Aisne flows into the Oise. The second, mostly Picards and led by Baudot de Noyelles, was at Margny, only one kilometre from Compiègne, and on the other side of the causeway leading from the town bridge. The third, which consisted of English soldiers, under Sir John Montgomery, was at Venette, two kilometres from

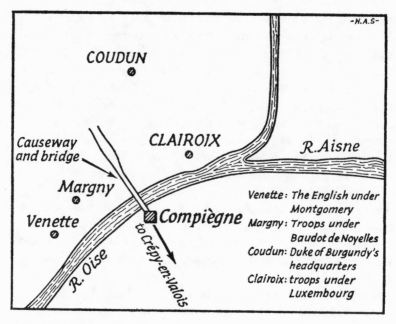

THE SIEGE OF COMPIÈGNE

Compiègne and further downstream from Margny. Venette lay on the road to Clermont. The aim of these dispositions was to prevent any communication between the town and the right bank of the Oise. The Duke of Burgundy was present at the siege, and had made his headquarters at Coudun,[25] a little further back.

When she got to Compiègne, Joan behaved with typical impetuosity. Having arrived at five in the morning, by five in the afternoon she was ready to make a sortie.[26] The object of her attack was the nearest of the Burgundian encampments, that of Baudot de Noyelles. With her she had about 500 men.[27] At first the sally seemed to take the Burgundians completely by surprise, though someone – Joan denied that it was she – had ordered the bells to be rung as her men came out.[28] Joan herself was mounted upon a dapple-grey horse, 'very beautiful and fiery'.[29] She afterwards specified that her mount was a 'demi-charger'.[30] It had obviously been chosen because a somewhat lighter horse would be handier in the boggy ground of the water-meadows beside the Oise. As she rode her standard fluttered in the wind.[31] The first rush carried Joan and her force right into the Burgundian camp, where the soldiers were mostly disarmed, and resting after the fatigues of the day. But then her luck ran out. Jean de Luxembourg, with several other captains, had left his quarters at Clairoix, and was on his way to visit Baudot de Noyelles. On the way, the group paused to reconnoitre, from a hillock somewhat to the rear. Thanks to this, they saw what was going on, and had time to send back for their own harness, and to order their troops to come up.[32] Despite this, Joan made two further assaults at the head of her men. They reached the camp at Margny for a second time, then, as the situation became more difficult, at least managed to push their opponents halfway back there.[33] But it was not only Luxembourg's men who had heard the alarm. The noise had roused the Duke of Burgundy's headquarters at Coudun,[34] and it also alerted Montgomery's English at Venette. It was the latter who cut Joan's line of retreat, and she found herself being pushed off the causeway.[35] She behaved with her usual superb courage, making tremendous efforts to cover the withdrawal.[36]

The French were now so hard pressed that the drawbridge had to be raised,[37] and several unfortunates were thrown into the water. Some of these were saved from drowning when the Burgundians took pity on them, and held out their lances to pull them from the Oise.[38] Joan herself was trapped in the boggy ground between the causeway and the river.[39] Here a Picard archer came up to her, and seizing her by the floating panels of her gorgeous gold and scarlet *huque*, the open surcoat which she wore over her armour, dragged her ignominiously from her horse. She was then taken prisoner by Guillaume de Wandonne, a man-at-arms serving under Jean de Luxembourg,[40] and in command of a company.[41] At the confused moment of her capture, there was some uncertainty as to whether Joan had actually given her parole or not. Wandonne apparently stated that she did, but was not altogether believed,[42] and Joan's subsequent conduct, as well as her assertions at her trial, indicate that she did not think herself bound by any oath or promise. Perceval de Cagny says that, when asked to surrender, she replied: 'I have sworn and given my oath to someone other than you, and I will keep my word.'[43]

It is true to say that, while those who were captured with

Joan could expect the usual treatment meted out to captives who were deemed worth a ransom, Joan herself was a different case. She had always particularly feared imprisonment, and had indeed prayed, when her voices warned her she would be taken, that she might die rather than suffer a long captivity.[44] It is improbable, however, that she had any idea of what was in store for her. This is one of the things which makes it unlikely that, when she was taken, she first tried to hide herself, and then attempted to conceal her identity until the imposture was revealed when they were taking off her armour.[45] Despite the fact that our authority is a bishop, the story does not carry conviction. Another reason for disbelieving it is the fact that Joan's standard, carried into battle with her, would already have announced her presence to her enemies. More often debated, but just as unlikely, is the theory that Joan was betrayed to the Burgundians by Guillaume de Flavy, captain of Compiègne, a theory which was aired in Flavy's own lifetime (he was a notorious bad hat) and which is repeated in several chronicles written only a little later. Not only is there no proof of this, but Flavy's subsequent resistance to the besiegers suggests that no such betrayal took place, as does the absence of any record of payment in the Burgundian archives. Such a record exists in the case of Guichard Bournel.[46] Joan's rashness was so much a part of her character that it is unnecessary to look for a more sinister explanation of her misfortune. The Duke of Burgundy arrived soon after Joan had been taken, and, according to Monstrelet, who claims to have been present, 'spoke several words to her, which I do not well remember'.[47] The confrontation is denied by two other sources, one of which is Pope Pius II. Yet one would be astonished if Philip the Good had failed to take a look at the famous Maid, now that she had fallen into Burgundian hands, though it is doubtful if he deigned to argue with her. The letter he wrote, upon the evening she was captured, to the inhabitants of Saint-Quentin, shows how much importance he attached to the event. He speaks of it as something which will make a great stir, and which will expose 'the error and foolish credulity of those who have been well disposed and favourable towards the doings of this woman'.[48]

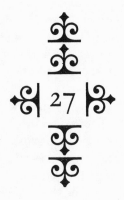

27

The news of Joan's capture brought some swift reactions. The swiftest was embodied in a letter written to Philip the Good from Paris, and dated 26 May 1430. It must have been composed as soon as the news of Joan's capture arrived in the city. The letter was written in the name of the Vicar General of the Inquisitor, but it was obviously inspired by influential members of the University of Paris. It demanded that Joan be sent to the city for trial, on the grounds that she was 'vehemently suspect of several crimes smacking of heresy'. And it promised that things would be done 'according to the good counsel, favour and help of the good doctors and masters of the University of Paris and other notable councillors of this place'.[1] The university had long been interested in Joan, but in no friendly spirit. In November 1429, for example, the Venetian letter-writer Pancrazio Giustiniani reported that it had sent to the Pope in Rome to accuse Joan of heresy, on the grounds that she sinned against the Faith 'in pretending to know and say the things that are to come'.[2] Pressure from the university was maintained thereafter. On 14 July, two further letters were delivered to the Burgundian camp before Compiègne. One was addressed to Philip the Good, and the other to Jean de Luxembourg, and now the University of Paris wrote in its own name, without bothering to shelter behind anyone else. Philip was reminded of the communication which had previously been sent to him, to which no reply had as yet been received. In both letters the doctors of the university expressed the fear that Joan might be freed 'by subtle means', and in writing to Luxembourg they specified that there had been talk of a ransom.[3] The two men were asked to hand Joan over for trial to the Bishop of Beauvais 'who has also asked for her, and within whose diocese she was apprehended'.[4]

Why should the University of Paris concern itself so closely with Joan's fate? It is difficult to realize today just how important this institution was, not only in the intellectual, but also in the political life of the time. Amidst the disorders of the early fifteenth century, it stood, or tried to stand, for good government and intellectual stability. It was proud of its own status, and resistant to any form of outside interference. The pope and the king found it equally recalcitrant in the face of their commands. Indeed, the great schism which rent the papacy had given the university the position of a quasi-independent power, one which it had no intention of surrendering now that the church was reunited under Martin V. For this reason, it had become the chief support of the conciliar theory which placed the ultimate authority of the church not with the pope at all, but with the collective wisdom of the Council. Quite apart from this, the tone of the university's teaching was authoritarian. In the late fourteenth century, it had come under the influence of Occam, and Occam's doctrines had had a twofold effect. On the one hand, the function of the will was exaggerated, and men were encouraged to take refuge in a kind of categorical imperative, and to accept blindly and without question the heritage of the faith. On the other hand, belief in the supernatural came to seem unreasonable, or at least beyond the scope of reason. The result of the conflict between these two ideas was a new kind of dogmatism. The leap of faith must be made, but men must nevertheless believe only what duly constituted authority told them to believe. In the eyes of the doctors, this authority rested with themselves, and they, more than any of their contemporaries, were suspicious of the visionaries who characterized the epoch. It did not help matters that many of these visionaries were women. The University of Paris was a masculine institution because those who governed it had taken Holy Orders, which were open only to men, and it was not merely male-dominated but deeply suspicious of the female sex. One of the witnesses questioned at the time of Joan's rehabilitation was the famous scholar Jean Beaupère, one of the principal ornaments of the university. He had been one of the judges at Rouen and even now, when he was summoned to the preliminary investigation of 1450, he was not inclined to retract the verdict he had given there. Joan, he said resentfully, was 'very subtle, with the subtlety of woman'.[5]

In 1430 the University of Paris had long been Burgundian in its sympathies. Like the rest of the kingdom, it had been divided into two camps by the rivalry between Louis of Orleans and John the Fearless, but even then it had tended to see the party of Burgundy as the party of reform, opposed to the rule of tyrants and favourites. In 1418, when Paris fell, it swung permanently into the Burgundian camp. Those members of the university who were favourable to the dauphin fled from Paris, and their opponents reigned supreme. When John the Fearless was murdered at Montereau, the University of Paris did not hesitate to declare itself. It wrote an official letter to his widow, in which they spoke of the dead duke as 'the prince of this century who, after the king our sovereign lord, has most cherished and loved us'.[6] Burgundian sympathies gradually came to involve an alliance with the English. When the Treaty of Troyes was made in 1420, the University of Paris solemnly adhered to it. Later, it asked Henry V to confirm its privileges. At Henry's entry into Paris, he was harangued by Nicolas Midi – later to be another of Joan's judges – who evoked the utopian dream of a true union of the kingdoms of England and France.

Inclined to be hostile to Joan from the first moment it heard of her, the university may have felt itself provoked by two things in particular. One was that many of those who had sat on the board of assessors in Poitiers were members of the exiled minority of dauphinist sympathizers. The second cause was nearer home. Joan's unsuccessful attack on Paris had given the doctors a real fright, while at the same time tending, as they saw it, to belie her prophecies, which had up to that time been fulfilled. Closely linked to the university, but no longer of it, was an individual who has already been mentioned – Pierre Cauchon, Bishop of Beauvais. On 14 July 1430, Cauchon appeared in person in the Burgundian camp outside Compiègne. He brought with him the letters to Philip the Good and Jean de Luxembourg whose contents I have described, but his real mission was to make a formal demand on his own behalf. He claimed that Joan had been taken 'in his diocese and within his spiritual jurisdiction',[7] and that she should be given over to him for trial.

Cauchon was linked, not only to the University of Paris, but to the English régime in France. Indeed, of all Frenchmen holding high positions, he was the one most closely identified with the invaders. Born at or near Rheims, about 1371, he was not of noble origin. He was a man who had risen through brains and force of personality. He studied at the University of Paris, where he was brilliantly successful, and in 1403 he became rector. He took an active part in the violent politics of the first two decades of the century. In 1420, two years after the Burgundian triumph, Cauchon became Bishop of Beauvais, having previously held a canonry there. Everyone recognized that his bishopric, which also made him an ecclesiastical peer of France, was Cauchon's reward for long fidelity to Burgundian interests.[8] In 1422, his importance in the new political structure was confirmed by the fact that, on the death of Charles VI, he was named as one of the king's testamentary executors. From this point onwards, Cauchon began to swing out of the Burgundian orbit, and into that of Bedford and the English occupying power. In 1423, he was named councillor of the young Henry VI, and in 1425 he did an important service to Bedford, when the latter was having difficulties with the Paris *Parlement*. The Regent was duly impressed by Cauchon's adroitness in handling a tricky issue.

With the resurgence of French power, things began to go wrong for the Bishop of Beauvais. He refused to attend the coronation and when, as Charles made his way towards Paris, his own see submitted to the king, Cauchon found himself excluded from it. The episcopal domain was promptly sequestrated by the dauphinists. Bedford tried to compensate Cauchon for his misfortune by getting him translated to the see of Rouen, and in December 1429 wrote to the Pope on the bishop's behalf. This move was blocked by the Rouen chapter, which feared Cauchon's already well-established reputation for high-handedness. In 1430, Cauchon's sympathies, connections and antecedents exactly qualified him to act as the intermediary between the English and the Burgundians in the matter of Joan of Arc, while the University of Paris could also feel confident that he would serve its interests. But he was far more than a mere intermediary. He had a personal interest in the business, as it was Joan, more than anyone else, who had been responsible for turning him out of Beauvais. His intelligence matched his lack of moderation, and he had a will as tremendous as Joan's own. In every way he was a dangerous opponent for the girl he was about to confront. It rapidly became clear that Joan's transfer from one authority to another would have to be the subject of a financial deal. Cauchon's summons to the Duke of Burgundy envisages this deal in some detail, though the terms proposed are interestingly ambiguous. The bishop began by saying that, though the prisoner could not properly be considered a prize of war, the king – by which he meant Bedford as regent for Henry VI – was nevertheless prepared to give those who had captured her the sum of 6,000 *livres*, together with a pension of 200 to 300 *livres* to Guillaume de Wandonne.[9] He then added that, should this sum be insufficient, the king was prepared to guarantee the sum of 10,000 francs 'according to the right, usage and custom of France'.[10] In making this alternative offer, Cauchon was basing himself upon an established royal privilege.[11]

Nevertheless negotiations took a considerable time. There were two basic reasons. One was the character of Jean de Luxembourg. A bluff warrior, who had lost an eye in battle, Luxembourg was already a pensioner of the king of England. A document dated ten days before Joan's capture at Compiègne shows him being given a pension of 500 *livres*.[12] Yet everything we know about him indicates that he was capable of driving an extremely hard bargain. Luxembourg's relationship to Joan is difficult to define. It seems to have had an element of sadism, but also one of guilt. After he had handed her over to the English, he visited her in prison at Rouen. It was when her trial had already been going on for some time. 'Joan,' said Luxembourg upon this occasion, 'I have come here to buy you back, on condition that you are willing to promise never to bear arms against us again.' Joan's reaction was predictably indignant. 'In God's name,' she said, 'you are making fun of me, for I well know that you have neither the power nor the will.' She repeated this reply several times, and as Jean de Luxembourg persisted in his proposal, she finished by saying: 'I know well that the English will put me to death, believing after my death to gain the kingdom of France. But, were there a hundred thousand more *godons* than there are at present, they would not have the kingdom.'[13] While feeling, with Joan, that Luxembourg's words to her on this occasion were little more than a cruel tease, it is also possible to think that they concealed a real uneasiness about the transaction which had taken place. It was believed at a reasonably early date that Luxembourg long resisted the idea of surrendering Joan for trial,[14] and no doubt this was a story he put about himself in the years that followed. Once the Church intervened, however, he had little choice.

The other obstacle to transferring possession of Joan was the condition of Bedford's exchequer. Jean de Luxembourg seems to have rejected as insufficient the mere guarantee that the money would be paid. He wanted cash, and he got his way. On 2 September 1430, the estates of Normandy were asked for an *aide* of 120,000 *livres tournois*, 10,000 of which were to be set aside specifically for 'the purchase of Joan the Maid, who is said to be a sorcerer, a warlike person, leading the armies of the dauphin'.[15] The *aide* came in with exceptional rapidity, but Joan's price had to be raised more rapidly still. It was paid in large part in gold specie advanced from the privy purse of the King of England.[16] This was a violation of the rule that the English dominions in France were expected to pay their own way, and the source of the money, even more than the cash payment, is a guarantee of English anxiety to have Joan.

It is clear that English attitudes towards Joan were based upon a series of false assumptions based on native English, rather than French, experience. The English experience of heresy, for example, was based on the struggle against the Lollards – who were not only heretics but radicals in revolt against the social order. The Lancastrian dynasty, always conscious of its own shaky claim to the English throne, was thoroughly paranoid about them. After persecutions under Henry IV and Henry V, the whole business was revived in 1428, when Cardinal Beaufort was charged by the pope to crusade against the Hussites and started to clean house before leaving home. In accusing Joan of heresy, the English authorities in France were marching in step with their colleagues across the Channel, and may have convinced themselves that they had got hold of someone who threatened the fabric of society in the same way as the Lollards with whom they were already familiar. But in many ways they were less interested in Joan the heretic than in Joan the witch. Their minds leapt to the subject of sorcery as soon as they heard of her existence. Joan's trial falls at a period when witch-persecution was quite rapidly on the increase, and accusations of witchcraft were common under the Lancastrian régime. In 1419, Joan of Navarre, widow of Henry IV and stepmother of Henry V, was arrested, apparently on charges of having practised witchcraft.[17] In the same year, Archbishop Chichele of Canterbury was ordered to have prayers said in all churches for the protection of the king against witchcraft. Bedford referred to Joan as a 'limb of the fiend', and may have had enough in common with his brother Henry V to share the latter's panic fear of witches.

The idea that Joan's trial was to some extent a personal misjudgement, or, rather, a collective misjudgement on the part of a small group of influential people connected with the English government in France, can be supported by negative evidence. It comes as a surprise, after learning of the high price that was paid for Joan, to discover that no chronicle completed in England before her rehabilitation makes any allusion to her in connection with the siege of Orleans or the battle of Patay, or says anything about her trial and execution. No attempt was made to inform and propagandize the people of England on the subject of her downfall. And even her impact upon the morale of the English soldiers in France seems to have been much less marked than is generally supposed.[18]

The bargain made for Joan's sale was almost a private undertaking, despite the use of public money for the purpose, and a witness at the Trial of Rehabilitation well described the atmosphere that surrounded it:

I saw [Cauchon] when he reported to the Regent and to Warwick upon his negotiations for buying Joan. He did not abstain from joy, and animatedly said to them some words which I did not well understand. After which he went to confer apart with the Earl of Warwick.[19]

Cauchon's part, and Bedford's, in the transaction are already clear, but what of Richard Beauchamp, Earl of Warwick? Warwick, not Bedford, was to be Cauchon's chief link with the English while the trial was going on. It was these two who stage-managed the business together, though not without a certain divergence of aims. Warwick may fairly be called one of the most puzzling characters in Joan's case. Everything we otherwise know about him makes the coarse brutality of his actions and attitudes, as they are reported to us by those who witnessed them, seem inexplicable. He was, for example, deeply religious, and had actually made the pilgrimage to Jerusalem in his youth. The *Dictionary of National Biography* calls him 'a brave and chivalrous warrior', and does not mention his connection with Joan. The best conclusion is that Warwick was a patriot and a puritan of a typically Lancastrian type, and that he must have borne more than a passing resemblance to Henry V, who also combined deep piety with self-serving cunning and savagery. Warwick had been one of the executors of Henry's will, and in 1428 had been given charge of the young Henry VI. This was the reason, indeed, why we find him in Rouen, since the king was also there. We must put Warwick's attitudes to Joan into the context of his responsibilities – everything the earl did was done to preserve the heritage of the young king, whose position Joan had so severely shaken. For the governing group, Joan had become a symbol of their undeserved humiliation after so many years of success, and it was they who saw in her the reason why 'the French prospered and went on prospering without cause'.[20]

28

After she was taken, Joan may have been kept at Margny for a few hours. Immediately after this she was held for three or four days in Luxembourg's own quarters at Clairoix.[1] But neither of these places was nearly secure enough to lodge so important a prisoner – one, furthermore, who might well be in possession of supernatural powers. She was therefore transferred to the château of Beaulieu-les-Fontaines near Noyon.

Beaulieu was an important fortress, though what remains of it does not look particularly impressive today, surrounded as it is by dense and melancholy trees. Beaulieu had been built in the twelfth century, and was octagonal in plan, with a donjon at least fifty feet high and several other towers. There was a deep moat, fed by one of the rivulets that give the place its name. The conditions of Joan's captivity were not at first too harsh. She was allowed the company of Aulon, who had been captured with her, and when the latter grew gloomy about the prospects for the besieged in Compiègne, she reproved him sharply.[2] She had by no means lost faith in her mission.

It was while she was at Beaulieu that she made her first attempt to escape. The room in which she was kept had a plank floor, and she prised part of this up, got into a lower room, and was just about to lock the guards in their own guardroom when she was surprised by the porter.[3] There is a tradition that she was imprisoned in the tower to the right of the gateway, as one looks at the present house, and this would fit the circumstances as Joan described them. As a result of this escape-attempt, she is said to have been thrown into a small, dark cell by the governor of Beaulieu, Jacobin Estobart.[4]

Later, when she was questioned about the incident, Joan was quite unrepentant. She said bluntly that 'she had never been a prisoner in any place from which she would not willingly have escaped'.[5] And a little afterwards she elaborated upon this, in terms of the circumstances in which she found herself at the moment she was speaking:

Asked if she would go, if she saw the chance, she replied that if she saw the door open, she would go; and this would be God's commandment to her. And she believes firmly that, if she saw the door open and the guards and other English were unable to bar her way, she would know that this was her permission to go and that God would send her help. But she would not go without permission – at least not making a sally as a test, as a means of knowing if God wanted her to go. And she quoted the proverb: 'God helps those who help themselves.'[6]

Joan's attitude was exactly that which she had expressed in Poitiers, when she said: 'In God's name, the soldiers will fight, and God will give the victory.' However much she may have been changed by experience, she retained to the very end the impress of the 'peasant morality'[7] in which she had been brought up.

Early in June, for greater security, Joan was transferred further north, to Luxembourg's principal stronghold, the château of Beaurevoir.[8] Beaurevoir, like Beaulieu, went back to the twelfth century, but had been largely rebuilt in the six years preceding Joan's arrival. It was a large castle, with many towers, in the latest style of military architecture. The only vestige of it which still remains is the detached watch-tower, which was about 500 metres away from the main building. The countryside is now rich agricultural land, but in the early fifteenth century it was largely forest.

At Beaurevoir, Joan found Jean de Luxembourg's wife, his aunt,[9] and also probably his stepdaughter. An immediate bond of sympathy sprang up between Joan and her hostesses. They tried to get her to wear women's clothes, and offered to give her these, or the cloth to make them. Joan made her stock answer, that 'she would not put off men's clothing without God's permission'.[10] But she added, when she recalled this, that 'she would rather have taken women's dress at the request of these two ladies than of any other woman in France, excepting her queen'.[11] One notes that, implicit in this, there is the idea that to wear women's clothes, or, on the contrary, not to wear them, was in Joan's eyes a strictly female decision. It is one of the moments at which she comes closest to feminism as we know it today.

Jeanne de Luxembourg, Luxembourg's aunt from whom he expected to receive a great inheritance, was apparently so much impressed with Joan that she interceded with her nephew upon the prisoner's behalf.[12] It has been thought that it was his aunt's opposition which delayed Luxembourg's decision to hand his prisoner over to the English, since the handover coincides with the formerly accepted date of Jeanne de Luxembourg's death in November 1430. In fact, the situation must have been slightly different. Joan and the Demoiselle de Luxembourg were in contact with one another for just short of three months. Joan arrived early in June, and was gone by the end of August. She herself asserted that she spent four months there,[13] but the period must be reduced in order to take account of a document which shows that she was already elsewhere before the beginning of September.[14] The Demoiselle de Luxembourg seems to have left Beaurevoir at almost the same time, and in fact she died in Avignon on 15 September – earlier than was once supposed, and too far away to affect the situation. What this suggests is that Jean de Luxembourg may have been sufficiently influenced by his aunt's feelings to keep Joan at Beaurevoir as long as the latter was present, but felt free to transfer the prisoner as soon as she departed. Circumstances, indeed, may have prompted him to send Joan away before the departure took place.

While Joan's stay at Beaurevoir is usually spoken of as the easiest and pleasantest part of her captivity – a respite before the rigours to which she was later subjected – there are reasons to think that much of her time there was spent in considerable distress of mind. The negotiations for her sale to the English, which have already been described, were only one aspect. When the news of Joan's capture was announced the reactions

217

of her enemies were, as we have seen, both purposeful and energetic. What about the reactions of her friends? 'Those of her party' was Joan's own, and perhaps more accurate, phrase for them. There was certainly popular consternation. Public prayers were said for Joan at Orleans, Tours and Blois. At Tours, there was a general procession. The canons of the cathedral church and the regular and secular clergy took part in it, all of them walking barefoot through the streets.[15] One of the surviving prayers for Joan's deliverance makes it plain that her mission was thought of as still being incomplete. It runs in part:

Oh! we implore Thee, through the intercession of the Blessed Virgin Mary and all the saints, to allow us to see her, without any harm done to her, free of their power, and accomplishing literally all that you have ordained as one single mission.[16]

The reaction elsewhere was less positive. Regnault de Chartres, writing to the people of Rheims to tell them what had happened, alleged that Joan 'had not wanted to take advice, but to do everything according to her own wishes'. He commended to them a new wonder-worker, a young shepherd from the mountains of Gévaudan, who 'said no more and no less than Joan the Maid had done; and who had God's command to accompany the king's troops'.[17] Regnault's letter (or rather the abstract of it which is all we possess) makes it clear that for him Joan's career had been no more than a propaganda exercise, and one propagandist would do as well as another. Charles VII's own reactions have long been the subject of controversy. True, there are the rumours of an attempt to ransom Joan alluded to in the letter which the University of Paris sent to Jean de Luxembourg. The *Morosini Chronicle* reports that the king sent an emissary to the Burgundian court, trying to prevent the sale of Joan to the English.[18] But there is no firm evidence that anything concrete was done. Inaction when friends or servants were in danger was typical of Charles's pattern of conduct. Jean Jouvenel des Ursins was later to reproach him with his unwillingness to help on such occasions:

Have I not seen your chancellors taken prisoner upon several occasions . . . and those nearest to you killed or made captive? And I never heard that justice had been done.[19]

An unfeeling detachment of this kind has sometimes been thought characteristic of the children of schizophrenics. Charles's subsequent conduct towards Joan's family, and those who had been closely associated with her, may be interpreted as showing that he later felt twinges of guilt. Her brothers Pierre and Jean retained their rank as noblemen, and continued to serve the king; and in 1437, when Charles at last made his solemn entry into Paris, it was Jean d'Aulon who held the bridle of the king's horse, walking beside his master.

While Joan was at Beaurevoir, she learned of the king's inaction, and of her bitterest enemies' attempt to get possession of her. She may even have met Cauchon, as he is known to have visited the castle during the course of the negotiations, as well as going to see Jean de Luxembourg at Compiègne.[20] But if she grew desperate, it was not only because of her situation, which was gloomy enough in itself, but because of the pressures of her own temperament. Her inability to form ordinary relationships of friendship or love was increased by her own inner uncertainty about which sex she belonged to. Her isolation as a prisoner must have brought home to her the isolation in which she had always lived. Her feelings exploded in a moment of fugue. What she did was to leap from the donjon of the castle. It has been estimated that this leap involved a fall of at least sixty or seventy feet.[21] She was knocked senseless, but survived with only bruises.

Joan's leap has been considered so astonishing that modern authors have often preferred to accept the account given in the *Chronique des cordeliers*, rather than the one she gave herself. According to this, she got out of a window, and was letting herself down by means of a rope, when the rope broke.[22] Though this story may look plausible, it is flatly contradicted by what we learn from the trial document:

Asked why she leaped from the tower of Beaurevoir, [she] replied that she had heard it said that those of Compiègne, everyone who had reached the age of seven years, would be put to fire and sword and she preferred to die rather than live after such a destruction of good people – and this was one of the causes of her leap. And the other was that she knew she had been sold to the English and she would have preferred to die rather than be in the hands of the English.[23]

Her judges were convinced that she had made a suicide attempt, and in the eyes of the medieval Church suicide was a particularly heinous sin. Joan, however, categorically denied that she had intended to destroy herself, but in terms which sound like a rationalization after the event. 'I did not do it out of despair,' she said, 'but in the hope of saving my body and going to help some good people who were in need.'[24] It is a statement which does not altogether match her own account of the incident, as set out above. The leap was certainly preceded by a period of intense inner conflict:

> St Catherine told her almost every day she should not jump and God would help those of Compiègne. And Joan said to St Catherine that, since God would help those of Compiègne, she herself wished to be there. Then St Catherine said to her: 'No mistake, you must take this patiently, and you will not be set free before you have seen the king of the English.' And Joan replied: 'Verily, I do not wish to see him; and I would rather die than be in the hands of the English.'[25]

As a result of her fall, Joan suffered a severe case of concussion:

> Asked if, when speech returned to her, she denied God and his saints – because, she was told, this had been established by information – [she] replied that she did not recall ever speaking ill of God and his saints, there or elsewhere, and she had not confessed it, for she had no memory of what she did or said.[26]

The interrogation seems certain of its ground, and one can readily imagine that, when Joan was picked up from the boggy castle ditch into which she had fallen, she gave vent to an outburst of rage and despair. But her physical strength soon reasserted itself, and, as she recovered, she came to terms with what she had done:

> After she fell from the tower, she did not wish to eat for two or three days, and she was overcome by this leap to the point where she could not eat or drink, but always she was comforted by St Catherine, who told her to confess and ask God's pardon. . .[27]

Joan's 'gamble with God',[28] as it has euphemistically been called, must have taken place sometime in August, by which time the main outlines of the bargain for her purchase would have been settled. Jean de Luxembourg clearly got a considerable shock. He had always had his prisoner carefully guarded, fearing she might escape 'by magic art, or by some other subtle means'.[29] But she had nevertheless nearly slipped through his hands, and the money with her. We need look no further for the main reason why Joan was now sent from Beaurevoir to Arras. She was too valuable a piece of property to lose.

29

At Arras, Joan was imprisoned in the Cour le Comte, the residence of the Dukes of Burgundy in the centre of the city. During
part of the time that she was there, Philip the Good was holding
his court in Arras, but there is nothing to show that he ever
went to see her, though they were housed in the same complex
of buildings. However, Joan was visited by a number of other
people. Two men from Tournai came, a priest and the *sergent de
la ville*, and gave her twenty *écus* 'for her necessities'.[1] She had
appealed to the city for this money when she was moved from
Beaurevoir. Another visitor was Jean de Pressy, councillor and
Chamberlain of the Duke of Burgundy.[2] He was familiar with
the ramifications of Joan's case, having been present when
Cauchon delivered his summons to the duke. Now he came
several times, and admonished her to resume women's dress.[3]
A third contact was with a Scotsman, who showed Joan a
picture of herself. She was represented wearing full armour,
upon bended knee, and presenting a letter to Charles VII.[4] We
have no information as to the purpose of this visit, which may
have been prompted by simple curiosity. Yet we do get a hint
that she had found well-wishers, even in Burgundian Arras, as
it seems to have been here that files were discovered on her
person during a search. These can only have been smuggled in
to her from outside.[5]

Meanwhile the negotiations for handing her over dragged on,
even though both the fact of purchase and the price itself had

now been agreed. On 21 November, the University of Paris wrote to Henry VI, which is to say to the English government in France, expressing its joy at the news that Joan was now in the king's power, and asking that she be handed over at once to ecclesiastical justice, more specifically to Cauchon and to the Inquisitor.[6] On the same day they wrote to Cauchon himself, to rebuke him for the long delay in the case, and to ask that Joan be sent at once to Paris for judgement.[7] They must have known this second demand was unlikely to be met, and the letter has the air of being a put-up job, written in collusion with the man they were supposedly reproaching.

The clerks of the university were a little sanguine. When they wrote their letter to Henry VI, Joan was technically in the power of the English, but had only got as far as Le Crotoy, on the Somme estuary. The castle had an English officer in charge of it – he was called Walter Cressoner, and he acted as lieutenant of the captain of Le Crotoy, Raoul Boutellier. Boutellier was also *bailli* of Rouen. At Le Crotoy there was a sympathizer among Joan's fellow-prisoners. His name was Nicolas de Queuville, and he was chancellor of the church at Amiens. He had recently plotted to deliver that city to Charles VII, and had been lucky to escape with his life, as two of his accomplices were executed. As an ordained priest, Queuville often celebrated mass in the castle chapel, and Joan was allowed to attend, and even to confess to him.[8] Such consolations were soon to be taken from her.

The next stage in Joan's journey was across the Somme to Saint-Valéry. The generally accepted date of her departure from Le Crotoy is 20 December 1430. From here she moved with a strong escort towards Rouen, and on the twenty-eighth of the month she is spoken of as being already in that town.[9] Her place of imprisonment was the castle, 'in a tower towards the fields',[10] and it was here that she was to be kept throughout her trial. It was a secular and not an ecclesiastical prison – a point which was afterwards to assume some importance. The fortress was already crowded, since it contained the infant Henry VI and his court. Despite this close propinquity, it is doubtful whether she ever saw the English king, any more than she saw Philip the Good at Arras.

Cauchon, meanwhile, was busy organizing matters to his own

satisfaction. During Joan's imprisonment at Le Crotoy, he had been in Amiens, conferring with Suffolk and Fastolf among others. It is thought that this meeting may have been to finalize the details of her journey to Rouen. Now, he was concerned with the pattern of the trial itself. With some justice, he considered himself an expert on such things, having presided over several criminal cases in the matter of heresy, most notably in 1426. He was determined that this should be exemplary in all respects. At the beginning of the proceedings, he said to Guillaume Manchon, one of the notaries, that it was intended 'to make a beautiful trial of this' – the phrase is even more expressive in Latin – *unum pulchrum processum*.[11]

He began, on 28 December, by getting the chapter of Rouen – the competent authority, since the archiepiscopal see was at that moment vacant – to make him a concession of territory, so that he could try Joan 'as if he was in his own diocese of Beauvais'.[12] The next step was to have Joan formally handed over to him for trial by the English authorities. This was done in a letter dated 3 January, though Joan, of course, remained where she was.[13] On 9 January, he appointed the various officials who would be necessary, among them the 'promoter' – we might say 'prosecutor', though the functions are not in fact identical – and also the notaries.[14] The promoter was called Jean d'Estivet. He was a canon of Beauvais, and had served Cauchon in the same capacity in his own see, where the ecclesiastical court was notably partisan and ferocious. On 13 January, Cauchon called a conference at his house in Rouen, and 'had read [to those present] the result of the inquiries made in the district of origin of the said woman, and also elsewhere, in several different places, as well as certain memoranda founded both upon the material of these inquiries and upon other points which common fame reported'.[15] The final clause was important, as inquisitorial proceedings could not begin upon the motion of the judge alone, but had to be based on previous, commonly reported bad reputation or *diffamatio*.[16] The preliminary inquiry, like most things connected with Joan, has been a subject of controversy. One notary claimed never to have seen the report and said he thought no inquiry had been made.[17] But in fact there is plenty of evidence to show that Cauchon's investigations were widespread. He was particularly persistent in his efforts to discover all he could about Joan before her journey to Chinon, and the man responsible for doing a large part of the work actually testified at the Trial of Rehabilitation. His name was Nicolas Bailly, and he was a royal official. He said that some twelve or fifteen witnesses were examined. Another witness, from Greux, claimed that he had seen Bailly and his men at work, and that they had been quite thorough in doing their task. Amongst those whom he names as having given evidence to them is Joan's godfather, Jean Morel.[18] The latter, also at the Trial of Rehabilitation, prudently said he knew nothing on the subject. But Nicolas Bailly and those who came with him were not the only ones who were commissioned to find out what they could. Dominique Jacob, a priest of the district, thought the friars minor had been mixed up in it.[19] And Jean Moreau, a citizen of Rouen, remembered that he had met a man 'from Lorraine', who came from near Domrémy and who had been given a special commission to gather information at Joan's place of origin and to learn what was said of her. Moreau recalled that the inquiry had taken place not only at Domrémy itself, but in five or six neighbouring parishes.[20]

If we want to reconstruct the kind of information which was brought together by this inquiry, however, all we have to do is to look at the list of seventy articles which formed the basis of Joan's interrogation, but which were afterwards discarded in favour of a briefer (and more deadly) list containing twelve articles only. We see from this that the net was widespread, but brought in material of very different kinds. Thus there is much about Joan's childhood, about the flight to Neufchâteau and the suit for breach of promise before the ecclesiastical court in Toul. All these are things which would have been turned up by the researches already described. But there is also material from Rheims, from Senlis, from the first visit to Compiègne and from Joan's recent imprisonment at Beaurevoir. The triviality of much of it, rather than its bias in Joan's favour, explains why Cauchon found the evidence disappointing. And we can also discern that one reason that these investigations, and especially those held in and round Domrémy, proved so unsatisfactory was that the investigators had been wrongly briefed. The questions they were told to ask were founded upon the presumption that Joan was a sorceress.

In addition to his failure to get the kind of information he hoped for, Cauchon ran into another snag. This was the attitude of the Vice Inquisitor, Jean Le Maître. Le Maître was a timorous man. He did not like the smell of the business at all. Summoned to Cauchon's residence in Rouen on 19 February, he at once raised objections to his competence to serve. Cauchon must have been much irritated: he needed the Vice Inquisitor because it was customary for any bishop who tried a case of heresy to sit with a representative of the Inquisition. In fact, these two were the only true judges, and any other clerics who sat with them were technically simply assessors. The bishop wrote to the Inquisitor for France, Jean Graverant, for an authorization which would allow Le Maître to sit, and decided that the business could at any rate start while they waited for a reply. Le Maître's resistance to the whole idea of taking part in Joan's trial is documented not only in the official record of the process, but by the statements of a number of witnesses at the Trial of Rehabilitation. Jean Massieu, appointed tipstaff for the duration of the trial, gives a vivid picture of the Vice Inquisitor's state of mind:

> He several times refused to take part, and did everything he could not to be mixed up with it. But those he knew told him that, if he persisted with his abstention, he would be in danger of death. In fact, he only decided under English pressure. I often heard him say to me: 'I see that, if this matter is not proceeded with as the English wish, it is all over with life.'[21]

The English influence seems in fact to have been all-pervasive, despite Cauchon's attempt to make the proceedings as regular and orthodox as possible. If Bedford was absent from Rouen for the duration of the trial, this was not so much because he wished visibly to dissociate himself from it, as one authority supposes,[22] but because the young Henry VI was there, and Bedford's functions lapsed in the presence of the king and his council. The notary Guillaume Manchon says flatly that 'If Joan was taken to Rouen and not to Paris, it was because the King of England and his principal counsellors were then at Rouen.'[23] This must have been the common opinion.

The English paid the expenses of the judges,[24] and, pandering to the curious double-think of the time, after Joan's death the

English government gave letters of guarantee to Cauchon and others who participated in the trial, to protect them against any consequences harmful to themselves.[25] These were signed by an Englishman, Laurence Calot, the king's secretary, and were later something of an embarrassment to those who had obtained them, as they confirmed not only their presence at the proceedings, but their doubts about their own part in them.[26] Not only did Cauchon consult frequently with Warwick and others, but these apparently put pressure on him to speed matters up. We learn that 'the English were discontented with the length of the trial, and grumbled that it did not finish quicker'.[27] Most telling of all is the situation with regard to Joan's custody. Not only did she remain in English hands, surrounded by English guards, even after she had been officially handed over to the bishop's jurisdiction, but the letter making the handover actually specified that, should she not be convicted, it was the king's intention 'to have her back and bring her before himself'.[28]

Very shortly after she arrived in Rouen, Joan was visited by the Regent's wife, Anne of Burgundy, or by women acting under her instructions. She underwent a new test for virginity, similar to the one she had undergone at Poitiers.[29] It was later rumoured that Bedford himself was so much overcome with prurient curiosity that he concealed himself in order to see what was done.[30] That such concealment was possible we know from the evidence of the notaries, who were later asked to record Joan's utterances when she was unaware of their presence.[31] If the story is true – and it seems not unlikely in view of Bedford's puritan temperament – then the examination took place before 13 January 1431, which was the day on which the regent left the city. He did not return until 10 September, long after Joan had been burnt. The examination showed that Joan was still *virgo intacta*, but that she had injured herself in some way by riding astride.[32]

Throughout her imprisonment in Rouen, Joan was shut up in the second largest tower of the castle, the Tour du Trésor, afterwards to be called the Tour de la Pucelle in her memory. It was near the back gate, and looked out, as we have heard, over the fields outside the city.[33] The room in which she was confined was reached by means of a short flight of stairs, and was on the first floor.[34] The tower was thirty-two feet in diameter, and the room itself must have been somewhat smaller than this. It resembled the chamber Joan had occupied at Chinon, in the Tour du Coudrai. The only piece of furniture seems to have been Joan's bed, and this, or at least the bedding, may have been removed during the day. She had her feet in leg irons,[35] and much of the time was chained by the waist to a great baulk of wood, some five or six feet in length.[36] Sometimes, however, she was released from the chain, especially if an important visitor like Cauchon came to see her.[37] Harsh as it was, her imprisonment was not as severe as it had at first been planned to make it. When negotiations for Joan's sale had been concluded, and her arrival at Rouen was imminent, an iron cage was ordered from a local locksmith. In this cage the prisoner would have been held upright, pinioned by neck, feet and hands, and unable to move a muscle.[38] The horrible device was indeed constructed – we have a report from a witness who saw it.[39] But no one made the claim that they had seen it in use, and it is improbable that it was employed. Its construction was a panicky reaction to Joan's reputation as a sorceress.

Joan was guarded day and night by a squad of English soldiers under the command of a captain called John Grey.[40] It was afterwards alleged that they were individuals of the lowest type, but this seems unlikely. The *bailli*'s guard, from which they were drawn, consisted of handpicked men. However, there is no doubt that they treated Joan badly. One of their tactics was to torture her with alternate hope and fear, at one moment telling her she was about to be freed, at another saying that her execution was imminent.[41] In spite of her reply to Jean de Luxembourg, Joan still at moments hoped that rescue was possible, even after she had actually been put on trial. One of her judges tells us:

In her simplicity she thought that the English must set her free in return for a ransom: she could not believe that they wished to kill her.[42]

Her guards' conduct in this respect probably had less effect on Joan than the atmosphere of sexual threat in which they forced her to live. We know that she had a marked squeamishness about any kind of physical contact. Following her visit, for example, Anne of Burgundy ordered that a woman's dress should be made for Joan, and the tailor, who was called Jeannotin Simon, came to make a fitting. While doing so, he fingered Joan's breast. Enraged, she pulled away from him and roundly boxed his ears.[43] She had done the same thing to Aimond de Macy at Beaurevoir, when he jokingly tried to touch her breasts.[44]

It cannot have taken those who guarded her long to find out about this phobia, and they used it to make her days, and especially her nights,[45] a misery. On one occasion she complained angrily to Warwick and Cauchon:

> I do not dare to take off these leggings, nor to wear them unless they are strongly laced. You both know that my guardians have several times tried to do violence to me. Once even as I cried out, you, Earl of Warwick, you came at my cries to help me; and, had you not come, I should have been the victim of my guards.[46]

Warwick became sufficiently concerned about what was going on to change some members of the guard, and to give a severe warning to the others.[47] But it is unlikely that this had much effect. Only a change in Joan's conditions of imprisonment would have made any difference. Those under which she was held made sadistic teasing, and even outright physical bullying, all too easy. It does not excuse the behaviour of these guards, but it does make their conduct explicable, when we consider that things were almost as nerve-wracking for the gaolers as they were for the prisoner.

Five guards were kept with Joan all the time, and the keys to the prison remained in the safest possible hands: with Cardinal Beaufort, then present in the castle with the king his great-nephew; with the Vice Inquisitor; and with Cauchon's lieutenant, the promoter Estivet.[48] Despite these precautions, there was constant anxiety that she would find the means to escape.[49] This nervousness, as well as Joan's complaints, led to constant changes of personnel.[50] The English soldiers, perhaps decent enough men, were locked up for long periods with a woman whom they feared might be a sorceress,[51] and whom they knew to be the implacable enemy of England and the architect of recent English defeats. No wonder they tormented her when they got the chance – and perhaps, despite Warwick's intervention, their superiors encouraged them to do so. To her gaolers' jibes, Joan returned as good as she got,[52] and we already know how fiercely her tongue could sting.

30

There has been much debate about the fairness or otherwise of Joan's trial. This ignores, as Cauchon and his colleagues sometimes seemed to ignore, the role of the English in the matter. The English authorities always intended to burn Joan, and they paid out 10,000 *écus* which they could ill spare in order to make sure it was done. The trial was merely to legitimize the burning, and it was quite an expensive extra, but nevertheless a sham. The debates about the legality of the proceedings at Rouen, which occurred at the time of the Trial of Rehabilitation, were also a sham. Once the inquiry into Joan's fate was undertaken officially, and upon a large scale, everyone knew that the original proceedings would eventually be quashed. In addition to this, modern discussions of the trial, and of the way in which Joan was treated by Cauchon, and by her judges in general, are prone to a quite special error, which is that they tend to ignore the nature of the crime of which she was accused. In the legal sense, heresy was always an exception to established rules. The chief reason was that it was an intellectual crime, not effaced or extenuated by apparent observance of the practices of the church. The aim of the judge, in a trial of this sort, was not as much to look for facts, as to search deep into the mind and heart of the accused, keeping always in his own mind the thought that error must be *knowing* in order to be heretical. And there was another point as well. If an accused person professed error out of ignorance, but refused to abandon that error when it was revealed by the Church, then he or she must be condemned. Because of the secret and intellectual nature of the crime, the principal aim of interrogation was always to persuade the accused person to confess, and confession alone was enough to bring about condemnation. The notion of *diffamatio* made a charge of heresy particularly difficult to rebut. There was always a presumption that the accused must be guilty, and, once again, the intellectual nature of the crime made it hard to supply satisfactory proof of innocence.

If we keep these points in mind, we begin to see that there is a paradox about the trial of Joan of Arc. It had its roots in partisan injustice of the crudest kind, but, as it proceeded, it moved closer and closer towards a concept of what was just, however twisted and hateful we may find such justice to be. The fact that it developed in this way is explained by the presence of a distinguished contingent from the University of Paris. Though Joan was tried under English auspices, she was condemned by Frenchmen. If we examine the long list of assessors who sat with Cauchon, we find very few Englishmen among them. The man who appeared most frequently at the sessions of the court was Nicolas Midi, who attended thirty-seven times. He was a canon of Rouen, and in 1433 he was to become rector of the University of Louvain. It was he who drew up the first draft of the twelve articles which have already been mentioned.[1] Amongst other assiduous attenders were Pierre Maurice, Jean Beaupère, Jacques de Touraine, and Thomas de Courcelles. They sat between twenty-three and nineteen times each. It was they who represented the collective wisdom of the University of Paris. And we may suspect it was they who had a marked influence upon the sequence of events.

It would be nice to know more about these Parisian intellectuals who were to play so large a part in deciding Joan's fate, but we do at any rate know something about one or two of them. Jean Beaupère, for example, had lost his right hand in 1423, when he was attacked by brigands between Paris and Beauvais. He had long been English-oriented. In 1420, he had been one of the councillors at the Treaty of Troyes, and in 1422 the university sent him to London to assure the government there of its inviolable loyalty. In September 1430 he was named canon of Rouen, and he was received by the chapter on 20 February 1431, during the course of Joan's trial.

Thomas de Courcelles was famous for his brilliance, and also for his modesty. Pius II described him as one who 'was always looking at the ground, as if he would fain pass unnoticed'. He refused a cardinal's hat. One reason for this, besides modesty, may have been the fact that he was an ardent supporter of the liberties of the French Church. He played an important role at the Council of Basel, and, by 1435, had become one of the supporters of Charles VII. He represented the king at the Congress of Arras, which led to the peace treaty with Burgundy. Despite the part he played in condemning Joan, he became a personal friend of the king, and, at the last, pronounced Charles's funeral oration.

The first session at which Joan herself appeared was on 21 February 1431. It took place in the chapel royal of the castle, which stood in the middle of the courtyard, and was unsatisfactory from many points of view. It is the notary Guillaume Manchon who reports what happened:

> At the first interrogation, in the chapel at Rouen, on the occasion of the first questions put to Joan, a great tumult arose. Joan was interrupted at every word when she spoke of her apparitions; and there were two or three secretaries of the English king who enregistered her declarations according to their own fantasy, omitting her excuses and all that pointed to her discharge. I complained and said that if things were not more orderly, I would not accept the responsibility of holding the pen.[2]

In fact the first session had immediately developed into a struggle over the the oath. Asked to swear to tell the truth, Joan replied: 'I do not know what you will ask me about. Perhaps you will ask me things which I shall not tell you.'[3] She meant to protect the revelations she had made to 'her king'. Finally, she consented to take a strictly limited oath. She was then questioned formally about her parentage, origins and religious education. Cauchon asked her to repeat the *Pater noster* and Joan refused, unless he heard her in confession. At the conclusion of the session, Cauchon forbade Joan to leave the prison assigned to her, on pain of being convicted of heresy:

> But she replied that she would not accept this prohibition, adding

that, if she escaped, no one could blame her for having infringed or broken her word, because she had never given her word to anyone. She then complained of being kept chained up and in irons.[4]

The bishop had failed to accomplish much, but he and Joan had given one another a taste of their metal.

Cauchon, however, had a weapon up his sleeve, in the form of a priest called Nicolas Loiselleur. Loiselleur had been a canon of Rouen since 1421, and was one of the assessors in the case. More important, he was a personal friend of Cauchon and was willing to serve as the latter's jackal. According to Manchon (and his testimony is supported by his fellow notary Boisguillaume, and also by Thomas de Courcelles), Loiselleur acted as a stool-pigeon. Manchon relates that he and Boisguillaume were ordered to place themselves in a room which was next to Joan's prison, and which communicated with it by means of a secret opening which enabled them to hear what was said. Loiselleur entered the prison, in lay dress, and probably additionally disguised, and the guards went out and left him and Joan together. He persuaded Joan that he was a dauphinist sympathizer and came from the same part of the country as she did, and drew her on to talk about her voices. Cauchon asked the notaries to enregister what was done, but they refused. Nevertheless, Loiselleur continued to visit Joan in this way, and saw to it that the notaries were kept in touch with what was said.[5]

Loiselleur's conduct can be related to standard inquisitorial practice. For example, the thirteenth-century Dominican Étienne de Belleville prescribed what should be done in such cases: 'Once you are convinced of his crime by witnesses, let no-one approach the heretic, unless it be, from time to time, two adroit members of the faithful, who warn him, with precaution and as if from compassion, to guarantee himself against death by confessing his errors; and who promise him that, if he does so, he can escape the punishment of fire.'[6] However, though this device was recommended in inquisitorial manuals, it made people uneasy. Courcelles said: 'I remember having advised Loiselleur to make himself known to Joan and tell her he was a priest.'[7] This conversation may have taken place on 13 February, when both men were present at one of the preliminary meetings held at Cauchon's residence. Loiselleur apparently took the advice he was given. He revealed his priestly status, but without losing Joan's trust, and heard her in confession. Manchon says:

Joan had great confidence in Loiselleur, so much so that several times he heard her in confession. In general, she was never brought before her judges if the said Loiselleur had not had converse with her before.[8]

One question that arises is of the time when these secret interviews took place. Loiselleur appeared openly at the trial from the time of the third session on 24 February. Are we to suppose that Joan was too bewildered to recognize him, or to see through the trick which had been played on her? It seems hardly likely, given what we know of her shrewdness and powers of observation. If, at a later stage of the trial, she 'was not permitted to confess to anyone but him',[9] as Manchon alleges, this may have been a way of preventing her from confessing at all. The context makes it seem that it was.

What we must picture is a number of these meetings in the prison, shortly before the first public hearing of 21 February, and forming part of the preliminary investigation which Cauchon had initiated. Indeed, the questions Loiselleur asked may well have been based upon information newly received from Domrémy. The promoter, Jean d'Estivet, another close friend of Cauchon, is also said to have visited Joan in disguise.[10] He, too, would have been recognized at once if the visit took place after the trial opened. Loiselleur and Estivet seem to have gone further than mere investigation. One witness at the Trial of Rehabilitation tells us, though on hearsay only, that 'they exhorted [Joan] not to submit to the Church, if she did not wish to incur an unfavourable judgement'.[11] Another says, less plausibly, that Loiselleur pretended to be St Catherine and 'induced Joan to say what he wished'.[12] We may surmise that Loiselleur's first appearance amongst the assessors was delayed for a few days, even though he had been connected with the trial from the very beginning, so that he might continue with the good work.

At the second session of the court, on 22 February, for example, there seems to have been a renewed attempt to make a record parallel to that undertaken by the official notaries. This time it was clandestine, and Loiselleur was in charge of it. Manchon was naturally indignant at this attempt to encroach on his domain:

At the beginning, by command of [Cauchon], the two clerics stationed themselves near a window behind a curtain, just by the place where the judges were, while [my fellow notary] and I were at the foot of the judges, in addition to Jean Monnet, secretary to Jean Beaupère. These two [hidden] clerks wrote while Joan spoke, and they reported what went against her and suppressed her excuses. I think Master Loiselleur kept himself hidden with them, to keep an eye on what they wrote. After dinner there was made, in the bishop's house, in the presence of several doctors, the collation of our writings. But as the two clerks reported things differently from me, and did not put in what excused Joan, [Cauchon] became very angry with me. It was represented to me that others had written differently, and people tried to get me to write what they did. But I replied that I had written faithfully and refused to change anything. At the same time, as I have said, I had marked with a *Nota* the points which were controversial, and where the interrogators should rebegin. The next day Joan was once more questioned about the doubtful points, and her replies confirmed exactly what I had written.[13]

Clearly one topic which came up during these conversations between Joan and Loiselleur was her longing to escape and the hopes which her voices held out to her on the subject. We may, thanks to this, be able to pinpoint exactly the moment when she knew she had been tricked. It occurred at the session of 24 February, the first at which Loiselleur appeared officially. The relevant fragment of dialogue is thus reproduced in the trial records:

Asked if her counsel had revealed to her that she would escape from prison, she replied:
'Have I to tell you that?'
Asked if the voice had not that night given her counsel and advice about which she should speak, she replied that if the voice had told it to her, she had not well understood.[14]

The name of the questioner is not recorded, but we may well imagine it to have been Loiselleur himself.

After the chaos of the first session, it was decided to move the hearings to the robing room behind the great hall of the castle, and to put two English guards on the door.[15] It was in this room that the next five sessions of the trial were held. They lasted from 22 February until 1 March.

Joan was taken to and from the room where she was imprisoned by Jean Massieu, the tipstaff appointed by Cauchon. Massieu's subsequent history shows that he was not altogether a man of good character. In 1438, he was prosecuted for a moral offence, and in 1458 for misconduct. Nevertheless, Joan aroused his sympathy. As he was taking her across the castle courtyard, she asked if the host was exposed in any accessible place. Massieu replied that this was done in the castle chapel, and Joan begged him to change their route so as to go past it.

I willingly agreed and let her kneel before the chapel. Bowing to the earth Joan devoutly made her prayer. This incident having come to the ears of the Bishop of Beauvais, he was displeased, and ordered me not to tolerate such prayers in future. The promoter, Estivet, addressed many reprimands to me. 'Recreant,' he said, 'what made you so bold as to allow this excommunicated whore to approach the church without permission? I'll have you put in a tower where you'll see neither moon nor sun, if you do anything else.' However, I did not listen to the threat. Estivet, perceiving it, several times placed himself before the doors of the chapel, between Joan and me, to stop her making her prayers there.[16]

The sessions themselves were gruelling. Joan sat alone at a table, confronted by a phalanx of churchmen.[17] The principal interrogators were the contingent from Paris – Jean Beaupère took a particularly prominent part. Massieu reports that Joan was bothered by the fact that they put their questions all at once, and interrupted her answers: 'Several times she said: "*Beaux seigneurs*, one after the other." '[18] On another occasion, when she was being questioned by Beaupère and the violently hostile Abbot of Fécamp, both at the same time, she protested more vehemently: 'Joan did not wish to reply to so many interrogations at once. She also told them that they did her great injustice to torment her so, and that she had already replied on all these matters.'[19] And even Beaupère himself became weary of so many interventions: 'Let her speak,' he said testily, 'it is I who have the job of interrogating her!'[20] At least one of the assessors, Jean de Châtillon, Archdeacon of Évreux, seems at this stage to have uttered a mild protest, not so much about the manner of the questioning, as at the content of some of the questions:

'In such a matter one must not act thus,' he said.
'You break our ears, leave us in peace,' said the other assessors to him several times.
'I must obey my conscience,' he replied.[21]

Massieu, who tells this story, believes that Châtillon was told not to return to the sittings of the court, but in fact he continued to attend, though there is other evidence that he remained mildly unhappy about the procedure.

Those who protested more seriously were treated with greater roughness. One such was Nicolas de Houppeville, a priest of the diocese of Rouen. According to his own evidence, Houppeville was summoned to the first session, but could not go. In the interim, he talked to the notary Boisguillaume, and told him 'there was great danger in undertaking such a trial, for several reasons'[22] – in that Joan had already been examined at Poitiers, and by the Archbishop of Rheims. Not content with having Houppeville chased away from the room when he turned up on the second day, Cauchon cited the offender to appear before him to answer for what he had said. Houppeville remained defiant, and told the bishop that he did not come under the latter's jurisdiction, since he did not depend from the diocese of Beauvais, but from that of Rouen. As a reward for this, he was locked up,[23] and only released at the intervention of the Abbot of Fécamp.

Discontent among the other assessors did not go further than a certain amount of grumbling. Jean Le Fèvre, who seems to have felt genuine sympathy for Joan, says that he disliked seeing Joan in lay hands, and above all in the hands of the English, and that 'many were of this opinion, but no-one dared to speak'.[24] At the five public sessions which took place from 22 February to 3 March, each lasting from eight until eleven in the morning,[25] the struggle about the oath was renewed each time, though with diminishing vigour. On 22 February Joan was chiefly interrogated about the beginning of her mission, her relations with Baudricourt at Vaucouleurs and her journey to Chinon. Her letter of summons to Bedford was read out to her and, as we have already seen, she contested some of the phrases in the copy. When the questioning moved to the subject of her voices, there were occasions when she refused point blank to reply, using a phrase which was to become familiar to her interrogators: 'Pass over that.'

On 22 February, a Saturday, the questioning went back to her voices, and the interrogation showed that the assessors were already aware that these had come to her in prison. But suddenly, in the midst of this, Joan rounded on Cauchon. 'You say you are my judge,' she told him. 'Take care as to what you do, for in truth I am sent from God and you are putting yourself in great danger.'[26] Reading the record, one hardly knows which to admire more, Joan's courage, or the savage arrogance of her tone. A little later came one of the best known of her ripostes. She was asked: 'Do you believe you are in a state of grace?' It was a trap question, on a level with the modern: 'Have you stopped beating your wife yet?' Either Joan admitted that she was *not* in a state of grace, or she claimed to know God's mind on the subject. One assessor, Jean Le Fèvre, thought it was so manifestly unfair to ask her this that he intervened: 'I remarked that this was a very large question and that Joan was not bound to reply to it.'[27] But Joan's answer was a masterpiece of adroitness: 'If I am not, may God put me in it; and if I am may God keep me in it.'[28] This derives from a prayer which was commonly used at the time,[29] but the judges were stunned, as one of the notaries reports.[30] Cauchon turned on Le Fèvre with the words: 'You, you would have done better to keep silent',[31] and the questioning turned to an easier topic, moving again to Joan's childhood at Domrémy.

On 27 February, after getting out of Joan the fact that on the preceding Saturday she had actually heard her voices in the room where she was being questioned (perhaps, in this, they sought an explanation for the readiness of her reply on the subject of grace), her interrogators again returned to the topic of her voices in general, and also asked her about the way in which her saints visibly manifested themselves. She was questioned about her refusal to cease wearing male dress, and made an answer which Cauchon must have noted:

Asked if it seemed to her that the commandment made to her to take male dress was lawful, she replied:

'All that I have done is by the commandment of the Lord: and, if he had commanded me to take another dress, I should have taken it, because it would have been by God's command.'[32]

The questioning then passed to her sword, her standard, her prediction that she would be wounded at Orleans, and finally to her refusal to accept the composition which Suffolk had offered at the siege of Jargeau. The questions put to her on the first three topics were connected with the hope – already diminishing in the minds of her more intelligent auditors – that a charge of witchcraft might be proven against her. The last subject was a different matter.

The trial record, which we must remember is not stenographic, but a revision made in the evening of notes taken during the day's session,[33] is comparatively laconic, but we can recover something which was said at this point by turning to a different source – one of the witnesses at the Trial of Rehabilitation. Jacques de Touraine, a friar minor, had taken over the questioning from Beaupère:

Jacques asked Joan if she had ever been in a place where the English were killed. She replied: 'In God's name, yes. How gently you talk! Why don't they leave France and go back to their own country?'[34]

Amongst those who were listening to the exchanges was 'a great English lord' – one of the members of Henry VI's suite with enough pull to get him past the sentries at the door. Hearing this, even he was tempted to applaud. His comment was: 'Really, this is a fine woman. If only she was English!'[35] Englishmen will recognize a thoroughly national reaction which has not changed much throughout the ages. By the end of this session, the general feeling seems to have been that Joan was doing astonishingly well. Massieu tells us:

The fourth or fifth day of the trial, as I was bringing Joan back from the tribunal to her prison, a priest called Master Eustace Turquetil, chorister in the King of England's chapel, interrogated me in these terms: 'How do her replies seem to you? Will she be burned? What will happen?' I replied: 'Up to now I have seen nothing but good and honour in her and know nothing reprehensible: but I do not know what will happen at the end. God knows.'[36]

This incautious reply was reported, and Massieu was summoned by Cauchon and vehemently rebuked. The session of 1 March shows the extent to which the trial had already begun to stagnate, though it did begin with some questions about the Count of Armagnac's letter concerning the pope, and Joan's reply to it. Otherwise, what was covered was familiar ground, though the questions and the replies to them add many details to our knowledge of Joan. The only moment at which the questioning shifted on to really dangerous ground was when she was again asked about the King's Sign.

On Saturday 3 March, Joan made her last public appearance for over three weeks. It is at this session that there occurs Joan's account of her meeting with Brother Richard outside Troyes, the story of the child who came to life again at Lagny – Joan specified that it was 'black as her doublet',[37] a detail which tells us that she was once more as soberly dressed as she had been when she came to Chinon – and the mention of the pair of gloves which was lost at Rheims. The tone adopted by Joan during this session was often impatient and sarcastic. Asked if the men-at-arms made pennons in imitation of the one she herself carried, she answered: 'It is good to know that the gentlemen continued to use their [own] coats of arms.'[38] Those who believe in Joan's consistent 'sweetness' and 'meekness' do so in defiance of the trial record.

What impressed those who were present at the trial was the strength of Joan's memory, and her ability to recall the replies she had already made. Both the official notaries, Manchon and Boisguillaume, stress this,[39] and they above all others were in a position to know. Boisguillaume has a charming story about Joan threatening to pull his ears, because of some mistake in the record.[40] Even in these extreme circumstances she could produce flashes of humour. Some felt, and here Manchon must again be included, that Joan had little chance against so many learned doctors, especially as she had no one to advise her.[41] Others thought that, despite being ignorant and simple, she often replied like the subtlest of scholars.[42] The collective reaction, even at this early stage, is perhaps best represented by the words of Jean Tiphaine who, despite the fact that he was a canon of the Sainte-Chapelle in Paris, was more expert in medicine than he was in theology. His verdict was that

In fact there is no doctor, however great or subtle, who, being interrogated by great doctors and amidst so large an assembly as Joan was, would not have been brought down and perplexed.[43]

Though Cauchon knew that he still had immeasurably the advantage, he was getting worried. Joan was proving a tough nut to crack. He decided to call a halt to the public sessions, to collate the information already gathered, and to continue the trial with a series of private interrogations in the prisoner's cell.[44] He may have felt, amongst other things, that Joan's self-esteem fed upon the attention she was receiving, and that the best way to break her was to shut her away.

31

On Sunday 4 March, and every day until the Friday following, Cauchon held a series of conferences at his residence. Those present formed a kind of 'steering committee' for the future conduct of the trial. In addition to the bishop himself, its members were the following: Beaupère, Jacques de Touraine, Midi, Maurice, Courcelles and Loiselleur.[1] Manchon took the minutes. It will be noticed that the proceedings had now fallen completely into the hands of the representatives of the University of Paris. It was decided to sift the record and to decide what questions should be asked in the sessions which were to follow. It also seems to have been decided that it would be useful to consult a well-respected priest and legal expert who had just arrived in Rouen. His name was Jean Lohier. Cauchon gave him a copy of the trial-minute as far as it had then progressed, and asked for his opinion. Lohier asked for a delay of two or three days to study it. His opinion, when it arrived, was a shock. He made the following points: that the form of the trial was irregular; that it was held in a 'closed and shut' place – i.e. the castle – where those present were not at liberty to give their real opinions; that the trial touched upon the honour of the King of France, who was neither present nor represented; and that no schedule of accusations had been given to the accused. For all these reasons he thought the trial invalid. Cauchon kept his temper sufficiently to ask Lohier to remain in Rouen and be a witness to the proceedings. Lohier refused. On 10 March –

immediately following the first of the new series of interrogations – a further and unofficial reunion of the steering committee was held[2] at which the bishop gave free rein to his indignation. On the morning following this outburst, Manchon met Lohier in Rouen cathedral:

I asked him what he thought of the proceedings against Joan, and he replied: 'You see how they are setting about it. They will catch her, if they can, through her own words, I mean thanks to those assertions where she says *I know for certain* about her apparitions. But if she said *It seems to me*, rather than *I know for certain*, then I am convinced that no man could condemn her. It looks as if they are proceeding more out of hatred than otherwise; and for this reason I will not remain here, because I do not want to be in this place any longer.[3]

The same day, so Manchon tells us, Lohier left the city. We certainly do not find his name listed among the judges.

At the first session in Joan's cell, the questioning was taken up by Jean de la Fontaine, whom Cauchon had appointed to deputize when he could not be present himself. Only four others were there, in addition to La Fontaine and the bishop. Once again, some of the questions revealed that Cauchon and his colleagues had knowledge of matters which they could only have drawn from Joan herself, by abusing her confidence. For example, she was asked, at one point, about the premonition of capture that had come to her at Melun – the first time the subject had been introduced.[4] The thing which must have given Cauchon greatest satisfaction on this occasion was that Joan, for the first time, showed some willingness to talk about the 'sign' to her king. Her tone combined vagueness and boastfulness. These moments of *folie de grandeur* were the first real indications she had given of vulnerability:

She was asked if [the sign] was gold, silver, a precious stone or a crown. She replied: 'I will tell you nothing else and no man could describe so rich a thing as the sign is: and in any case the sign you need is that God should deliver me from your hands, and it is very certain that he knows how to send you packing.'[5]

Despite having refused to enter into further descriptions, Joan, by the end of the session, had begun to elaborate her fantasy about the angel.

At the second session in the new series, on the morning of Monday, 12 March, the questioning about the sign began again, but the interrogation soon veered off on to the subject of Joan's voices in general. One question prompted a strange answer, which again seems to hint at mental instability:

Asked if she had had letters from St Michael or from her voices, she replied: 'I do not have permission to tell you, and eight days from now I will willingly tell you what I know.'[6]

That day, the questioning was continued during the afternoon. Cauchon was absent, and Jean de la Fontaine was left to conduct the interrogation without him. Amongst the things Joan spoke of were her father's dream that she would go away with the men-at-arms, and her own intention to bring the captive Duke of Orleans back from England.

The reason for Cauchon's absence was probably that he was busy receiving the Vice Inquisitor, Jean Le Maître, who had at last arrived to show his letter of commission from Jean Graverant. The bishop must have been sardonically amused by his co-adjutor's quaking reluctance, which had become notorious in Rouen.[7] The following morning, Le Maître duly presented himself to listen to the next stage of the questioning. With him was a monk of his own order, the Dominicans, called Isambard de la Pierre. They arrived at a dramatic moment, for this was the occasion upon which Joan told in full the story of the angel bearing the crown, who came to the king at Chinon in her presence. Those present must have felt that it weighed heavily against her, as a string of obvious and provable lies.

The morning session of 14 March began with a discussion of Joan's leap from the tower at Beaurevoir. The transition is interesting: having explored what he took to be one of the weakest points in Joan's position, Cauchon was now intent upon exploring another. As the questioning wore on, Joan began to reveal her anguish more and more openly. At one point she made the pathetic request that, if she was sent to Paris after having been questioned at Rouen, she might be given a copy of the notaries' record of what had been said, 'so that she could give [this] to the people in Paris and say to them: "Here is how I was questioned in Rouen and how I replied", so that she might be no more tormented with so many demands.'[8] Here the simplicity of the illiterate peasant-girl appears very clearly. At another moment, Joan spoke of her 'martyrdom', calling it thus 'because of the pain and adversity she suffers in prison'.[9] By the end of the session she had been led on to very dangerous ground:

Asked if, since her voices had told her that at the end she would enter Paradise, she believed she was sure of being saved and would not be damned in hell, she replied that she firmly believed what the voices told her, to wit that she would be saved, as firmly as if she was there already.

Asked if, after this revelation, she believed she could commit a mortal sin, she replied: 'I do not know, but in everything submit to God.' When it was said to her that this was an answer that carried great weight, she replied that she too held it to be a great treasure.[10]

There were four more such interrogations in the chamber where Joan was confined, following that which has just been recorded. They introduced ideas and themes which were to be extremely important in sealing Joan's fate. On the afternoon of 14 March, for example, Joan was questioned once more about her insistence on wearing men's clothing; and the topic returned the next day, now linked to the request she had made to be allowed to go to mass. After several uneasy exchanges with Cauchon, Joan finally said: 'I will take counsel upon the subject, and then I will answer you.'[11] Before this an even more important topic had been introduced, that of submission to the church.[12] Though this was the first time Joan had been asked about it, she was to be questioned upon the subject nearly twenty times thereafter, and it became, indeed, the crux of the whole business. Cauchon soon sensed that he had gained an important advantage:

Asked if, concerning what she had done and said, she wished to submit to and accept the opinion of the church, she replied: 'Everything I have said or done is in the hand of God and I submit to Him. And you may be certain that I have no wish to say or do anything, which is against the Christian faith; and if I have said or done anything, or if anything can be attributed to me, which the clerks think can be said to be against the Christian faith as Our Lord has established it, then I do not wish to maintain it, but will reject it.'

Asked if upon this point she was willing to accept the church's ruling, she replied: 'I will not now say anything more to you; but on Saturday send me your clerk if you do not wish to come yourself, and I will answer with God's aid upon this subject, and the answer can be written down.'[13]

According to the trial record, it was on this occasion that Joan was apprised of the difference between the Church militant and the Church triumphant – that is between the Church on earth, and the Church already possessed of celestial bliss. Evidently she did not fully understand what had been said to her. The Vice Inquisitor's assistant, Isambard de la Pierre, later recalled:

The ignorance in which Joan found herself as to what the Church was provided, I think, the reason why she sometimes made difficulty about submission. During a large part of the trial, when she was questioned about submission to the Church, Joan understood by 'Church' the gathering of judges and assessors there present.[14]

Isambard tells us that Joan was at last indoctrinated by Pierre Maurice, which would put off the moment of her enlightenment until at least 31 March. Maurice was not present at the interrogation of the fifteenth.

Saturday 17 March saw a return, during the morning session, to Joan's insistence upon wearing men's clothing. Joan's answers exhibited a strange mixture of resignation and unconquerable hope:

Asked what she had to say about the women's clothes that had been offered to her so that she might go and hear mass, she replied that, as to women's clothing, she would not wear it yet, so long as it pleased God. But if it so happened that she was condemned, then she requested the gentlemen of the church to allow her to have a woman's shift and a kerchief on her head. She said she would rather die than go back on what God had made her do; and that she believed firmly that God would not let it come to pass that she would be brought so low that she would not soon have help, and miraculously.[15]

At the afternoon session, Cauchon, who had briefly been away from the interrogations, was once again present. Halfway through the session, a dramatic clash took place between the bishop and Isambard de la Pierre. The Dominican reported the incident as follows:

On one occasion, several others and myself being present, Joan was being pressed to submit to the church. She replied that she would willingly submit to the Holy Father, and asked to be taken to him, but she did not wish to submit to those who were there, because they were her principal enemies. I intervened to advise her to submit to the Council General at Basel, which was at that moment assembled. Joan asked me what a Council General was. I answered that it was a congregation of the universal Church, and that in this council of prelates and doctors of Christianity there were as many of her party as of the party of the English. Hearing this, Joan began to say: 'Oh! because in that place there are some who belong to our party, I should like to go and submit to the Council of Basel.' Immediately, reproaching me with great spite and indignation, the Bishop of Beauvais cried: 'Be silent, for the devil's sake.'[16] Then the notary, Guillaume Manchon, asked if he should enregister this submission of Joan to the Council. The bishop told him no, it was not necessary, and he must be careful not to write it down. At which Joan said to the bishop: 'Ha! you write well enough what goes against me, and you do not write what is for me.' I believe that, in fact, Joan's declaration was not enregistered, and there was a great murmur amongst those present.[17]

Isambard's recollections are supported by the trial record, which confines itself to the following:

Asked if it did not seem to her that she was bound to tell the truth to our Lord the Pope, Vicar of God, upon everything that might be asked of her concerning the faith and the state of her conscience, more fully than she replied to ourselves; she answered that she demanded that she be taken before the pope and that before him she would reply to all that she ought to reply to.[18]

Joan was thereafter cautious when the council was mentioned. On 2 May, when she was asked about it, and when the answer was officially recorded, she replied sullenly: 'You will get nothing else from me on that.'[19]

After 17 March, Cauchon decided that matters had, for the time being, gone far enough, and that it was time to collate Joan's answers, and to reduce them to a number of specific propositions or 'articles'. On 24 March, the record of her answers was read back to Joan, and she made a few corrections. She also took the opportunity to ask that she should be allowed to hear mass next day, Palm Sunday, 'because of the solemn nature of the days and of the time'.[20] This request, repeated on Palm Sunday itself, when Cauchon again came to see her, escorted by Beaupère, Midi, Maurice and Courcelles, was summarily refused unless Joan agreed to don women's dress. But on that she remained obdurate.

32

On 27 March, Joan made her first appearance in public for more than three weeks. The scene was the robing room, where all but one of the first series of interrogations had taken place. She was now to have read to her the seventy articles of accusation which had been compiled by the promoter Estivet. It has often been remarked that he did not make a very good job of them. Though they were closely tied to the preliminary information which had been gathered concerning Joan, they often either ignored or distorted the replies she had made during the interrogations. Even amongst the assessors at the trial, Estivet's work aroused criticism. Though the seventy articles were supposed to unite things which were 'confused and scattered',[1] they were scarcely less disorderly than the materials from which they were drawn. The Parisian doctors were especially discontented with the work which the promoter had done. In any case, they seem to have regarded him as a crude provincial ignoramus.

Before the reading began, Estivet addressed the assembly. Joan, he said, should be required to reply according to established canonical procedure, answering each article either with the words 'yes, I believe it to be thus', or 'no, I do not believe it to be thus'.[2] Cauchon asked the opinion of the assessors, then admonished Joan formally, and asked her to choose, or to permit that there should be chosen for her, 'one or several of those present',[3] to advise her on her replies. Joan, however, was unwilling to accept advice. Laying her hand on the gospels, she said:

First, I thank you and all the company also for admonishing me upon the subject of my well-being and of our faith. As for the counsel you offer me, for that I thank you too; but I have no intention of departing from the counsel of God. And as for the oath you wish me to take, I am ready to swear to tell the truth in everything to do with your trial.[4]

Though she rejected the proffered advisers, Joan did, nevertheless, receive clandestine help as the articles were read. Her ally was Isambard de la Pierre, the Inquisitor's assistant. A colleague of Isambard, another Dominican called Guillaume Duval, tells us what happened. We know that his account refers to this day, as he was present at the trial upon one occasion only:

Because there was no place to seat ourselves in the assembly of councillors, we went, according to our custom, to sit at the table near the Maid. There, while Joan was being examined, Brother Isambard warned her what to say, jogging her with his elbow.[5]

Another witness tells us that Isambard 'directed Joan in her responses, at the same time as he repeated them to the notary'.[6]

Naturally, these activities were noticed. On the evening of 27 March, after thirty of the articles had been read and the day's session was over, Duval, Isambard and Cauchon's deputy Jean de la Fontaine were sent by some of the other assessors to see Joan, in order to counsel her if she had changed her mind about taking advice. When they arrived at the castle, they were confronted by the Earl of Warwick:

[He] assailed Brother Isambard with biting insults and invectives. 'Why,' he said, 'did you this morning support that bad woman by making signs to her? *Par la morbleu*, rogue, if I again see you taking trouble to help her and to warn her to her profit, I will have you thrown in the Seine.'[7]

On this occasion, Isambard and those who accompanied him were not admitted,[8] and the news of Warwick's threats was soon passed round among the other clerks connected with the trial.

The next day, the remaining forty articles were read, and Joan replied. On this occasion Isambard de la Pierre was not present, but he persisted in his mission to advise Joan, and on 30 March, Good Friday, he succeeded in getting in to see her, bringing with him Jean de la Fontaine and Ladvenu. They warned her that

She ought to believe and hold that the Church was our Holy Father the Pope, and those who preside in the Church militant; and that she should not hesitate to submit herself to the Sovereign Pontiff and the Holy Council, as there were notable clerics there, as many of her party as otherwise; and that if she did not do so, she would put herself in great danger.[9]

Joan paid some heed to the warning, and when, on the thirty-first, Cauchon, Le Maître and a group of assessors visited her in her cell, to clear up certain points upon which she had reserved her replies, she offered a somewhat qualified submission to 'the Church of God which is upon earth, that is to say to our lord the Pope, to the cardinals, archbishops, bishops and other prelates of the Church'.[10] Cauchon was both disconcerted and angry. He summoned the English guards to find out who had spoken to Joan the preceding day. His wrath fell particularly upon his deputy, La Fontaine, who was forced to make himself scarce. Isambard and Ladvenu were protected by Le Maître.[11] The Inquisitor had probably been responsible for sending them in the first place. We are told that, after this, Warwick 'forbade anyone to see the Maid, save the Bishop of Beauvais or someone who came from him'.[12]

On Easter Sunday, the holiest and most solemn of the feasts of the Church, Joan was not permitted to hear mass or take communion. She was also effectively prevented from confessing herself, since Cauchon insisted that any confession must be made to Loiselleur, whom she now recognized as her mortal enemy.[13] Joan must have understood that her position was now dangerous indeed, since Easter was the time at which all Christians were required to demonstrate their membership of the Church by receiving the sacraments. As soon as Easter was over, Cauchon, urged forward by the dissatisfaction of the Parisian doctors with Estivet's work, decided that the seventy articles must now be reduced to something more concise. The work was done during the three following days.

The first draft of the new articles, at first eleven then twelve in number, was produced by Nicolas Midi,[14] but he was assisted by others. At the Trial of Rehabilitation, for example, five sheets of paper were produced. They contained a version of the articles in the hand of Jacques de Touraine, so loaded with alterations and additions that it was impossible to transcribe them.[15] On the same occasion, a sheet of notes in Manchon's hand was produced. This listed a number of corrections which were to be made. Most of these were in fact incorporated in the final version – of the fifteen proposed, five were made, and four more were accepted in modified form. Only four were entirely rejected.[16]

Though the twelve articles are far more moderate than Estivet's seventy, they are partial, and not always in complete conformity with Joan's replies. This fact was stressed by Manchon when he appeared as a witness at the Trial of Rehabilitation, but at the time he made no protest. His excuse was that the drafting was done by 'people he dared not contradict'.[17] The striking thing about these accusations, when we read them now, is not so much their unfairness – though there are certainly things in them which will strike us as unfair – as the way in which the prosecution has shifted its ground. Apart from one mention of the Fairies' Tree in the first article, all mention of witchcraft has disappeared. Instead of this, we have a series of propositions drawn from what Joan herself had said to her interrogators, culminating in this:

Item: this woman says and confesses that if the Church wished her to do something contrary to the commandment which she says she has had from God, she would not do it whatever it was, affirming that she well knows that what is contained in her process comes from God's command and that it would be impossible for her to do the contrary of that. And, where these things are concerned, she does not wish to submit herself to the judgement of the Church militant or to that of any man in the world, but to God alone, whose commandments she will always obey, above all in what concerns her revelations and what she says she has done thanks to these revelations.[18]

The twelve articles were not read to Joan, and she had no opportunity at this stage to contradict them.[19] Nevertheless, while we may quibble over certain points of accuracy, and also over some details of interpretation, in essence what they contained was drawn from the mass of her own statements as the notaries had recorded them. As such, they were deadly.

Having got what he wanted, Cauchon sent the list of propositions which had been compiled to a long list of advisers, to the cathedral chapter in Rouen, and the faculties of law and of theology at the University of Paris. He can have had little doubt as to what the reactions would be. Yet he believed in making assurance doubly sure. To the articles themselves he usually added another document – the minutes of a discussion held between 9 and 12 April between twenty-two of the theologians present in Rouen. Their verdict was severe. Joan's revelations they characterized as 'fictions of human invention', or else as things that 'proceeded from an evil spirit'. She herself they called 'blasphemous towards God' and 'in error as to the faith'.[20] Satisfactory as this was from Cauchon's point of view, it was not as good as an admission of guilt from Joan herself. An opportunity to exert further pressure on her soon arose. In the middle of April she fell ill, and for a moment alarmed those who kept her in captivity. The cause of her sickness is not known, but it is likely to have been food-poisoning. Joan was visited by several physicians. The promoter Estivet accompanied them to the room where Joan was kept. One asked Joan what was wrong with her:

She replied to me that, a carp having been sent her by the Bishop of Beauvais, she had eaten some of it, and that she was sure this was why she was ill. Whereupon Estivet attacked her. He complained of her evil words [the implication that Cauchon had tried to poison her] and called her 'camp-follower', using these terms: 'It is you, camp-follower, who have eaten herrings and other things which upset you.'[21]

Estivet's dislike of Joan was notorious,[22] and it was returned in full measure. A violent altercation broke out between the two. The bewildered doctor managed to get from the guards that Joan had been afflicted with severe vomiting. Meanwhile, two of his colleagues succeeded in conducting a brief physical examination: 'We palped her on the right side and found that she was feverish.'[23] The advice of the physicians was that Joan should be bled. When they told Warwick this, he was doubtful. He remembered her leap from the tower at Beaurevoir.

'Bleeding?' he said, 'Take care. She is cunning and might well kill herself.'[24] The physicians insisted, and Joan began to recover.

While she was on the mend, but still weak, Cauchon appeared in her cell, with an entourage of assessors. They began to exhort Joan upon 'what she should do, hold and believe'.[25] She was depressed and at first her responses were despairing. She was convinced that she was about to die of her sickness, even though she was in fact getting better, and could only think of burial in holy ground. As the interview proceeded, however, she revived, and as she did so her resistance began to stiffen. In the matter of her revelations and her voices her egocentricity was particularly apparent:

She was asked: 'Suppose some good woman came, who said she had a revelation from God concerning your case, would you believe it?' She replied that no Christian in the world could come to her and say he had had a revelation, without her knowing if he was telling the truth or not; and she would find out through St Catherine and St Margaret.

She was asked: 'Do you not think that God could reveal to some good woman a thing unknown to you yourself?'

She replied that of course this was possible. 'But,' she said, 'I would not believe either man or woman, unless I had been given some sign.'[26]

Summoned to submit to the church militant, she showed herself even more obdurate than formerly. 'Whatever may happen to me,' she declared, 'I will not say or do anything other than what I have said before during the process.'[27]

On 2 May, Joan was subjected to a public admonition, once more in the robing room where the public sessions had been held. Sixty-three assessors were present, and the address was delivered by Jean de Châtillon, now restored to Cauchon's favour. The tone he adopted was harsh and menacing and she reacted violently against it. Seeing the way things were going, Cauchon felt emboldened to make her certain offers. Should they consult, he asked (and one can imagine the irony of the tone), those such as Clermont, La Trémoille and Regnault de Chartres, whom she claimed had been present when the angel brought the crown to her king? Did she want to ask three or four clerics of her party to come to Rouen under safe-conduct, to say what they knew about her apparitions? Did she wish to refer or submit to the churchmen of Poitiers, the place where she had been examined? To this last question, Joan replied, in a burst of ill-timed exasperation: 'Do you think you can catch me this way and thus draw me towards you?'[28]

A week later, she was again taken from her cell, but now she was brought to the *donjon* of the castle and shown the instruments of torture, there and ready to be used, with the executioner and his companion awaiting orders. Faced with this threat, her attitude was a mixture of courage and contempt:

Truly, if you tear my limbs away and separate my soul from my body, I shall not say anything different to you; and, if I do say something, then afterwards I will always aver that you forced me to say it.[29]

It was upon this occasion, when faced with the torturer and his tools, that she had her last word on the subject of Regnault de Chartres: 'He would not dare to say the contrary of what I have told you'.[30] Those present recoiled from her intransigence:

Seeing then the hardness of her soul and her manner of replying, we the judges aforesaid, fearing that the pains of torture would be of but little profit to her, decided for the moment that they should not be applied, until we had been able to take more ample advice upon the subject.[31]

One could hardly hope to find a statement which more accurately reflected a certain aspect of the times in which Joan lived.

The maturer deliberation of the assessors was also opposed to the use of torture, but not from any feeling of mercy. Three voted in favour, at a meeting held three days later, and eleven against. The opinions against are well represented by the following:

Raoul Roussel: It seems to me that she should not be tortured, so that a process as well conducted as this one cannot be calumniated.
Guillaume Érard: There is no point in torturing her, since there is enough important material, even without.[32]

The three votes in favour of torture included those of Thomas de Courcelles (who was to display an extremely uneasy conscience at the Trial of Rehabilitation) and Nicolas Loiselleur.

The next day, Sunday 13 May, Cauchon dined with Warwick.

His fellow guests were the Earl of Stafford, Jean de Luxembourg, Louis de Luxembourg and the Bishop of Noyon. The Beauchamp household book tells us that they ate strawberries,[33] and no doubt Joan was the principal topic of conversation. It seems to have been upon this occasion, either before or after the meal, that Jean de Luxembourg was taken to see the prisoner. In the context, Luxembourg's offer to buy Joan and have her freed takes on a particular tinge of cruelty, as things had already gone a long way beyond the stage when such an arrangement would have been possible, if, indeed, it had ever been possible at all.

The process was now moving rapidly to its close. On 19 May Cauchon had the conclusions of the University of Paris read aloud to the assembled doctors, and on the twenty-third Joan was brought before a smaller assembly to be yet again admonished. Those before whom she appeared included the bishops of Thérouanne and of Noyon, in addition to Cauchon himself. The admonition, upon this occasion, was delivered by Pierre Maurice, and, after making known to her the twelve articles and the inferences which had been drawn from them, he made an appeal of considerable eloquence. Its tone, very different from that adopted by Jean de Châtillon, can be judged from the following excerpt:

To take an example, if your king, from his authority, gave you the guard of some fortress, forbidding you to receive anyone who came to it, and someone came, saying that he did so upon your king's order; then you ought not to believe or receive him, unless he at least brought with him letters or some other certain sign. Thus, too, when our Lord Jesus Christ, ascending into Heaven, gave the government of his Church to the blessed apostle Peter and his successors, he forbade that thenceforth it should receive those who came in His name, if this were not sufficiently demonstrated by something other than their own affirmations. Certainly you ought not to believe in those who you say have in such fashion come to you: and we ought not to believe in you, since God commands the contrary.[34]

Joan remained unmoved. 'If I were to be condemned,' she declared, 'and I saw the fire lit, the wood prepared, and the executioner or the man whose duty it was to light the fire ready to do so, and if I myself were in the fire, I would nevertheless say nothing different and would maintain what I have said during the trial until my death.'³⁵ After this, little more could be said. Both sides had made their positions clear, and the consequences for Joan were now apparently inevitable.

What were the considerations which now influenced Joan's judges? As men of the Church, living in the France of the early fifteenth century, they had complex loyalties. First, to the Church itself as an overriding ideal, the source of salvation and the fountainhead of right conduct. Secondly to the pope as head of the Church – but chiefly of the Church as a terrestrial institution. Here their loyalty was shaken by several factors – by the recent schism, which had given men a choice of popes to obey; by the attraction of the conciliar theory, which seemed to push the pope into second place, and to give collective pre-eminence to doctors such as themselves; and by deep-rooted Gallicanism, which wished to see the French Church as an independent body. As soon as Joan touched on the question of papal supremacy, she raised a number of extremely touchy issues.

But those who confronted Joan, in addition to being churchmen, were also, for the most part, Frenchmen, caught up in the throes of a complex civil war. Though the sense of nationality was not so clearly developed as it was to become in the nineteenth century, it was nevertheless beginning to stir, as we can see from Joan's own utterances. The assessors at Rouen had chosen the English side, or rather the choice had been made for them, by imperceptible degrees, by the events of the preceding decade. They owed much to English (and to Burgundian) patronage, but we cannot dismiss their motivations as being entirely venal. To choose Bedford and Philip the Good, as against Charles VII and Georges de La Trémoille, was to choose order and justice in preference to chaos and caprice. Or so it still seemed to many Frenchmen in the spring of 1431.

Finally they were males, middle-aged and scholarly, by their profession men of peace, confronted by a young female who seemed to them the declared adherent of violence and everything that was irrational. She seemed to lay claim to the masculine potency which they had renounced by their clerical vows, but which they were unwilling to concede to a usurper such as this. At the same time Joan confused them because of her confident claims to be in direct touch with God, and to know God's wishes. Their profession and their epoch taught them to believe that supernatural intervention of this kind was perfectly possible. What they were unwilling to concede was the notion that it could happen to her, that this man-woman could be the channel through which divine orders were conveyed. And yet, at the same time, they seem to have been impressed by Joan in spite of themselves. Her myth had preceded her, and when the judges confronted the prisoner in Rouen they had already formed an impression of what she was like. The unflattering picture drawn by the Bourgeois of Paris in his journal gives us an idea of how they may have thought of her. The reality contradicted many of their expectations. In particular, Joan put forward an idea of what was good which was in apparent harmony with their own, but which had led her into actions which they considered deplorable. Worse still, she put it forward with stubborn sincerity. What the judges resented most of all in Joan's attitudes – or so we may suspect – was the implication that they themselves were in danger of being judged, and unfavourably, by a higher power. When Joan told Cauchon that he stood in great danger, she threatened the whole body of assessors.

And yet, in a narrow sense, the trial was properly conducted. Perhaps, indeed, the confused resentment which Joan aroused made the proceedings in some respects more meticulous. For example, though the notaries who were responsible for the trial record describe attempts to make them write things other than those they believed to be correct, they also assert, with a good deal of professional pride, that these attempts were successfully resisted. A small number of Joan's statements – favourable to her but marginal to the main thrust of the case – were probably not enregistered. This is the worst we can say about the main body of the trial record. There is no evidence of wholesale falsification.

Though the record is accurate, there was nevertheless a good deal of pressure put upon some of the judges – those who showed an inclination to help Joan during her interrogations. Their descriptions of the way in which they were threatened by Warwick and Cauchon are often dismissed as self-justifying exaggerations, if not outright falsehoods. Yet, as we have seen, their statements can be fitted without difficulty into the framework of the trial record. How much difference did this intimidation make? We may guess that it made very little, and may have even been marginally favourable to Joan. Cauchon's tactics were self-defeating. Those who aided Joan seem to have done so more because they resented the bishop than because they sympathized with the prisoner. Joan was tried for political motives. As the notary Manchon knew, those who brought her to judgement not only feared Joan herself,[36] but wished to strike a blow at Charles VII.[37] But there were reasons why the assessors could often blot the political nature of the trial out of their collective consciousness. Joan was certainly not guiltless of transgressions against the things which ecclesiastical law upheld. Granted the contemporary definition of heresy, it is difficult indeed to say that she was not heretical. She was condemned, not upon the evidence of others, but out of her own mouth. As the Parisian doctors took control of what was happening, the kind of trial the English seem to have envisaged was abandoned, and a quite different affair took its place. The twelve articles, as we have seen, tacitly acquit Joan of the charge of sorcery. Cauchon, the servant of the English, was also the child of the university, and followed the intellectual lead offered by his colleagues – followed it so far, indeed, that he was eventually to find himself in a dilemma.

Even after the machinery for exonerating Joan had been set in motion, some of those who had acted as assessors in the trial of 1431 found trouble in withdrawing their original verdict. And it was not merely the unwillingness to admit they had been wrong which bothered them, but a genuine moral difficulty. In 1450, Beaupère, who clearly detested Joan, still maintained that there was 'more human intention and natural cause' in her apparitions 'than supernatural cause'.[38] Ladvenu thought that when speaking of the kingdom and the war she 'seemed inspired by the Holy Spirit', but that, in speaking of herself, she 'feigned many things'.[39] Pierre Miget remarked: 'It seemed to me that she insisted too much on the visions she said that she had had.'[40] Thomas de Courcelles noted that Joan 'obstinately maintained that she could not submit to the Church'.[41] And in 1452, another assessor called André Marguerie declared that, far from recognizing that Joan had replied as she should and catholically, 'he believed rather the contrary'.[42] He repeated this declaration more or less word for word in 1456.[43] Joan's

260

support of Charles VII was not the only factor in her condemnation. She died, too, for her defiance of the established theological orthodoxy of her time. One may wonder if fairer treatment would have made any difference to her eventual fate.

Once the process began Joan was doomed for two reasons, and it is impossible to say which was the stronger. One was that the English had bought her, and their only motive for buying her was to have her publicly burnt. The other was that, being what she was, any trial upon matters of faith would inevitably lead her to condemn herself.

Joan's tragedy culminates in two intensely dramatic public scenes – her abjuration and her execution. Between these lies the hugger-mugger business of her relapse into heresy. Cauchon's 'beautiful process' loses its dignity, and becomes the very thing the bishop had sought to avoid – a thing so troubled, controversial and doubtful that Joan's spirit was bound to rise again to haunt those who had conducted it.

On 24 May, Joan made her first appearance in Rouen outside the walls of the castle. She was brought to the cemetery on the south side of the abbey church of Saint-Ouen, one of the few spaces in the city which was large enough to accommodate a really large crowd. This crowd was both expected and desired by the organizers of the trial. They knew that Joan's presence in the castle had aroused immense curiosity, while few people had had any opportunity to see her because of the conditions of strict security under which she was kept. And they hoped to humiliate her so thoroughly that her reputation would be destroyed past hope of recovery.

The population of Rouen was a desirable audience for the scene which Cauchon and Warwick had planned between them. The city had surrendered to the English in December 1419, and had since then become the headquarters of the occupying power. The siege of 1418–19 had been bitterly contested, and even in 1431 Rouen had not yet fully recovered from its effects. The ruins of the buildings destroyed more than ten years before were still visible in many places. The Abbey of Saint-Ouen, where Joan was now to be shown, had suffered particularly in the course of the siege and its aftermath.

After the siege, Rouen was forced to produce a heavy indemnity. It had only just finished paying this off at the time of Joan's trial. The new masters of the city also imposed certain fairly onerous duties upon its citizens. Though they were exempted from military service, they were obliged to keep the watch, and every night 240 of them manned the walls. This was not an idle precaution. The town of Louviers, which was only seven leagues from Rouen, had been surprised and captured by La Hire on 8 December 1429, and ever since then his troops had made continual raids upon the surrounding countryside. Louviers did not again fall to the English until 25 October 1431. In May of that year Rouen therefore had a little of the atmosphere of a city which was itself under siege. Yet, despite a long series of Armagnac plots during the period of the English domination, we must not conclude that the citizens of Rouen were immediately ready to take Joan's part.

Bedford's government recognized how important Rouen was to them, and the English looked after its interests very carefully. The population might have sunk to about 15,000, from a high point of 40,000 reached during the thirteenth century, but the city remained an extremely important commercial centre. The port of Rouen was busy throughout the English occupation, and luxury trades, such as embroidery, continued to flourish. Banking was also important in Rouen – a good indication of the continuing vigour of its commercial life. The inhabitants were aware of the benefits which the occupiers brought them, and they particularly appreciated the good discipline of the English garrison. Like other French cities, Rouen was terrified of the greed and turbulence of the Armagnac forces. In 1432, there was a moment of truth. Rouen castle – the very spot where Joan had so recently been imprisoned – was surprised and taken by a handful of Charles's men. The Earl of Arundel, then the English commander, appealed to the bourgeois of Rouen for their support, and got it without hesitation. The castle was retaken, and Rouen did not fall to the king for some years. Those who came to Saint-Ouen to catch a glimpse of Joan were therefore curious, but they were not necessarily sympathetic.

Before she appeared, a last effort was made to change her attitudes. This time it was Jean Beaupère who, in the early morning, came in alone to see her:

I warned her that she would soon be taken to the scaffold to be preached, and said to her that, if she was a good Christian, she would say at the said scaffold that she submitted all her words and deeds to the judgement of our mother Holy Church, and more especially to that of the ecclesiastical judges.[1]

According to Beaupère, Joan declared to him that she would do so. In view of what followed, we may doubt if her declaration was particularly heartfelt, though her voices apparently prophesied to her that she would submit.

Because of the crowd, Joan seems to have been taken into the church, and to have emerged into the churchyard of Saint-Ouen by a side door. She came out accompanied by Loiselleur, who was saying:

Joan, believe me, for, if you wish, you can be saved. Put on the clothes of your sex, and do everything prescribed to you. Otherwise you are in danger of death. If you do what I tell you, I repeat, you are saved; no ill will happen to you, and much good; and you will then be rejoined to the church.[2]

Jean de Châtillon and Pierre Maurice added their solicitations to Loiselleur's[3] before Joan mounted the scaffold. This was a high platform, made so that everyone could see both Joan and the preacher. Facing it there was another scaffold upon which sat Cauchon, Cardinal Beaufort and Jean de Mailly, Bishop of Noyon, among others. The sermon, which was an essential part of the ceremony, whether it ended with Joan's abjuration or her execution, was to be preached by Guillaume Érard, a theologian from Paris who had taken very little part in the trial proceedings. In fact, his only previous confrontation with Joan had been upon 9 May, upon the occasion when she was threatened with torture. His servant, Jean de Lenozoles, later deposed that Érard viewed the task of preaching the sermon with distaste. 'I would much prefer to be in Flanders,' he said pettishly. 'This affair is most disagreeable to me.'[4] However, it is clear that he understood what was required of him.

Érard's sermon is now lost. It was a sufficiently striking performance, however, for various phrases and sentences to stick in his listeners' minds. The text he chose came from the Gospel according to St John: 'As the branch cannot bear fruit in itself, except it abide in the vine.'[5] But though he stuck to it sufficiently to refer to 'the pride of this woman',[6] the main weight of Érard's attack fell upon Charles VII. It is Massieu who gives us the fullest account of what he said:

> Ha, France! You are much abused, you who have been the most Christian house. Charles, who calls himself king, and your governor, has attached himself as a heretic and schismatic to the words and deeds of an evil, infamous woman; and not only he, but all the clergy of his obedience and seigneury, by whom she has been examined and not rejected, as she herself has said.

Having repeated this attack on the king some two or three times, Érard finally turned to Joan, who was standing beside him, and said to her, wagging his finger: 'It is to you, Joan, that I speak, and I tell you your king is heretic and schismatic.'[7]

The provocation was too much. Whatever Joan's intentions had been when she arrived, she now said, according to Massieu's account: 'By my faith, sirs, in all reverence, I dare say and swear, on pain of my life, that he is the most noble Christian of all Christians, the one who best loves the faith and the Church, and he is not what you call him.'[8] Another witness leads us to think that she was less elaborately polite. She turned on Érard and said: 'Do not speak of my king. He is a good Christian.'[9] Érard cried to the tipstaff Massieu, who was also standing on the same raised platform: 'Make her be silent!'[10] Everyone understood what was going on. The sermon showed, more clearly than anything which had preceded it, that the motivation of Joan's trial was to discredit Charles VII.[11] When he had finished, Érard again turned to Joan and said:

> Here present you see the judges who upon different occasions have summoned and required you to submit all your words and deeds to our holy mother the Church. They have remonstrated with you, and have explained to you, that according to churchmen, there were many things amongst those you have said and done which are false and erroneous.

Joan replied:

> In what concerns submission to the Church, I have already replied to them. Let the record of everything I have said and done be sent to

Rome, to our lord the Sovereign Pontiff. I submit myself to him and in the first place to God. And as to my words and my actions, I said and did them moved by God. I charge no man with them, not my king nor any other: and, if there is some fault, then it is mine and no one else's.[12]

This formal appeal to the pope seems to have caused a moment of consternation. Those around Joan again started to press her to submit fully, and she remarked ironically: 'You take great pains to seduce me.'[13] Cauchon asked her if she wished to abjure whatever the churchmen had condemned, and she answered once more: 'I submit to God and to our Lord the Pope.'[14] But Cauchon was having none of this. He knew that, under standard inquisitorial procedure, the ecclesiastical judge was within his rights if he himself rejected an appeal to Rome, on the grounds that there was insufficient cause. He told Joan it must be a full submission, or he would proceed to sentence.

The delay was making the crowd restless, and there were also mutterings in the group where Cauchon sat. The loudest came from Laurent Calot, the secretary of the King of England.[15] Cauchon had had two sentences prepared, one condemning Joan outright, the other to be used if she abjured. He pulled the sentence of condemnation from his sleeve and started to read it.[16] Even after the reading had begun, Loiselleur and Érard were pressing Joan to recant. Érard told her that 'she should do as she was advised and she would be delivered from prison'.[17] He had with him a copy of the articles Joan would be required to sign, and started to read them to her. Joan replied that she did not know what it all meant,[18] and Érard passed the parchment to Massieu, who once more began to explain. According to his later recollection, the formula was quite short. There were, he said, 'only seven lines, or eight at the most'.[19] The stir around Joan was now becoming so marked that there was a great murmuring among the spectators,[20] and Cauchon paused in his reading. Calot, enraged beyond measure at this hitch in the proceedings, shouted to the bishop that he was a traitor.[21] 'You'll pay for that!' Cauchon retorted, and then said, to the world at large: 'I have just been insulted. I will go no further forward until I have received an apology.'[22] Érard seized the opportunity to say to Massieu: 'Advise her to abjure.' Massieu again takes up the story:

First I tried to get out of it. Then I said to Joan: 'You must understand – if you go against any of these articles, you will be burned. I advise you to appeal to the universal Church as to whether you must abjure these articles or not.'[23] Guillaume Érard said to me: 'What are you saying to her?' I replied: 'I am making the text of the abjuration formula known to Joan, and inviting her to sign, but she declares she does not know how to do it.'[24] To which Érard replied: 'Do it now, or you will be burned this very day.' Joan then said she would rather sign than be burned.[25]

She had every reason to be conscious of her peril. Near by she could see the executioner with his cart, waiting to receive her.[26]

The pause prolonged itself, the murmuring in the crowd grew louder, and stones were starting to fly.[27] Joan joined her hands and cried in a loud voice that she submitted to the judgement of the Church. Then she prayed to St Michael to direct and advise her.[28] Apparently taken aback by the turn of events, though he had sedulously prepared for it, Cauchon turned to Beaufort and asked what ought to be done. The latter knew the answer as well as Cauchon knew it himself. The aim of the inquisition was not to destroy the body but to save the soul. The cardinal therefore advised that Joan, even at this eleventh hour, must be received into penitence.[29] Calot, however, was still discontented, and told Cauchon roundly: 'You are acting with too much leniency, and show yourself favourable to Joan.'[30] 'You lie!' said Cauchon. 'By my profession, I must seek the safety of her soul and body.'[31]

There has always been a dispute about the formula that Joan signed, there amid the confusion in the cemetery of Saint-Ouen. At the Trial of Rehabilitation, the promoter, Simon Chapitault, spoke of 'this pretended abjuration which, though forming part of the trial record, was fabricated after the trial was over. It is long out of measure, artificially made so that an innocent and ignorant girl could not have comprehended it.'[32] The evidence is indeed overwhelming that the abjuration presented to Joan was very short. Pierre Miget says that it 'lasted as long as a *Pater Noster*'.[33] In all probability what happened is that the record was 'perfected' after the event by inserting a more elaborate and specific formula in place of the shorter one which was actually signed.[34] The essential points were the same in both versions – disavowal of Joan's voices, the renunciation of male dress, and full submission to the Church.

The signature itself poses an interesting problem. At the preliminary inquiry of 1450, Massieu, who was in a position to know, said that she signed with a cross.[35] Boisguillaume, who was one of the notaries, and may have handled the document afterwards, says that she 'signed, and made a cross'.[36] This is indeed the form in which her signature appears in the trial record – first Joan's name, then a cross after it.[37] Joan's own letters – the originals where they survive – are signed 'Jehanne',

and it is generally thought that these signatures are authentic, and that she knew how to write her name. It has even been recently argued, though I think very unconvincingly, that at some point she learned how to read.[38] One thing which historians seem to have overlooked, however, is what Joan herself had to say about the use of a cross in her letters. Sometimes, she told her judges, she put a cross 'as a sign to those of her party to whom she was writing that they should not do what she wrote'.[39]

Two witnesses tell us that Joan seemed to take her surrender extremely lightly, after resisting for so long. Jean de Mailly, Bishop of Noyon, says: 'It seemed to me . . . that Joan hardly took her abjuration seriously, nor laid much weight upon it.'[40] Another of Joan's judges remembered that, as she repeated the prescribed formula after Massieu, 'she spoke several words of it laughing'.[41] This inappropriate burst of laughter has been dismissed as a nervous and e..entially mirthless *fou rire*, prompted by the horror of her circumstances. But it is tempting to see it also as the spontaneous reaction to a piece of peasant trickery. In her own mind, by signing this, she had not committed herself. And no doubt she thought she had given her judges fair warning thanks to what she had said at the trial. Cauchon was unaware of all this, and in the face of further protests he proceeded to read the second of the two sentences that had been prepared. Joan's excommunication was lifted, but she was condemned to perpetual imprisonment. Joan had no doubt thought that, if she recanted, she would be taken to an ecclesiastical prison. As they left Saint-Ouen, Massieu, who still had charge of her, advised her to ask that she 'be taken to the prisons of the Church, because the Church had condemned her'. Several others, amongst those who were present, made the same request to Cauchon, who abruptly refused.[42] He knew that the English would never allow it; the very letter which handed her over to him for judgement made this plain. Meanwhile, his allies found the position extremely unsatisfactory. Another witness tells us that

When Joan was being taken back from Saint-Ouen to prison, the soldiers insulted her, and their officers let them do it. In fact, the English leaders were mightily indignant at the Bishop of Beauvais, because Joan had not been pronounced guilty, condemned and given up for execution. Their indignation was such that, at the moment when the bishop and doctors returned to the castle, some of the English, saying they had ill-earned the king's money, raised their weapons to strike them. They did not strike them, however.

I also heard that the Earl of Warwick complained to the bishop and the doctors. 'The king is ill-served,' he said, 'since Joan is escaping.' To which one of them replied: 'Messire, don't worry. We will certainly entrap her again.'[43]

Whether or not one accepts this exchange between Warwick and the judges as authentic, there can be no doubt that to condemn Joan to perpetual imprisonment, and then to return her to Rouen castle and the mercies of her English gaolers, created a situation which could not be sustained for long. Cauchon was too intelligent not to recognize this, but we must not at once conclude that he meant to create the impasse from the beginning.

The Bishop of Beauvais, despite his love of power, his partisanship, and the innate violence of his nature, was a man of God, and one, perhaps, more God-fearing than many. When he died in 1442, he did not leave a great deal of money, and most of it went in pious legacies and foundations. It is also clear that he genuinely believed Joan to be guilty. His weaknesses seem to have been exhibitionism and vanity. When Cauchon spoke of making a beautiful process he seems to have been using these words in several senses. In the first place, it would be beautiful because it reached the right, the fore-ordained conclusion. The English purchase of Joan would be justified. In the second place, it would be an exemplary trial of its sort – a model for future generations to look back upon when proceedings against a heretic were contemplated. In the third place, Cauchon envisaged for himself, though less precisely than he might have done, a striking and creditable role in the drama which was about to unfold. He would not appear as the ally of the English, but simply as the defender of the faith against an impertinent and mendacious person, who also happened to have hoodwinked the chief of his political enemies.

When Joan recanted at Saint-Ouen, Cauchon may not immediately have seen the trap he had prepared for himself, but he certainly grasped his position within moments of the event. The declared aim of inquisitorial procedure was self-accusation and repentance. This had been publicly achieved. But now what was to be done with the convicted woman? Cauchon suddenly realized that the terms of his bargain with those who held Joan captive prevented him from acting as the beauty of the process required. By allowing him to triumph, Joan had in fact fatally botched his design. Once that was spoilt, he cared little about how things concluded. His one concern was that they should be settled quickly, and the business put out of the way.

ᛞ 34 ᛞ

On the afternoon of Thursday, 24 May, soon after she had been brought back from the tumult of Saint-Ouen, Joan was visited in prison by the Vice Inquisitor, Jean Le Maître, accompanied by Midi, Loiselleur, Courcelles, Isambard de la Pierre and several others. She was given female clothes and immediately put them on; and her hair, which was still cut pudding-basin fashion above her ears, as she had worn it ever since leaving Vaucouleurs, was now completely shaved off.[1] Having seen to this the men of God departed and left Joan to the mercy of her guards. No one will ever know precisely what happened during the next few days, in the privacy of the room where Joan was confined. It seems that she immediately began to be persecuted, not only by the gaolers, but by those voices she had just renounced in public, though not in her heart. Here is what she said to Cauchon on the subject, the following Monday.

We asked her if, since Thursday, she had heard the voices of St Catherine and St Margaret. She replied that she had. Asked what they said, [she] replied that God had told her, through St Catherine and St Margaret, of the great pity of this signal treason to which she, Joan, had consented in making the abjuration and recantation in order to save her life. She said that, before Thursday, her voices had told her what she would do that day, and she had then done it. She said, in addition, that her voices told her, when she was on the scaffold, before the people, that she should reply boldly to the preacher who was then preaching. And Joan said he was a false preacher who said that she did several things which she had not done. She said that, if she declared God had not sent her, she would damn herself, and that God had in truth sent her. She said that her voices had told her, since Thursday, that she had committed a great crime in confessing that what she had done was not well done.[2]

In fact Joan seems to have made no effort to conceal the return of her voices.[3] Those around her knew that they had come back immediately she heard them herself. And, by the Friday or the Saturday, so Beaupère tells us, it was already being reported to the judges that she repented having left off men's clothes.[4] The actual resumption does not seem to have occurred until the Sunday. It is Massieu who gives the most detailed account of what happened, an account which he says that he got from Joan when they were for a moment left alone together:

The men's clothing was put in a bag, in the same room where Joan was kept prisoner. She remained under the guard of five Englishmen. At night, three remained in the room with her, and two outside, at the door. Joan, in bed, had her legs held by two pairs of irons and her body by a chain which, crossing the foot of her bed, was fastened by a long piece of wood and locked with a key. Chained thus, she could not move. The following Sunday, which was Trinity Sunday, here is what took place. Morning having come, Joan said to the English, her guards: 'Take off my irons, so that I can get up.' Then one of these English took off the women's clothes she was wearing. They emptied the sack in which was men's clothing, saying to her: 'Get up,' and they put the women's clothes in the bag. Joan covered herself with the men's clothes given to her. At the same time she said: 'Messieurs, you know that this is forbidden to me. Without fault, I cannot wear it.' But they did not wish to give her other clothes, and the debate lasted until midday. In the end, out of physical necessity, Joan was forced to leave the room and take these clothes: and after she had come back they would not give her others, no matter what supplication or request she made.[5]

Other sources suggest that the male clothes which Joan had worn were, after being taken away, dishonestly made available to her again. Jean de Mailly, Bishop of Noyon, claims that they were handed in through a window.[6]

If everything indicates that there was a plot to get Joan to return to the dress which had been forbidden, whom are we to blame for it? Beaupère reports that, when Joan was said to be wavering, he and Midi were sent by Cauchon to the castle, to admonish her and get her to stick to her good resolution. He continues:

But we could not find the man who had the key to the prison. While we awaited the warder, some Englishmen who were in the courtyard of the castle spoke menacing words concerning us. It was Midi who reported them to me. They said: 'If we threw them both in the river, that would be well done.' Hearing this, we turned back. As we were once more crossing the castle bridge, the said Midi heard and reported to me similar, or nearly similar threats, made by other Englishmen. This frightened us and we left without talking to Joan.[7]

When the news came that Joan had definitely resumed the forbidden dress, another delegation was sent to the castle, on Cauchon's orders, and also on Warwick's. Manchon accompanied it. The garrison rioted as soon as the French priests appeared.

When we arrived in the main courtyard, in the absence of Monseigneur de Beauvais, the English in arms came to assail us. They were at least fifty, perhaps eighty, perhaps even a hundred. They shouted abuse at us, saying all we men of the church were false, traitors, Armagnacs and evil counsellors, and that we had spoilt the trial. They were angry, I think, because Joan had not been burnt after the first preaching and the first sentence. It was with difficulty, and not without terror, that we managed to escape from their hands and get out of the castle. For that day, we did nothing.[8]

Massieu reports having met the party of clerics as they emerged from the castle, all quaking and terrified.[9] He also reports that André Marguerie in particular was threatened for saying that 'it was not enough to see Joan in men's clothes, but it was also necessary to know the motives which had led her to retake this habit'.[10]

Both Isambard de la Pierre and Martin Ladvenu report Joan's complaints that she was 'molested and beaten'[11] by her guards; and they both report a story (claiming to have had it from Joan's own lips) that 'a great English lord had tried to rape her'.[12] This story has sometimes been dismissed as a fantasy on their part or, more probably, on Joan's. A serious attempt at rape, made when she was chained up as Massieu describes, would certainly have succeeded. But may there not have been an assault of this kind which deliberately stopped halfway? And if so, what prompted it? The only answer is that it was a calculated attempt to get Joan to resume the costume which would be fatal to her.

If those active in the conspiracy were the English garrison and some of their commanders, are we also to blame Cauchon? It has generally been assumed that he stage-managed everything that led to Joan's downfall, but, on this occasion, it seems unnecessary to blame him for anything more than a passive acceptance of what was going on. Passivity was not the bishop's strong suit, but he had little room for manoeuvre.

On Monday, Cauchon went to see Joan himself. Manchon joined him in Joan's cell. The notary says that he only reached it thanks to an escort provided by Warwick, which took him right to the prison.[13] The account he gives of what Joan said on this occasion differs considerably from the trial-record which he signed as notary. At the Trial of Rehabilitation he claimed that

In my presence she was asked why she had resumed men's clothing. She replied that she had done so to defend her modesty, because she was not safe in women's dress, in the company of guards who had tried to violate her modesty, something about which she had complained several times to the bishop and the earl. She also said that the judges had promised her that she would be in the hands and in the prisons of the church, with a woman for companion. She added that, if it was the pleasure of the judges to put her in a safe place, where she need not fear, then she was ready to take woman's clothes.[14]

The record of Joan's interrogation, on the other hand, reads as follows:

Asked why she had taken men's clothing and what had led her to take it, she said that she had taken it of her own free will, without being forced to do so by anyone, and that she preferred this dress to a woman's. She was then reminded that she had promised and sworn not to resume men's clothing, but she replied that she had never understood that she had taken an oath not to resume men's clothing. Once more interrogated: why had she done so? she replied that she had done so because it was more licit and proper to wear men's dress when she was among men, rather than wearing women's dress. She said too that she had taken men's dress because the promise made to her had not been kept – that is that she should go to mass, receive the body of Christ and be released from irons.[15]

If Joan's decision to resume men's clothing was initially forced upon her by her guards, it soon became, as the interrogation of 28 May suggests, a matter of deliberate choice. Massieu tells us that.

After Joan had been seen, throughout Trinity Sunday, in the men's clothing she had resumed, the next day they again gave her women's clothes.[16]

Having once more donned the forbidden garments, her obsession returned in all its force. When Cauchon appeared, she was still clad in them.

Her true attitude during that crucial Monday interview is probably summed up in this statement, which she made as it was coming to an end: 'She said that she preferred to do her penitence once and for all, that is to say by dying, than to endure longer her pain in prison.'[17] We seem to catch, here, an echo of the mood she had been in at Beaurevoir, when she hurled herself towards what seemed certain destruction from the summit of Jean de Luxembourg's keep. At the very end, however, she once more began to waver, saying that: 'If the judges wished it, she would again wear women's clothes, but for the rest she would do nothing more.'[18] By this time, however, she had already given Cauchon everything he needed in order to condemn her. In particular, she had made one fatal admission: 'She said that, whatever she had said and recanted upon the Thursday in question, she had said and done it solely from fear of the fire.'[19] Manchon, however much his account might vary in other respects, was also constrained to recall her answer at the Trial of Rehabilitation: 'Everything she had done, she had done from fear of fire, having before her eyes the executioner and his cart.'[20] It was this, far more than the resumption of male clothing, which made it inevitable she would be executed. Even as she said the words, she must have known their effect. To that extent, her death was her own decision.

Coming out of the prison, Cauchon ran into Warwick, who was waiting, surrounded by a crowd of English, to discover what had taken place. The bishop greeted the earl in his own language. 'Farewell,' he said, 'be of good heart, it is done.'[21] One would give much to know the precise tone of voice in which these few words were spoken.

Only the formalities remained to be completed. The next day, Cauchon summoned to the chapel of the archbishopric of Rouen a representative selection of those who had acted as assessors during the course of the trial. The verdict could not be in doubt. Joan must be abandoned to secular justice. Thomas de Courcelles and Isambard de la Pierre, usually so different in their viewpoints, both added the rider that 'the said woman should be once more charitably admonished for the safety of her soul, and told that she had nothing more to hope for in what concerned her temporal life'.[22]

35

For our knowledge of what went on in Joan's prison on the morning of 30 May, before she was brought out to die, we have two different sources, the so-called 'Posthumous Information' attached to the trial document, and the depositions made at the Trial of Rehabilitation. They sometimes seem to contradict one another, and the Posthumous Information has been further doubted because the official notaries refused to swear to it, as they swore to the rest. The real reason for their refusal, however, was that they were not present at these last interviews. And the contradictions between the two sources are not as fundamental as they look.

The first people to arrive in her cell on that last day were Pierre Maurice and Nicolas Loiselleur. They had come to exhort her once again, and also to make a final attempt to discover the truth about her apparitions. To Maurice Joan admitted that the story she had told about the way a crown was brought to the king had been a lie, and that 'she herself was the angel'. But she was vehement about the reality of her visions. 'Whether they were good or evil spirits they appeared to me,' she said. Maurice remarked that they seemed to have deceived her, and she half-admitted that they had.[1] But inwardly, she was still certain of the justice of her cause. She asked Maurice: 'Master Peter, where shall I be this evening?' He replied with another question: 'Do you not have good hope in God?' Joan answered: 'Yes, and with God's help, I shall be in Paradise.'[2] Martin

Ladvenu and Jean Toutmouillé then joined the others in Joan's cell. Toutmouillé was a Dominican, who had taken no part in the trial. Ladvenu, who belonged to the same order, had brought him along for moral support in what he suspected would be an unpleasant ordeal. They told Joan the final decision of her judges, and, faced with the horror of her fate, she suddenly broke down:

Alas! Am I to be treated so horribly and cruelly that my body, which has never been corrupted, must today be consumed and reduced to ash! Ah! Ah! I would seven times rather be beheaded than be thus burned. Alas! If I had been in the ecclesiastical prison to which I submitted myself, and if I had been guarded by men of the Church, and not by my enemies and adversaries, this misfortune would not so miserably have come to me. Oh, I appeal before God, the great judge, the great wrongs and injustices done to me![3]

At this moment Cauchon arrived, accompanied by Le Maître, Courcelles and others. Joan turned on him, saying: 'Bishop, I die through you.' He answered her smugly: 'Ah! Joan, take all things patiently. You die because you have not kept your promises to us, and have returned to your former wrong-doing.' Joan once more reverted to her grievances about the conditions in which she had been kept: 'Alas! If you had put me in the prisons of the ecclesiastical court and the hands of competent and proper ecclesiastical guardians, this would not have happened, and this is why I appeal to God against you.'[4] The bishop ignored these remonstrances, for he saw that she was at last in a condition of extreme physical terror. Joan had none of the masochism which has often marked the temperament of martyrs. She never embraced suffering for its own sake, and she seems, indeed, to have had unusual sensitivity to physical pain. In addition, the idea of fire was terrible to her, as we have seen, because it was not a 'clean' death, but meant the soiling of the flesh she had so carefully kept immaculate.

Seeing his advantage, Cauchon began to press her on the subject of the veracity or otherwise of her voices. He knew from the secret interviews which Loiselleur had had with her, and later from her own mouth, that these had promised that she would escape. As the projection of her own wishes, how could they do otherwise? 'Come now, Joan,' Cauchon said, 'you always told us that your voices said you would be set free; now tell us the truth.' Joan had no fortitude left to resist the attack. 'In truth,' she cried, 'I see that they have deceived me.'[5] It was an important admission, and Cauchon made certain that the others who were present had heard it.

Loiselleur, who had been one of the most active of Joan's persecutors, now felt a stirring in his long-dormant conscience. When he left Joan, he was weeping, and these tears were ill received by the English troops who were assembled in the courtyard, waiting to escort Joan to the stake. They began to jeer at Loiselleur and to threaten him, and the miserable priest had to run to Warwick for protection.[6] Having failed to get anything more out of the prisoner, Cauchon and most of his entourage departed. Joan then made two successive confessions to Martin Ladvenu. She begged that she might receive communion before she died. Massieu was sent to find Cauchon and get an answer from him on this subject. Cauchon consulted the group of doctors who were still with him, and sent his reply: 'Tell Brother Martin to give her communion and everything she asks.'[7] The bishop's willingness to allow Joan to receive the Eucharist is something which has aroused controversy. Some authorities have seen in it a sign that Joan made a second and formal abjuration. But the public sentence which Cauchon pronounced a few hours later in the Place du Vieux-Marché makes no mention of this. Indeed, the trial record, after telling us the theme of the sermon preached on the same occasion, insists that Joan never truly disavowed her errors.[8] It therefore seems likely that, when Cauchon gave his permission, he imposed no terms.

The resolution of the difficulty may possibly be found in the fact that inquisitorial procedure was capable of making a distinction between avowals made under the seal of the confessional, and those made for all to hear. Medieval thinking was perfectly capable of supporting this paradox, which served to protect the guardians of the faith, themselves only human, from their own fallibility. In any case, there are two pieces of evidence which seem to confirm the theory I have put forward. One comes from the notary, Manchon, who at this moment was with the bishop and the others. He says that the judges decided that 'if Joan asked for the Eucharist, it should be given to her, and that she should be absolved at the tribunal of penitence'.[9]

This declaration was made at the Trial of Rehabilitation, when Manchon was asked how it was that Joan, then being supposedly heretic and excommunicate, was allowed to receive the sacraments. He might in any case have added that it was customary to allow relapsed persons to receive them, if repentance seemed probable.

The other piece of evidence is to be found in the record of Posthumous Information. A witness who was present after Cauchon departed, and who saw communion administered to Joan, records what he overheard. Holding the host in his hands, Ladvenu asked her: 'Do you believe this to be the body of Christ?' Joan answered: 'Yes, and it is the one thing that can save me; I ask that it be given to me.' Then Ladvenu said: 'Do you still believe in your voices?' And Joan answered: 'I believe in God alone, and no longer wish to put my faith in these voices, because they have thus deceived me.'[10] It was as near as Cauchon could come, in an official document, to betraying the secret of the confessional.

The confusion about Joan's status was reflected in the way the Eucharist was brought to her. At first it came 'extremely irreverently, in a paten enveloped in the cloth with which the chalice is covered, without surplice or stole'.[11] Ladvenu was having none of this, and he sent it back.[12] On the second occasion it came properly escorted, with many torches, and liturgies were sung.[13] The priest did not want it said, on some future occasion, that he had administered communion to a relapsed heretic upon his own responsibility, and without anyone knowing about it. He also wanted to make the point that respect was due to the body of Christ, even if none was owed to Joan.

Just before 9 a.m. the procession set out for the Vieux-Marché. As Joan was put in the cart, Loiselleur tried to get into it to ask her pardon, and the soldiers chased him away.[14] The escort consisted of the entire garrison of the castle, about eighty men with swords and staves.[15] Joan was wearing a black shift,[16] and a kerchief on her head, and was weeping abundantly.[17] With her were Martin Ladvenu and Jean Massieu. They came out of the castle by a small gate on the west side, called the *porte de derrière*, and moved through the narrow streets towards the place of execution.

In the Vieux-Marché four scaffolds had been erected – one

for the judges, as formerly at Saint-Ouen, one for Joan and the preacher, one for the *bailli* and the council of the secular court, and finally one for the stake, which was inserted into a high plaster base – high enough for the whole of the huge crowd to savour the agonies of the victim. Nailed to the stake was a sign, which read:

Joan, who had herself called the Maid, a liar, pernicious deceiver of the people, sorceress, superstitious, blasphemer of God, defamer of the faith of Jesus Christ, boastful, idolatrous, cruel, dissolute, invoker of demons, apostate, schismatic and heretic.[18]

The sermon, on this occasion, was preached not by Érard but by Nicolas Midi, who took for his text the words from the First Epistle to the Corinthians: 'Whether one member suffer, all the members suffer with it.'[19] The sermon went on for a long time, but Joan listened without attempting to interrupt.[20] When it was finished, Cauchon exhorted her to think of the salvation of her soul, and to attend to the counsel of the two Dominicans who were with her – Ladvenu had been joined by Isambard de la Pierre.[21] The bishop then read the definitive sentence of the church casting Joan off and abandoning her to the secular authorities. Midi too turned to the prisoner and said, 'Joan, go in peace. The Church can protect you no longer and delivers you up to the secular arm.'[22] And it seems to have been at this point that Joan was crowned with a mitre, which proclaimed her to be: 'Heretic, relapsed, apostate, idolator.'[23] She knelt and began to pray, asking pardon of 'her judges, the English, the king of France and all the princes of the kingdom'.[24] She was still, however, careful to exonerate Charles VII from responsibility for her actions.[25]

We are told by Massieu, who was standing beside her, that these prayers and lamentations continued for another half-hour after the conclusion of the sermon.[26] Many of those present were moved to tears, but the tight phalanx of English guards surrounding Joan – there may have been as many as 200 of them – greeted her conduct with derisive laughter.[27] At length Joan was taken to where the *bailli* sat by two sergeants. Here she remained for some time, but there is no record of what was said.[28] Contrary to the usual practice, no secular sentence was pronounced. The *bailli* suddenly made a sign with his hand, saying: 'Take her, take her', and at once Joan was dragged to the stake,[29] where all was prepared. The omission of a secular sentence was irregular, and was much commented upon afterwards. Louis de Luxembourg noted it, and on a subsequent occasion sent Martin Ladvenu to the *bailli* to warn him that the same slapdash mode of procedure was not to be followed a second time.[30] It was at this point that most of the clerics who were present withdrew. The claim was later made that they went because they were too much moved to watch the last moments of the tragedy.[31] But in fact it would not have been customary for them to stay. Joan was no longer anything to do with them.

As Joan was being chained to the post, she invoked St Michael in particular.[32] It seems clear that he, who had come to her in the beginning, was also with her at the last. Though she had renounced her voices only a moment before, their hold upon her was too strong to be thus shaken off, and now they returned to her as comforters, just as they had soothed and reassured her when she felt the pain of her wound at Orleans. If she was still fearful and troubled, the trouble had started to change its form. One of the spectators heard her exclaim 'Rouen, Rouen, shall I die here?'[33] as if still incredulous that her apparitions did not come to save her. And then she said 'Ha! Rouen, I have great fear that you will suffer for my death!'[34] Though they could not rescue her, the voices might be tempted to avenge her. Joan's sense of her own importance also endured until the end. She asked, while her arms were still free, if she might have a cross, and one of the English soldiers near by pitied her sufficiently to make a small one from two pieces of stick. This she kissed and thrust into her bosom, under her shift.[35] Massieu had climbed up on to the scaffold itself, and was still trying to comfort her, but the guards were becoming impatient, and started to harass him, saying 'What, priest, will you make us dine here?'[36] Thanks to the inordinate length of the sermon, added to Cauchon's exhortation and sentence, and the time Joan had spent in prayer, it must by now have been nearly noon. After three hours, the English soldiers were hungry and impatient to be done.

Joan begged Isambard de la Pierre to go to the near-by church of Saint-Sauveur, and to bring the processional cross. She wanted him to hold this before her eyes until she died. He and Massieu went to get it, and Joan embraced it passionately until it was taken from her, and her hands were bound.[37] The fire was lit, and the flames and smoke began to envelop the victim until she was almost hidden from view. Joan took some time to die, so long that the executioner afterwards said to Ladvenu that the execution had been exceptionally cruel. Since the scaffold had been built so high, he could not climb up to dispatch her, as was usual, and he was therefore forced to leave her to the fire.[38] The spectators heard her calling upon God and the saints, particularly upon St Michael and St Catherine.[39] As the pyre blazed up, she cried for holy water.[40] And at last, as she was released, she uttered a great cry of 'Jesus!', and then dropped her head.[41]

✦❦ Bibliography ❧✦

BOOKS

AYROLES, JEAN BAPTISTE J., *La Vraie Jeanne d'Arc*, 5 vols., Paris, 1890–1902.

BAILLY-MAÎTRE, L., *L'Arrivée de Jeanne d'Arc à Rouen*, Longuyon, 1932.

BASIN, THOMAS, *Histoire de Charles VII*, Charles Samaran (ed. and trans.), 2 vols., Paris, 1933, 1944.

BATAILLE, GEORGES, *Le Procès de Gilles de Rais*, Paris, 1965.

BEAUCOURT, G. DU FRESNE DE, *Histoire de Charles VII*, 6 vols., Paris, 1881–91.

BELLOC, HILAIRE, *Joan of Arc*, London, 1929.

BILLARD, ANDRÉ, *Jeanne d'Arc et ses juges*, Paris, 1933.

BOUCHER DE MOLANDON, *La Famille de Jeanne d'Arc*, Orleans, 1878.

BOUCHER DE MOLANDON and DE BEAUCORPS, ADALBERT, *L'Armée anglaise vaincue par Jeanne d'Arc*, Orleans/Paris, 1892.

BOUCHET, JEAN, *Annales d'Aquitaine*, Paris, 1644; *Panégyrique du chevalier sans reproche, Louis de La Trémoille*, Michaud and Poujolat, série 1, tom. 4, Paris, 1837.

BOURGEOIS DE PARIS, *Journal d'un Bourgeois de Paris, 1408–1499*, Alexandre Tuetey (ed.), Paris, 1881.

DE BOUTELLIER, E., and DE BRAUX, G., *Nouvelles recherches sur la famille de Jeanne d'Arc*, Paris, 1879.

BRACHET, AUGUSTE, *Pathologie mentale des rois de France*, Paris, 1903.

BRUGIÈRE DE BARANTE, AMABLE DE, *Histoire des ducs de Bourgogne*, new edition, Gachard (ed.), 2 vols., Brussels, 1838.

BRUN, FÉLIX, *Jeanne d'Arc à Soissons*, Soissons, 1920.

BURNE, A. H., *The Agincourt War*, London, 1956.

DE CASTELNAU, JACQUES-TH., *Le Paris de Charles V*, Paris, 1930.

DE CAUZONS, TH., *La Magie et la sorcellerie en France*, Paris, n.d. (1910).

CHAMPION, L. G. M., *Jeanne d'Arc écuyère*, Paris, 1901.

CHAMPION, PIERRE, *Guillaume de Flavy*, Paris, 1906; *Procès de condamnation de Jeanne d'Arc*, 2 vols., Paris, 1921; *Splendeurs et misères de Paris, XIVe–XVe siècles*, Paris, 1934.

CHAPOY, HENRI, *Les Compagnons de la Pucelle*, 2nd ed., Paris, 1898.

CHARPENTIER, PIERRE, and CUISSARD, C., *Journal du Siège d'Orléans*, Orleans, 1896.

CHARTIER, ALAIN, *Les Croniques du feu roi Charles septièsme*, Paris, 1528.

CHARTIER, JEAN, *Chronique*, A. Vallet de Viriville (ed.), Paris, 1858.

CHASTELLAIN, GEORGES, *Œuvres*, Kervyn de Lettenhove (ed.), 8 vols. Brussels, 1863–8.

CHÉRUEL, ADOLPHE, *Histoire de Rouen sous la domination anglaise*, Rouen, 1840.

CHÉVELLE, C., *Jeanne d'Arc à Burey-le-Petit ou Burey-en-Vaux – la famille Laxart*, Nancy, 1899.

CHRISTIE, MABEL E., *Henry VI*, London, 1922.

CLAUSEL DE COUSSERGUES, *Du Sacre des Rois de France*, Paris, 1825.

COUSINOT, J., *Chronique de la Pucelle ou chronique de Cousinot*, Vallet de Viriville (ed.), Paris, 1859.

DAVID-DARNAC, MAURICE, *Histoire véridique et merveilleuse de la Pucelle d'Orléans*, Paris, 1965.

DEBOUT, HENRI, *Jeanne d'Arc, prisonnière à Arras*, Arras, 1894; *Jeanne d'Arc et les archives anglaises*, Paris, 1895.

DEFOURNEAUX, MARCELIN, *La Vie quotidienne au temps de Jeanne d'Arc*, Paris, 1953.

DENIS, F. A., *Le Séjour de Jeanne d'Arc à Lagny*, Lagny, 1896.

DIGOT, AUGUSTE, *Histoire de Lorraine*, Nancy, 1856.

DOINEL, JULES, *Jeanne d'Arc, telle qu'elle est*, Orleans, 1892.

DONCOEUR, PAUL, *La Minute française des interrogatoires de Jeanne la Pucelle*, Melun, 1952.

DONCOEUR, PAUL, and LANHERS, YVONNE, *Instrument public des sentences portées les 24 et 30 mai 1431 par Pierre Cauchon et Jean le Maître, O.P., contre Jeanne la Pucelle*, Paris, 1954; *L'Enquête ordonnée par Charles VII en 1450 et le codicille de Guillaume Bouillé*, Paris, 1956; *L'Enquête du Cardinal Estouteville en 1452*, Paris, 1958; *La Rédaction episcopale du procès de 1455–6*, Paris, 1961.

DOUGLAS, MARY (ed.), *Witchcraft Confessions and Accusations*, London, 1970.

DUBOSC, GEORGES, *Autour de la vie de Jeanne d'Arc*, Rouen, 1920.

EDWARDS, J. G., GALBRAITH, W. H., and JACOB, E. F., *Historical Essays in Honour of James Tait*, Manchester, 1933.

FABRO, JOSEPH, *Procès de réhabilitation*, Paris, 1913.

DE FAUQUEMBERGUE, CLÉMENT, *Journal*, Tuetey (ed.), Paris, 1903–15.

FAVIER, JEAN, *Paris au XVe siècle*, Paris, 1974.

FLAMMERMONT, CHARLES JULES, *Senlis pendant la seconde partie de la Guerre de Cent Ans*, Paris, 1879.

DE FOULQUES DE VILLARET, AMICIE, *Louis de Coutes*, Orléans/Château-dun, 1890; *Campagnes des anglais dans l'Orléannais*, Orleans, 1893.

FRANCE, ANATOLE, *Jeanne d'Arc – édition définitive*, Paris, 1910.

FÜGEL, J. C., *The Psychology of Clothes*, London, 1930.

Vie de Guillaume de Gamaches, Paris, 1786.

GORCE, MATHIEU MAXIME, *Saint Vincent Ferrier*, Paris, 1924.

GRUEL, GUILLAUME, *Chronique d'Arthur de Richemont*, Achille Le Vasseur (ed.), Paris, 1890.

GUÉRIN, ANDRÉ, and PALMER WHITE, JACK, *Operation Shepherdess*, London, 1961.

GUILLEMIN, HENRI, *Jeanne dite 'Jeanne d'Arc'*, Paris, 1970.

GUITTON, JEAN, *Problème et mystère de Jeanne d'Arc*, Paris, 1961.

HARMAND, ADRIEN, *Jeanne d'Arc, ses costumes, son armure*, Paris, 1929.

HEIM, MAURICE, *Charles VI, le Fol*, Paris, 1955.

HOLLAND-SMITH, JOHN, *Joan of Arc*, London, 1973.

HUGUET, ADRIEN, *Jeanne d'Arc au Crotoy*, Amiens, 1929.

JACOB, E. F., *The Fifteenth Century*, London, 1961.

JACOMET, D., *Jehanne d'Arc. Quarante-cinq documents originaux et iconographiques*, Paris, 1933.

JADART, HENRI, *Jeanne d'Arc à Reims*, Reims, 1887.

JENY, LUCIEN, and LANÉRY D'ARC, PIERRE, *Jeanne d'Arc en Berry*, Paris, 1892.

JOLLOIS, J. B., *Histoire du Siège d'Orléans*, Paris, 1833.

Le Jouvencel, Paris, 1493.

JUVENEL DES URSINS, *Histoire de Charles VI*, J. A. C. Buchon (ed.), Paris, 1875.

KIECKHEFER, RICHARD, *European Witch Trials*, London and Henley, 1976.

DE LANCESSEUR, PIERRE, *Jeanne d'Arc, Chef de Guerre*, Paris, 1961.

LANDRY, A., *Essai économique sur les mutations des monnaies de l'ancienne France, de Philippe le Bel à Charles VII*, Paris, 1910.

LANÉRY D'ARC, PIERRE, *Le Culte de Jeanne d'Arc au XVe siècle*, Orleans, 1887.

LANG, ANDREW, *The Maid of France*, London, 1908.

LA TRÉMOILLE, *Les La Tremoille pendant cinq siècles*, Nantes, 1890.

LEA, HENRY CHARLES, *History of the Inquisition*, London, 1888.

LE BRUN, EUGÈNE, *Une Étape de Jeanne d'Arc en Bourbonnais*, Paris/Moulins, 1912.

LE CACHEUX, PAUL, *Rouen au temps de Jeanne d'Arc*, Rouen/Paris, 1931.

LECHLER, PROFESSOR, *John Wycliffe and His English Precursors*, London, 1904.

LECLERCQ, J., VERDERBROUKE, F., and BOUCHER, L., *La Spiritualité du moyen âge*, Paris, 1961.

LEDAIN, BÉLISAIRE, *Jeanne d'Arc à Poitiers*, Paris/Poitiers, 1894.

LEDIEU, A., *Esquisses militaires de la Guerre de Cent Ans*, Lille/Paris, 1906.

LE FÈVRE, JEAN, *Chronique*, 2 vols., F. Morand, Paris, 1876, 1881.

LEFÈVRE-PONTALIS, GERMAIN, *Un Détail du Siège de Paris par Jeanne d'Arc*, Nogent-le-Rotrou, 1885.

LEFF, GORDON, *Heresy in the Later Middle Ages*, Manchester/New York, 1967.

LE MOYNE DE LA BORDERIE, L. A., *Une Prétendue Compagne de Jeanne d'Arc*, Pieronne et Perrinaic, Paris, 1894.

DE LETTENHOVE, KERVYN, *Chroniques relatives à l'histoire de la Belgique sous la domination des ducs de Bourgogne*, Brussels, 1876.

LEUBA, JAMES H., *The Psychology of Religious Mysticism*, London and New York, 1929.

LHERMITTE, JEAN, *Les Hallucinations*, Paris, 1951.

LIGHTBODY, CHARLES WAYLAND, *The Judgements of Joan*, London, 1961.

LOMIER, EUGÈNE, *Les Prisons de Jeanne d'Arc*, Paris, 1938.

LONGNON, AUGUSTE, *Paris pendant la domination anglaise*, Paris, 1878.

LOT, FERDINAND, *L'Art militaire et les armées au moyen âge*, Paris, 1946.

LOTTIN, DENIS, *Recherches historiques sur la ville d'Orléans*, Orleans, 1836–42.

LOWELL, FRANCIS C., *Joan of Arc*, Boston/New York, 1896.

LUCE, SIMÉON, *Jeanne d'Arc à Domrémy*, Paris, 1886.

MARTY, ANDRÉ, *L'Histoire de Jeanne d'Arc d'après les documents originaux*, Paris/Orleans, 1907.

MICHELET, JULES, *Vie de Jeanne d'Arc*, Gustave Rudler (annotated edition), Paris, 1925.

Les Miracles de Madame Sainte Katherine de Fierboys, Abbé J. J. Bourassé (ed.), Tours, 1858.

Le Mistère du Siège d'Orléans, F. Guéssard and E. de Certain (eds.), Paris, 1862.

MONSTRELET, ENGUERRAND DE, *Chronique*, L. Douët d'Arcq (ed.), Paris, 1857–62.

Chronique du Mont-Saint-Michel, Siméon Luce (ed.), 2 vols., Paris, 1879.

MOROSINI, ANTONIO, *Chronique d'Antonio Morosini. Extraits relatifs à l'histoire de France*, Germain Lefèvre-Pontalis (introduction and commentary), Léon Durez (ed. and trans.), 4 vols., Paris, 1898–1902.

DU MOTEY, H. I. F. R., *Jeanne d'Arc à Chinon*, Paris, 1927.

MOUGENOT, LÉON, *Jeanne d'Arc, le duc de Lorraine et le sire de Baudricourt*, Nancy, 1895.

PAINE, ALBERT BIGELOW, *Joan of Arc, Maid of France*, New York, 1925.

PARISH, EDMUND, *Hallucinations and Illusions*, London, 1897.

PERNOUD, RÉGINE, *Jeanne d'Arc par elle-même et par ses témoins*, Paris, 1962; *La Libération d'Orléans*, Paris, 1969; *Jeanne devant les Cauchons*, Paris, 1970.

PERROY, E., *The Hundred Years War*, London, 1962.

DE PHARES, SYMON, *Recueil des plus célèbres astrologues*, Ernest Wickersheimer (ed.), Paris, 1929.

PIUS II, *Commentaries*, Florence Allan Gragg (trans.), Northampton, Mass., 1950.

QUENEDEY, RAYMOND, *Les Étapes de la vie douloureuse de Jeanne d'Arc à Rouen*, Rouen, 1931.

287

QUERCY, PIERRE, *Les Hallucinations*, Paris, 1936.

QUICHERAT, JULES, *Procès de condamnation et de réhabilitation de Jeanne d'Arc*, 5 vols., Paris, 1841–9; *Aperçus nouveaux sur l'histoire de Jeanne d'Arc*, Paris, 1850; *Rodrigue de Villandrando*, Paris, 1879.

RAKNEM, INGVALD, *Joan of Arc*, Oslo, Bergen and Tromsö, 1971.

DE RARÉCOURT, MARQUIS DE PIMODAN, *La Première Étape de Jeanne d'Arc*, Paris, 1890.

DE ROBILLARD DE BEAUREPAIRE, CHARLES, *Mémoire sur le lieu de supplice de Jeanne d'Arc*, Rouen, 1867; *Recherches sur le procès de condamnation de Jeanne d'Arc*, Rouen, 1869.

RUSSELL, JEFFREY BURTON, *Witchcraft in the Middle Ages*, Ithaca and London, 1972.

RUTTER, OWEN, *The Land of St Joan*, London, 1941.

RYNER, J. H., *Jeanne d'Arc et sa mère*, Paris, 1950.

SACKVILLE-WEST, VITA, *Saint Joan of Arc*, London, 1936.

DE SAINT-JAMES, E., MARQUIS DE GAUCOURT, *Les faits relatifs à Jeanne d'Arc et au sire de Gaucourt*, Paris, 1857.

SAMARAN, CHARLES, *La Maison d'Armagnac au XVᵉ siècle*, Paris, 1907.

SARRAZIN, ALBERT, *Pierre Cauchon, juge de Jeanne d'Arc*, Paris, 1901; *Le Bourreau de Jeanne d'Arc*, Rouen, 1910.

SCOTT, WALTER SIDNEY, *Jeanne d'Arc*, London, 1974.

SELLER, P., *Vie de Sainte Colette*, Amiens, 1853.

SEPTET, MARIUS, *Jeanne d'Arc*, Tours, 1885.

DE SERMOIZE, *Joan of Arc and Her Secret Missions*, London, 1973.

SETH, RONALD, *Witches and Their Craft*, London, 1967.

SOREL, ALEXANDRE, *La Prise de Jeanne d'Arc devant Compiègne*, Paris and Orleans, 1889.

STEVENSON, JOSEPH, *Letters and Papers Illustrative of the Wars of the English in France, During the Reign of Henry VI*, 3 vols., London, 1861–4.

THIBAULT, MARCEL, *Isabeau de Bavière*, Paris, 1903.

TISSET, PIERRE, and LANHERS, YVONNE, *Procès de condamnation de Jeanne d'Arc*, vol. I, Paris, 1960; vol. II, trans., Paris, 1970; vol. III, intro., Paris, 1971.

TRÉBUCHET, L., *Un Compagnon de Jeanne d'Arc, Artur III*, Paris, 1897.

VALE, M. G. A., *Charles VII*, London, 1974.

VALLET DE VIRIVILLE, A., *Histoire de Charles VII*, 3 vols., Paris, 1862–5.

VALOIS, NOEL, *Le Conseil du roi au XIVᵉ, XVᵉ et XVIᵉ siècles*, Paris, 1888; *Un Nouveau Témoignage sur Jeanne d'Arc*, Paris, 1907.

VARIN, PIERRE, *Archives de la ville de Reims*, 10 vols., Reims, 1839–53.

VAUGHAN, RICHARD, *Philip the Good*, London, 1970.

VEITH, ILZA, *Hysteria, the History of a Disease*, Chicago and London, 1965.

VERGNAUD-ROMAGNÉSI, C. F., *Examen des apparitions et de la mission divine de Jeanne d'Arc*, Orleans, 1861.

VICKERS, K. H., *Humphrey, Duke of Gloucester*, London, 1907.

DE VIGNEULLES, GÉRARD, *Jeanne d'Arc dans les chroniques messines de Philippe de Vigneulles*, E. de Bouteiller (ed.), Orleans, 1878.

WALDMAN, MILTON, *Joan of Arc*, London, 1933.

WALLON, HENRI, *Jeanne d'Arc*, Paris, 1876.

WEST, LOUIS JOLYON (ed.), *Hallucinations*, New York and London, 1962.
WILLIAMS, CHARLES, *Witchcraft*, London, 1941.
WILLIAMS, E. CARLETON, *My Lord of Bedford*, London, 1963.
WINDECKEN, EBERHARD, *Les Sources allemandes de l'histoire de Jeanne d'Arc – Eberhard Windecken*, Germain Lefèvre-Pontalis (ed.), Paris, 1903.
WINWAR, FRANCES, *The Saint and the Devil*, London, 1948.

ARTICLES

BEAUCOURT, G. DU FRESNE DE, '*Jeanne d'Arc trahie par Charles VII*', *Revue des questions historiques*, vol. 2, 1867, pp. 286–91; '*La Conspiration du duc d'Alençon*', *Revue des questions historiques*, vol. 49, 1896, pp. 410ff.

DE BOISMARIN, '*Mémoire sur la date de l'arrivée de Jeanne d'Arc à Chinon*', *Bulletin du comité des travaux historiques*, 1892, pp. 350–59.

BOISSONADE, PAUL, '*Une Étape capitale de la mission de Jeanne d'Arc*', *Revue des questions historiques*, July 1930, pp. 17–67.

BOUCHER DE MOLANDON, '*Jacques Boucher*', *Mémoires de la société archéologique et historique de l'Orléannais*, vol. 22, 1899, pp. 373ff.

DE BOUTEILLER, F., '*Quelques Faits relatifs à Jeanne d'Arc et à sa famille*', *Revue des questions historiques*, vol. 24, 1878, pp. 241–9.

CAROLUS-BARRÉ, LOUIS, '*Jeanne, êtes-vous en état de grâce?*', *Bulletin de la société des antiquaires de France*, 1958, pp. 204–8.

COHN, A., '*Le Pont des Tournelles*', *Mémoires de la société archéologique et historique de l'Orléannais*, vol. 26, 1895.

DENIFLE, P. H., and CHÂTELLAIN, E., '*Le Procès de Jeanne d'Arc et l'Université de Paris*', *Mémoires de la société de l'histoire de Paris et de l'Ile de France*, vol. 74, 1897, pp. 1–32.

DESAMA, CLAUDE, '*La Première Entrevue de Jeanne d'Arc et de Charles VII à Chinon (mars 1429)*', *Analecta Bollandiana*, vol. 84, fasc. 1–2, 1966, pp. 133ff.

DODU, GASTON, '*La Folie de Charles VI*', *Revue historique*, vol. 150, 1924, pp. 161–88; '*Le Roi de Bourges*', *Revue historique*, vol. 159, 1928, pp. 38ff.

FFOULKES, CHARLES, 'The Armour of Jeanne d'Arc', *Burlington Magazine*, vol. 16, December 1909, pp. 141–6.

DE FLORIVAL, A., '*Le Passage de Jeanne d'Arc dans le Ponthieu*', *Bulletin de la société d'émulation d'Abbeville*, vol. 6, 1905, pp. 200ff.

GAILLY DE TAURMES, CH., '*Jeanne d'Arc à Saint-Denys de la Chapelle*', *Revue des deux mondes*, vol. 14, April 1923, pp. 900–920.

GOMART, CHARLES, '*Jeanne d'Arc au Château de Beaurevoir*', *Mémoires de la société d'émulation de Cambrai*, vol. 28, part 2, 1865.

HUGUET, ADRIEN, '*Le Passage de Jeanne d'Arc dans le Vimeu*', *Bulletin de la société d'archéologie du Vimeu*, 1907.

JOLY, HENRI, '*La Psychologie de Jeanne d'Arc*', *Études*, vol. 119, April 1909, pp. 158–83.

LA FONS DE MÉLICOCQ, '*Document nouveau sur Jeanne d'Arc*', *Bulletin de la société de l'histoire de France*, 1857–8, pp. 102–4.

LEFÈVRE-PONTALIS, GERMAIN, '*La Panique anglaise en mai 1429*', *Le Moyen Âge*, vol. 7, 1894, pp. 81–95.

LUCE, SIMÉON, 'Deux Documents inédits relatifs à Frère Richard et à Jeanne d'Arc', Revue bleue, vol. 50, 1892, pp. 201ff.

MONEY-KYRLE, ROGER, 'A Psychoanalytic Study of the Voices of Joan of Arc', British Journal of Medical Psychology, vol. 13, 1933.

DE POLI, OSCAR, 'Jean d'Aulon', Annuaire du conseil héraldique de France, 14e année, 1901, p. 1ff; 'Les Pages de Jeanne d'Arc', Annuaire de conseil héraldique de France, 15e année, 1902, pp. 3ff.

DE PUYMAIGRE, COMTE, 'La Chronique espagnole de la Pucelle d'Orléans', Revue des questions historiques, vol. 29, 1881, pp. 553ff.

QUICHERAT, JULES, 'Une Relation inédite sur Jeanne d'Arc', Revue historique, vol. 4, 1877, pp. 327ff; 'Supplément aux témoignages contemporaines sur Jeanne d'Arc', Revue historique, vol. 19, 1882, pp. 60–83.

REINACH, SALOMON, 'Observations sur le texte du procès de condamnation de Jeanne d'Arc', Revue historique, vol. 148, 1925, pp. 200ff.

SEPTET, MARIUS, 'Jeanne d'Arc au cimitière de Saint-Ouen', Revue des questions historiques, vol. 73, 1903, pp. 586–606; 'Observations critiques sur l'histoire de Jeanne d'Arc: la lettre de Perceval de Boulainvilliers', Bibliothèque de l'école de Chartres, vol. 77, 1916, pp. 439–47.

THOMAS, A., 'Le "Signe Royal" et le secret de Jeanne d'Arc', Revue historique, vol. 103, 1910, pp. 278–82.

VALSAN, MICHEL, 'Remarques occasionelles sur Jeanne d'Arc et Charles VII', Études traditionelles, nos. 412–13, 1969, pp. 112–37.

VALLET DE VIRIVILLE, A., 'Un Épisode de la vie de Jeanne d'Arc', Bibliothèque de l'école de Chartres, vol. 4, pp. 486–91; Revue archéologique, new series, June 1861, pp. 434–7.

◆❧ References ❧◆

By far the largest number of the references listed here are to the three volumes of the new edition of the *Procès de condamnation*, edited by Pierre Tisset and Yvonne Lanhers; and to the five volumes of documents and other material to do with Joan edited by Jules Quicherat. These are referred to here as T/L I, T/L II and T/L III; and as Q I to Q V. In the case of the Tisset/Lanhers edition, I have given combined references to the original text (T/L I) and to the translation (T/L II). Quicherat's old edition of the *Procès de réhabilitation* was used not only because it was more conveniently available to me, but because it was in many ways better arranged than the recent publications of Doncoeur and Lanhers. The text is to be found in volumes II and III of Quicherat's great work. I have also made extensive use of his collection of excerpts from contemporary chroniclers, which comprises his fourth volume; and references are, again for convenience sake, generally made to this rather than to separate editions of the same texts. References to this collection (Q IV) are accompanied not only by the page number, but by the name of the chronicler or diarist concerned.

INTRODUCTION

1. Ingvald Raknem, *Joan of Arc*, Oslo/Bergen/Tromsö, 1961, p. 1.
2. Pius II, *Commentaries*, Florence Allen Gragg (trans.), Northampton, Mass., 1950, Book VI, pp. 442–3.

CHAPTER 1

1. Thomas Basin, *Histoire de Charles VII*, Charles Samaran (ed. and trans.), 2 vols., Paris, 1933, 1944, vol. 1, p. 160.
2. ibid.
3. T/L I, p. 126 – T/L II, p. 114.
4. Bourgeois de Paris, *Journal d'un Bourgeois de Paris, 1408–1449*. A. Tuetey (ed.), Paris, 1881, p. 269.
5. Q III, p. 51.
6. Q II, pp. 191, 375.
7. Q II, p. 7.
8. Q II, p. 352.
9. Q II, p. 372.
10. Q V, p. 116.
11. *Bibliothèque de l'École de Chartres*, 2nd series, vol. 3, p. 116.
12. T/L I, p. 41 – T/L II, p. 41.
13. Q V, p. 116.
14. T/L I, p. 181 – T/L II, p. 148.
15. Q III, p. 101.
16. T/L I, p. 41 – T/L II, p. 41.
17. T/L I, p. 65 – T/L II, p. 64.

CHAPTER 2

1. Q II, p. 444.
2. Q II, p. 430.
3. Q II, p. 404.
4. ibid.
5. Q II, p. 430.
6. T/L I, p. 66 – T/L II, p. 67.
7. Q V, p. 115.
8. T/L I, p. 45 – T/L II, p. 45 and n. 2.
9. T/L I, p. 65 – T/L II, p. 64.
10. T/L I, p. 65 – T/L II, p. 65.
11. T/L I, p. 64 – T/L II, p. 64.
12. Q II, p. 398.
13. Q II, pp. 418, 430.
14. Q II, pp. 425, 427.
15. Q II, p. 425.
16. Q II, p. 420.
17. T/L I, p. 46 – T/L II, p. 45.
18. Q II, p. 30.
19. Q II, p. 390.
20. Q II, p. 424.
21. Q II, p. 413.
22. Q II, p. 459.
23. Q II, p. 439.

24. Q II, pp. 389–90.
25. Q II, p. 420.
26. Q II, p. 433.
27. Q II, p. 427.
28. T/L I, p. 46 – T/L II, p. 46.
29. Q II, p. 390.
30. Q II, p. 430.
31. T/L I, p. 150 – T/L II, p. 129.
32. Q II, pp. 402, 433.
33. T/L I, p. 47 – T/L II, pp. 46–7.
34. T/L I, p. 128 – T/L II, p. 115.
35. Edmund Parish, *Hallucinations and Illusions*, London, 1897, pp. 82–4.
36. ibid., p. 107.
37. Otto Allen Will Jr., 'Hallucinations: Comments Reflecting Clinical Observations of the Schizophrenic Reaction', *Hallucinations*, Louis Jolyon
West (ed.), New York/London, 1962, p. 71.
38. T/L I, p. 162 – T/L II, p. 137.
39. T/L I, p. 418 – T/L II, p. 364.
40. T/L I, p. 419 – T/L II, p. 364.
41. Jean Lhermitte, *Les Hallucinations*, Paris, 1951, pp. 55–6.
42. T/L I, p. 146–T/L II, p. 127.
43. T/L I, p. 70 – T/L II, p. 70.
44. T/L I, p. 419 – T/L II, p. 365.
45. T/L I, p. 122 – T/L II, pp. 112–13.
46. Q III, p. 204.
47. T/L I, pp. 84–5 – T/L II, p. 85.
48. ibid.
49. Lhermitte, op. cit., p. 171.
50. T/L I, p. 165 – T/L II, p. 173.
51. T/L I, p. 162 – T/L II, p. 136.
52. T/L I, p. 176 – T/L II, p. 144.
53. T/L I, p. 84 – T/L II, p. 84.
54. ibid.
55. T/L I, p. 86– T/L II, p. 87.
56. T/L I, p. 87– T/L II, p. 87.
57. ibid.
58. T/L I, p. 91 – T/L II, p. 91.
59. T/L I, p. 177 – T/L II, p. 145.
60. T/L I, p. 74 – T/L II, p. 73.
61. T/L I, p. 92 – T/L II, p. 91.
62. T/L I, p. 163 – T/L II, p. 137.
63. ibid.
64. ibid.
65. T/L I, p. 48 – T/L II, pp. 47–8.

CHAPTER 3

1. Q II, p. 396.
2. Q II, p. 427.
3. T/L I, p. 63 – T/L II, p. 63.
4. T/L I, p. 64 – T/L II, p. 64.
5. ibid.

6. T/L I, p. 124 – T/L II, p. 113.
7. T/L I, pp. 124–5 – T/L II, pp. 113–14.
8. T/L I, pp. 126–7 – T/L II, p. 115.
9. T/L I, pp. 200–201 – T/L II, p. 167.
10. T/L I, p. 200 – T/L II, p. 167.
11. T/L I, p. 46 – T/L II, p. 45.
12. T/L I, p. 127 – T/L II, p. 115.
13. T/L I, p. 123 – T/L II, p. 113.
14. T/L I, p. 123 – T/L II, p. 113.
15. Q II, p. 441.
16. Q II, p. 447.
17. Pierre Champion, *Procès de condamnation de Jeanne d'Arc*, Paris, 1921, vol. 2, p. 179.
18. Q II, p. 423.
19. Q II, p. 440.

CHAPTER 4

1. Q II, pp. 428, 430, 434.
2. T/L I, p. 49 – T/L II, p. 49.
3. Q II, p. 444.
4. T/L I, p. 49 – T/L II, p. 49.
5. Q II, pp. 446–7.
6. For this interpretation see T/L II, p. 49, n.3.
7. Q II, p. 444.
8. Léon Mougenot, *Jeanne d'Arc, le duc de Lorraine et le sire de Baudricourt*, Nancy, 1895, p. 73, n.1.
9. Q IV, p. 95, *Chronique de la Pucelle*.
10. Q II, p. 455.
11. T/L I, p. 49 – T/L II, pp. 49–50.
12. Q II, pp. 436, 448.
13. Q II, p. 456.
14. Q II, p. 436.
15. Q II, p. 448.
16. Q II, p. 447.
17. Q II, p. 446.
18. Q II, p. 461.
19. Q II, p. 444.
20. Q II, p. 445.
21. T/L I, p. 48 – T/L II, p. 48.
22. Q III, p. 92.
23. T/L I, p. 75 – T/L II, pp. 73–4.
24. T/L I, p. 95 – T/L II, p. 93.
25. T/L I, p. 153 – T/L II, pp. 131–2.
26. T/L I, p. 182 – T/L II, p. 149.
27. Q II, pp. 436–7.
28. Q II, p. 437.
29. Q III, p. 100.
30. Q III, p. 319.
31. Bourgeois de Paris, op. cit., p. 268.
32. Adrien Harmand, *Jeanne d'Arc, ses costumes, son armure*, Paris, 1929, p. 15, quoting the *Chronique des cordeliers*.

33. T/L I, p. 205 – T/L II, pp. 171–2.
34. T/L I, p. 207 – T/L II, p. 174.
35. Q IV, p. 427.
36. Q II, p. 437.
37. T/L I, p. 49 – T/L II, pp. 51–2.
38. Q III, p. 87.
39. Q II, p. 444.
40. Q II, pp. 391, 406.
41. T/L I, p. 49 – T/L II, p. 50.
42. Q II, p. 446.
43. T/L I, p. 49 – T/L II, p. 50.
44. T/L I, p. 50 – T/L II, p. 54.
45. T/L I, p. 50 – T/L II, p. 52.
46. Q II, p. 437.
47. T/L I, p. 50 – T/L II, p. 54.
48. Q II, p. 437.
49. Q II, p. 449.

CHAPTER 5

1. Auguste Brachet, *Pathologie mentale des rois de France*, Paris, 1903, p. 637, quoting the *Réligieux de Saint-Denis*, vol. II, p. 405.
2. ibid., p. 632 and facing plate.
3. *Comptes d'Isabeau*, Vallet de Viriville, Chartier III, p. 276.
4. Georges Chastellain, *Œuvres*, Kervyn de Lettenhove (ed.), Brussels, 1863–5, vol. II, p. 185.
5. *Jouvenel des Ursins*, p. 336.
6. Georges Chastellain, op. cit., vol. II, p. 179.
7. ibid., p. 178.
8. ibid., p. 179.
9. Jean Chartier, *Chronique*, Vallet de Viriville (ed.), Paris, 1858, vol. III, p. 129.
10. Basin, op. cit., vol. I, p. 111.
11. ibid., p. 102.
12. *Jouvenel des Ursins*, p. 335.
13. Chastellain, op. cit., vol. II, p. 182.
14. ibid., p. 185.
15. ibid., p. 181.
16. G. du Fresne de Beaucourt, *Histoire de Charles VII*, Paris, 1881–91, vol. II, p. 193, n.2.
17. ibid., p. 639 and n.6.
18. ibid., p. 195 and n.2.
19. Enguerrand de Monstrelet, *Chronique*, L. Douët d'Arcq (ed.), Paris, 1857–62, vol. IV, p. 30.
20. Quoted by Beaucourt, op. cit., vol. II, p. 260.
21. Guillaume Gruel, *Chronique d'Arthur de Richemont*, A. le Vasseur (ed.), Paris, 1890, p. 54.
22. Jean Bouchet, *Panégyrique du chevalier sans reproche, Louis de La Trémoille*, Michaud and Poujolat, série 1, tom. 4, Paris, 1837, p. 411.
23. La Trémoille, *Les La Trémoille pendant cinq siècles*, Nantes, 1890, pp. xiiiff.
24. ibid., p. 196.

CHAPTER 6

1. Q II, pp. 437, 457.
2. Q II, p. 457.
3. Q II, p. 438.
4. ibid.
5. Q II, p. 457.
6. Q III, pp. 86-7.
7. Q II, pp. 457-8.
8. Q II, pp. 437-8.
9. Q II, p. 438.
10. Q II, p. 458.
11. T/L I, p. 51 – T/L II, p. 53.
12. P. de Lancesseur, *Jeanne d'Arc, Chef de Guerre*, Paris, 1961, p. 12.
13. Q III, p. 3.
14. Symon de Phares, *Recueil des plus célèbres astrologues*, E. Wickersheimer (ed.), Paris, 1929, pp. 255-6.
15. Q III, pp. 3-4.
16. Q III, p. 203.
17. Q III, p. 199.
18. ibid.
19. T/L I, p. 51 – T/L II, p. 55.
20. T/L I, p. 76 – T/L II, p. 75.
21. ibid.
22. T/L I, p. 51 – T/L II, p. 55.
23. Q III, p. 115.
24. ibid.
25. ibid.
26. ibid.
27. Now the generally accepted date, rather than 6 March, which is the one given in the *Chronique de Mont-Saint-Michel*. For the arguments in favour of 23 February, see T/L II, p. 55, n.3.
28. Q III, p. 102.
29. Q III, p. 103.
30. T/L I, p. 76 – T/L II, p. 74.
31. See Richard Vaughan, *Philip the Good*, London, 1970, pp. 119-20, on the visit paid by Isabel of Portugal, Duchess of Burgundy, to Queen Marie of Anjou, wife of Charles VII.
32. *Livre noir de la Rochelle*, Jules Quicherat (ed.), in the *Revue historique*, vol. IV, pp. 336-7.
33. Q IV, pp. 52-3, Jean Chartier.
34. T/L I, pp. 51-2 – T/L II, p. 56.
35. Q III, p. 17.
36. Q IV, p. 52 Jean Chartier.
37. Q IV, p. 205, *Chronique de la Pucelle*.
38. Q IV, p. 523, Philippe de Bergame.
39. Q V, p. 120, Perceval de Boulainvilliers.
40. Q III, p. 116.

CHAPTER 7

1. T/L I, p. 76 – T/L II, p. 75.
2. T/L I, p. 88 – T/L II, p. 89.

3. T/L I, p. 273 – T/L II, p. 230.
4. T/L I, pp. 417–18 – T/L II, p. 364; T/L I, p. 419 – T/L II, p. 365; T/L I, p. 421 – T/L II, p. 367.
5. Q III, p. 103.
6. ibid.
7. Q III, p. 209.
8. Basin, op. cit., vol. I, p. 132.
9. Q III, p. 3.
10. Antonio Morosini, *Chronique d'Antonio Morosini – Extraits relatifs à l'histoire de France*, G. Lefèvre-Pontalis (ed.), Paris, 1898–1902, vol. III, pp. 346–9.
11. Q IV, pp. 208–9, *Chronique de la Pucelle*.
12. Q IV, p. 280, Pierre Sala.
13. J. B. J. Ayroles, *La Vraie Jeanne d'Arc*, Paris, 1890–1902, vol. III, p. 281, L'Abréviateur du Procès.
14. ibid., p. 288, Alain Bouchard, *Grandes Annales de Bretagne*.
15. Q III, pp. 91–2.
16. Q III, p. 85.
17. T/L I, p. 52 – T/L II, p. 56.
18. T/L I, p. 53 – T/L II, p. 56.
19. Q V, pp. 342ff.
20. T/L I, p. 134 – T/L II, p. 120.
21. T/L I, pp. 135–8 – T/L II, pp. 121–2.
22. T/L I, p. 418 – T/L II, p. 364.
23. Ayroles, op. cit., vol. I, pp. 57–8.
24. T/L I, p. 350 – T/L II, p. 302.
25. Q III, p. 17.
26. Q III, p. 66.
27. Q III, p. 92.
28. ibid.

CHAPTER 8

1. Q III, p. 103.
2. T/L I, p. 75 – T/L II, p. 76.
3. T/L I, p. 71 – T/L II, p. 71.
4. T/L I, p. 72 – T/L II, p. 72.
5. T/L I, p. 93 – T/L II, p. 91.
6. Q III, p. 203.
7. Q III, p. 204.
8. Q III, pp. 204–5.
9. Q III, p. 86.
10. Q III, p. 74.
11. Q III, p. 83.
12. Q IV, pp. 209–10, *Chronique de la Pucelle*.
13. Q III, p. 75.
14. Q III, p. 84.
15. ibid.
16. Q IV, p. 211, *Chronique de la Pucelle*.
17. *Livre noir de la Rochelle*, loc. cit., p. 338.
18. Q V, p. 119.
19. Q III, p. 75.

20. Q III, p. 82.
21. Morosini, op. cit., vol. III, pp. 100–10.
22. ibid., pp. 54–5, 58–9.
23. Q III, pp. 209–10. See also Q III, p. 102.
24. Q IV, p. 102, *Journal du siège*.
25. Q III, p. 205.
26. T/L I, p. 344 – T/L II, p. 298.
27. Morosini, op. cit., vol. III, pp. 96–7.
28. T/L I, p. 214 – T/L II, p. 179.
29. Q III, p. 5.
30. Q IV, p. 10, Perceval de Cagny.
31. T/L I, p. 141 – T/L II, p. 124.
32. Q III, pp. 20, 205.
33. Q III, p. 74.
34. T/L I, pp. 221–2 – T/L II, pp. 185–6.
35. T/L I, p. 82 – T/L II, p. 83.
36. Francis Lowell, *Joan of Arc*, Boston/New York, 1896, p. 76.
37. T/L I, p. 78 – T/L II, p. 77.
38. ibid.
39. Q III, p. 205.
40. Q IV, p. 427, Le Greffier de la chambre des comptes de Brabant.
41. Bourgeois de Paris, quoted Q III, p. 4, n.l.
42. T/L I, p. 82 – T/L II, p. 82.
43. Jules Quicherat, *Aperçus nouveaux sur l'histoire de Jeanne d'Arc*, Paris, 1850, pp. 132–3.
44. For example Q III, p. 116.
45. T/L I, p. 82 – T/L II, p. 82.
46. P. Seller, *Vie de Sainte Colette, réformatrice des trois ordres de Saint François*, Amiens, 1853, vol. I, pp. 246–8.
47. T/L I, p. 176 – T/L II, p. 144.
48. Q IV, p. 480, Walter Bower.
49. Q III, p. 205.
50. Q IV, p. 10, Perceval de Cagny.
51. Q III, p. 96.
52. Jean Bouchet, *Annales d'Aquitaine*, Paris, 1644, p. 246.

CHAPTER 9

1. Q III, p. 67.
2. Q III, p. 216.
3. Q III, p. 101.
4. ibid.
5. ibid. and Q III, p. 102.
6. Q III, p. 67.
7. Q V, p. 120.
8. T/L I, p. 76 – T/L II, p. 75.
9. ibid.
10. T/L I, p. 77 – T/L II, p. 76.
11. T/L I, p. 171 – T/L II, p. 144 and Q IV, p. 129.
12. Gérard de Vigneulles, *Jeanne d'Arc dans les chroniques messines de Philippe de Vigneulles*, E. de Bouteiller (ed.), Orleans, 1878, p. 14.
13. John Holland-Smith, *Joan of Arc*, London, 1973, p. 58.

14. T/L I, p. 77 – T/L II, p. 76.
15. Q III, p. 103.
16. Morosini, op. cit., vol. III, pp. 110–11.
17. T/L I, p. 78 – T/L II, pp. 77–8.
18. de Vigneulles, op. cit., p. 13.
19. Q IV, p. 12, Perceval de Cagny.
20. *Livre noir de la Rochelle*, p. 338.
21. T/L I, p. 78 – T/L II, p. 78.
22. Q IV, p. 152, *Journal du siège*.
23. ibid., p. 153.
24. Q V, p. 258.
25. Q V, pp. 154–6.
26. Q III, p. 93.
27. Q IV, p. 54, Jean Chartier.
28. ibid., pp. 55–6.
29. Q III, p. 67.
30. Q III, pp. 104–5.
31. Q III, p. 67.
32. Q IV, p. 215, *Chronique de la Pucelle*.
33. ibid., p. 217.
34. ibid., p. 215.
35. Q III, p. 104.

CHAPTER 10

1. Q IV, p. 130, *Journal du siège*.
2. Morosini, op. cit., vol. III, pp. 18–19.
3. ibid., pp. 20–22.
4. Q IV, pp. 146–7, *Journal du siège*. See also Morosini, op. cit., vol. IV, appendix XIV, pp. 310–12.
5. E. Carleton Williams, *My Lord of Bedford*, London, 1963, p. 165.
6. Q IV, pp. 149–50, *Journal du siège*.
7. Beaucourt, op. cit., vol. II, p. 174.

CHAPTER 11

1. T/L I, p. 78 – T/L II, p. 78.
2. Q III, p. 4.
3. Quoted by A. Ledieu, *Esquisses militaires de la Guerre de Cent Ans*, Lille/ Paris, 1906, p. 114.
4. *Chronique de la Pucelle*, Vallet de Viriville (ed.), (Paris, 1852, p. 246.
5. Ledieu, op. cit., pp. 76–7.
6. Q IV, p. 327, le Doyen de Saint-Thibaud de Metz.
7. Georges Bataille, *Le Procès de Gilles de Rais*, Paris, 1965, p. 41.
8. ibid., p. 79.
9. ibid., p. 36.
10. Ayroles, op. cit., vol. III, p. 221, *Chronique de Tournai*.
11. Q III, p. 67.
12. T/L I, p. 76 – T/L II, p. 78.
13. Q IV, p. 152, *Journal du siège*.
14. Q III, pp. 5–6.
15. Q III, p. 105.
16. Q IV, p. 152, *Journal du siège*.

17. Q III, p. 105.
18. Q III, p. 18.
19. Q III, p. 6.
20. Latin Chronicle of Jean Chartier, quoted by Ayroles, op. cit., vol. III, p. 163.
21. Q III, p. 78.
22. Q IV, p. 231, *Chronique de la Pucelle.*
23. Q III, p. 210.
24. Q III, p. 67.
25. Q III, p. 105.
26. Q IV, p. 152, *Journal du siège.*
27. ibid.
28. ibid.
29. Hall, *Chronicle*, fol. 127, quoted by W. S. Scott, *Joan of Arc*, London, 1974, p. 50.
30. Q IV, pp. 152–3, *Journal du siège.*
31. Q III, p. 78.
32. Q IV, p. 153, *Journal du siège.*
33. ibid.
34. Q III, p. 27.
35. Q IV, p. 219, *Chronique de la Pucelle.*
36. Q V, p. 290, *Chronique de l'établissement de la fête du 8 Mai.*
37. Q III, p. 67.
38. Q IV, p. 219, *Chronique de la Pucelle.*

CHAPTER 12

1. Q III, p. 68.
2. Q IV, p. 154, *Journal du siège.*
3. Q III, p. 7.
4. Q III, p. 24.
5. Q III, pp. 26–7.
6. Q IV, p. 221, *Chronique de la Pucelle.*
7. Q IV, p. 42, le Hérault Berri.
8. Q IV, p. 154, *Journal du siège.*
9. Q IV, p. 42, le Hérault Berri.
10. Q III, p. 68.
11. Q IV, p. 155, *Journal du siège.*
12. Q V, p. 290, *Chronique de l'établissement.*
13. ibid., p. 291.
14. Q III, p. 8.
15. Q III, p. 211.
16. Q IV, p. 155, *Journal du siège.*
17. ibid., p. 156.
18. ibid., p. 156.
19. Q.IV, p. 222, *Chronique de la Pucelle.*
20. Q IV, p. 156, *Journal du siège.*
21. Q III, p. 211.
22. *Chronique de Tournai*, quoted by Ayroles, op. cit., vol. III, p. 232.
23. Q III, pp. 105–6.
24. Q III, p. 212.
25. Q V, p. 291, *Chronique de l'établissement.*

26. Q IV, p. 6, Perceval de Cagny.
27. Q III, p. 212.
28. ibid.
29. Q III, p. 69.
30. Q III, p. 124.
31. Q III, p. 212.
32. Q IV, p. 157, *Journal du siège* and Q IV, p. 223, *Chronique de la Pucelle.*
33. ibid.
34. Q IV, p. 7, Perceval de Cagny.
35. Q III, p. 213.
36. Q IV, p. 224, *Chronique de la Pucelle.*
37. Q III, p. 69.
38. Q IV, p. 224, *Chronique de la Pucelle.*
39. Q III, p. 106.

CHAPTER 13

1. Q III, p. 106.
2. Q IV, p. 57, Jean Chartier.
3. T/L I, p. 99, T/L II, p. 95.
4. Q IV, p. 158, *Journal du siège.*
5. Q IV, p. 57, Jean Chartier.
6. Q IV, p. 158, *Journal du siège.*
7. Q IV, p. 58, Jean Chartier.
8. ibid., p. 59.
9. Q III, p. 7.
10. *Vie de Guillaume de Gamaches*, Paris, 1786, p. 43.
11. Q IV, p. 59, Jean Chartier.
12. Q III, pp. 107–8.
13. ibid.
14. Q III, p. 69.
15. Q III, p. 214.
16. Q IV, p. 158, *Journal du siège.*
17. Q IV, p. 226, *Chronique de la Pucelle.*
18. ibid. and Q III, p. 214.
19. Q III, p. 214.
20. Q IV, p. 226, *Chronique de la Pucelle.*
21. Q IV, pp. 60–61, Jean Chartier.
22. T/L I, p. 79 – T/L II, p. 78.
23. Q III, p. 214.
24. Q III, p. 79.
25. Q IV, p. 226, *Chronique de la Pucelle.*
26. ibid., p. 227.
27. Q III, pp. 214–15.
28. Q V, p. 292, *Chronique de l'établissement.*
29. Q III, p. 215.
30. ibid.
31. Q IV, p. 159, *Journal du siège.*
32. Q IV, p. 227, *Chronique de la Pucelle* and Q IV, p. 365, Monstrelet.
33. Q III, p. 79.
34. Q IV, p. 227, *Chronique de la Pucelle.*
35. Q III, p. 108.

36. Q III, p. 109.
37. Q III, p. 117. Deposition of Simon Charles. He misplaces the incident by one day and says that the guard was put on the day that the Augustins was taken. The guarding of the gates is confirmed by Louis de Coutes, Q III, p. 69 and by the *Chronique de la Pucelle*, Q IV, p. 227.
38. Q V, pp. 292–3, *Chronique de l'établissement*.
39. Q IV, p. 159, *Journal du siège*.
40. Q IV, p. 227, *Chronique de la Pucelle*.
41. Q V, p. 293, *Chronique de l'établissement*.

CHAPTER 14

1. Q III, p. 109.
2. Q V, p. 295, *Chronique de l'établissement*.
3. ibid.
4. Q III, pp. 124–5. See also Q IV, p. 227, *Chronique de la Pucelle*.
5. Q III, p. 70.
6. Q IV, p. 227, *Chronique de la Pucelle*.
7. Q III, p. 117.
8. ibid.
9. Q IV, p. 227, *Chronique de la Pucelle*.
10. ibid., pp. 227–8.
11. Q III, p. 70.
12. Q IV, p. 159, *Journal du siège*.
13. Q III, p. 215.
14. Q IV, p. 8, Perceval de Cagny.
15. Q IV, p. 160, *Journal du siège*.
16. ibid.
17. Morosini, op. cit., vol. III, pp. 30–31.
18. Q III, p. 109.
19. T/L I, p. 79 – T/L II, p. 78.
20. Q IV, p. 228, *Chronique de la Pucelle*.
21. T/L I, p. 79 – T/L II, p. 79.
22. Q IV, p. 426, le Greffier des Chambres de Comptes de Brabant.
23. Q III, p. 109.
24. Ayroles, op. cit., vol. III, p. 223, *Chronique de Tournai*.
25. Q III, pp. 109–10.
26. Q IV, p. 228, *Chronique de la Pucelle*.
27. Q III, p. 8.
28. Q III, pp. 216–17.
29. Q III, pp. 70–71.
30. Q IV, p. 161, *Journal du siège*.
31. ibid., p. 162. See also Q IV, p. 229, *Chronique de la Pucelle*.
32. Q III, p. 110.
33. Q V, pp. 293–4, *Chronique de l'établissement*.
34. Q V, p. 294, *Chronique de l'établissement*.
35. ibid.
36. Q III, p. 9 and Q IV, p. 230, *Chronique de la Pucelle*.
37. Q IV, p. 162, *Journal du siège*.
38. Q IV, p. 230, *Chronique de la Pucelle*.
39. T/L I, p. 79 – T/L II, p. 78.
40. Q IV, p. 9, Perceval de Cagny.

41. Q IV, p. 62, Jean Chartier.
42. Q IV, p. 163, *Journal du siège.*
43. Q III, p. 9.

CHAPTER 15

1. Q IV, p. 231, *Chronique de la Pucelle.*
2. Q III, p. 110.
3. Q III, p. 9.
4. Q IV, p. 62, Jean Chartier and Q IV, p. 231, *Chronique de la Pucelle.*
5. Q IV, p. 231, *Chronique de la Pucelle.*
6. Q IV, p. 45, le Hérault Berri.
7. Q III, p. 9.
8. Q IV, p. 63, Jean Chartier.
9. Q IV, p. 9, Perceval de Cagny.
10. Q IV, p. 63, Jean Chartier.
11. Q IV, p. 164, *Journal du siège.*
12. Q IV, p. 366, Monstrelet.
13. Q IV, p. 164, *Journal du siège.*
14. ibid.
15. Q IV, p. 232, *Chronique de la Pucelle.*
16. ibid.
17. Q IV, p. 63, Jean Chartier and Q IV, pp. 232–3, *Chronique de la Pucelle.*
18. ibid.
19. Q IV, p. 164, *Journal du siège.*
20. ibid.
21. Q III, p. 110.
22. Q IV, p. 165, *Journal du siège.*
23. ibid., pp. 166–7.
24. Morosini, op. cit., vol. III, pp. 36–7.
25. Q IV, p. 366, Monstrelet.
26. Jules Quicherat, *Revue historique*, vol. XIX, p. 66.
27. Q V, pp. 275–6.
28. Q V, pp. 275–7.
29. Q V, pp. 274–5.
30. Q V, p. 317.
31. ibid.
32. Q V, p. 316.

CHAPTER 16

1. Q IV, pp. 496–7, Eberhard de Windecken.
2. Q III, p. 80.
3. Q III, pp. 11–12.
4. Q IV, pp. 169–70, *Chronique de la Pucelle.*
5. Q V, p. 262.
6. ibid., n.107.
7. ibid., pp. 108–9.
8. ibid.
9. Q IV, pp. 169–70, *Journal du siège.*
10. ibid., p. 167.
11. Q III, p. 94.
12. Q IV, p. 12, Perceval de Cagny.

13. Q III, p. 95.
14. ibid.
15. ibid.
16. Q IV, p. 171, *Journal du siège*.
17. ibid.
18. Q III, p. 96.
19. Q IV, p. 171, *Journal du siège*.
20. Q III, p. 95.
21. Q IV, p. 12, Perceval de Cagny.
22. Q III, p. 95.
23. T/L I, p. 79 – T/L II, p. 79.
24. Q III, p. 95.
25. T/L I, p. 79 – T/L II, p. 79.
26. Q III, pp. 95–6 and Q IV, p. 12, Perceval de Cagny.
27. Q III, p. 96.
28. Q IV, p. 13, Perceval de Cagny.
29. Q IV, pp. 171–2, *Journal du siège*.
30. Q III, p. 97.
31. Harmand, op. cit., p. 250.
32. Q III, p. 97.
33. Q IV, p. 65, Jean Chartier and Q IV, p. 172, *Journal du siège*.
34. Q IV, p. 45, Le Hérault Berri and Q IV, p. 174, *Journal du siège*.
35. *Livre noir de la Rochelle*, loc. cit.
36. Q IV, p. 235, *Chronique de la Pucelle*.
37. Q IV, p. 13, Perceval de Cagny.
38. Q IV, p. 174, *Journal du siège*.
39. ibid.
40. Q IV, p. 13, Perceval de Cagny.
41. ibid., p. 12.

CHAPTER 17

1. Q IV, p. 173, *Journal du siège*; Q IV, p. 13, Perceval de Cagny.
2. Q IV, pp. 173–4, *Journal du siège*.
3. Q IV, p. 13, Perceval de Cagny.
4. ibid.
5. Q IV, p. 174, *Journal du siège* and Q IV, p. 240, *Chronique de la Pucelle*.
6. ibid.
7. Q III, p. 97.
8. Q IV, p. 14, Perceval de Cagny.
9. F. Guessard and É. de Certain (eds.), *Le Mistère du siège d'Orléans*, Paris, 1862, pp. 697–8.
10. Q IV, pp. 174–5, *Journal du siège*.
11. Q IV, p. 14, Perceval de Cagny.
12. Q III, p. 98.
13. Q IV, p. 318, Guillaume Gruel.
14. Q III, p. 98.
15. Q IV, p. 319, Guillaume Gruel.
16. Q III, p. 98 and Q IV, p. 239, *Chronique de la Pucelle*.
17. Q III, p. 98.
18. Q IV, p. 417, Wavrin.
19. Q III, p. 11.

20. Q IV, p. 417, Wavrin.
21. ibid.
22. Q IV, p. 318, Gruel (he misplaces the confrontation by a day).
23. Q IV, p. 417, Wavrin.
24. Q IV, p. 318, Gruel.
25. Q IV, p. 317, Gruel.
26. Q IV, p. 175, *Journal du siège* and Q IV, p. 241, *Chronique de la Pucelle.*
27. Q IV, p. 318, Wavrin.
28. Q IV, p. 412, Wavrin.
29. Q IV, p. 14, Perceval de Cagny.
30. Q IV, pp. 319–20, Gruel.
31. Q IV, p. 370, Monstrelet.
32. Q IV, pp. 175–6, *Journal du siège.*
33. Q IV, p. 67, Jean Chartier.
34. Siméon Luce, 'Deux Documents inédits relatifs à Frère Richard et à Jeanne d'Arc', *Revue bleue*, vol. L, 1892, p. 201.
35. Q IV, p. 15, Perceval de Cagny and Q IV, p. 241, *Chronique de la Pucelle.*
36. Q III, p. 98.
37. ibid.
38. ibid.
39. Q IV, p. 318, Gruel.
40. Q IV, p. 419, Wavrin.

CHAPTER 18

1. Q IV, p. 239, *Chronique de la Pucelle* and Q IV, pp. 413–14, Wavrin.
2. Q IV, p. 416, Wavrin.
3. ibid., p. 420.
4. ibid., p. 421.
5. ibid., p. 420.
6. Q III, p. 71 and Q IV, p. 419, Wavrin.
7. Q IV, p. 420, Wavrin.
8. Q IV, p. 177, *Journal du siège.*
9. Q IV, p. 68, Jean Chartier.
10. Q III, p. 71.
11. Q III, p. 120.
12. Q IV, p. 371, Monstrelet.
13. Q IV, p. 422, Wavrin.
14. ibid.
15. ibid.
16. ibid. See also Q IV, p. 319, Gruel.
17. Q IV, p. 423, Wavrin.
18. Q IV, p. 319, Gruel.
19. Siméon Luce, *Revue bleue*, vol. L, p. 203.
20. Q IV, p. 423, Wavrin.
21. ibid.
22. ibid.
23. ibid., p. 424.
24. Q IV, p. 374, Monstrelet.
25. Vigneulles, op. cit., p. 20 and Ayroles, op. cit., vol. III, p. 457.
26. Q IV, p. 423, Wavrin.
27. Q V, p. 120.

28. Q III, pp. 71–2.
29. Q IV, p. 244, *Chronique de la Pucelle*.
30. Q IV, p. 177, *Journal du siège*.
31. Q IV, p. 424, Wavrin.
32. Q IV, pp. 375–6, Monstrelet.
33. Q IV, p. 424, Wavrin.
34. Q IV, p. 319, Gruel.
35. Q III, p. 99.
36. Q IV, p. 16, Perceval de Cagny.
37. ibid.
38. Q IV, p. 245, *Chronique de la Pucelle*.
39. ibid.
40. ibid., pp. 244–5.
41. ibid., p. 245.
42. Q IV, p. 70, Jean Chartier.
43. Q IV, pp. 319–20, Gruel.
44. Q III, p. 116.
45. Q IV, p. 71, Jean Chartier.
46. ibid.
47. ibid.

CHAPTER 19

1. Q IV, p. 245, *Chronique de la Pucelle*.
2. Q IV, pp. 16–17, Perceval de Cagny.
3. Q IV, p. 246, *Chronique de la Pucelle*.
4. ibid., p. 247.
5. Q IV, p. 18, Perceval de Cagny.
6. Q V, p. 125.
7. Q IV, p. 18, Perceval de Cagny.
8. Q IV, p. 248, *Chronique du la Pucelle*.
9. Q IV, p. 180, *Journal du siège*.
10. Q IV, p. 71, Jean Chartier.
11. Q IV, p. 17, Perceval de Cagny.
12. Q IV, p. 377, Monstrelet.
13. Q IV, p. 70, Jean Chartier.
14. ibid., p. 72.
15. Q IV, pp. 377–8, Monstrelet.
16. Q IV, p. 72, Chartier.
17. Q IV, p. 181, *Journal du siège*.
18. Q IV, p. 72, Jean Chartier and Q IV, p. 181, *Journal du siège*.
19. *Livre noir de la Rochelle*, loc. cit., p. 341.
20. Q IV, p. 191, *Journal du siège*.
21. *Livre noir de la Rochelle*, loc. cit., pp. 341–2.
22. T/L I, p. 98 – T/L II, p. 94.
23. Bourgeois de Paris, op. cit., p. 233.
24. ibid., p. 234.
25. ibid., p. 235.
26. ibid.
27. ibid., pp. 232–3.
28. ibid., p. 235.
29. ibid., p. 237.

30. T/L II, p. 94, n.1.
31. Bourgeois de Paris, op. cit., p. 235.
32. Q IV, p. 377, Monstrelet.
33. *Livre noir de la Rochelle*, loc. cit., p. 342.
34. ibid.
35. Bourgeois de Paris, op. cit., pp. 242–3.
36. T/L I, p. 102 – T/L II, p. 97.
37. Q II, p. 450.
38. Q IV, p. 474, Bourgeois de Paris.
39. ibid.
40. T/L I, p. 105 – T/L II, p. 100.
41. Q IV, p. 382, Monstrelet.
42. Q IV, p. 290, Jean Rogier.
43. Q IV, p. 182, *Journal du siège*.
44. ibid.
45. Q IV, p. 73, Jean Chartier.
46. ibid. See also Q IV, p. 182, *Journal du siège*.
47. Q IV, p. 183, *Journal du siège*.
48. Q IV, p. 75, Jean Chartier.
49. Q III, p. 13.
50. Q IV, p. 75, Jean Chartier and Q IV, p. 183, *Journal du siège*.
51. Q IV, p. 76, Jean Chartier.
52. Q III, p. 13.
53. ibid. and Q IV, p. 295, Jean Rogier.
54. ibid.
55. Q III, p. 117.
56. Q IV, p. 184, *Journal du siège*.
57. Q IV, p. 252, *Chronique de la Pucelle*.
58. *Livre noir de la Rochelle*, loc. cit., p. 342.
59. Q IV, p. 253, *Chronique de la Pucelle*.
60. Q III, p. 117.
61. Q IV, p. 184, *Journal du siège*.
62. T/L I, p. 100 – T/L II, pp. 96–7.
63. ibid.
64. Q IV, p. 184, *Journal du siège*.
65. Q IV, p. 297, Jean Rogier.
66. Q IV, p. 251, *Chronique de la Pucelle*.
67. *Livre noir de la Rochelle*, loc. cit., p. 343.

CHAPTER 20

1. Q II, p. 391.
2. Q II, p. 423.
3. Q IV, p. 182, *Journal du siège*.
4. Q IV, p. 285, Jean Rogier.
5. Q IV, pp. 293–4, Jean Rogier.
6. Q IV, pp. 184–5, *Journal du siège*.
7. ibid.
8. ibid.
9. Q IV, p. 514, Pope Pius II.
10. ibid.
11. Q IV, p. 185, *Journal du siège*.

12. Q IV, p. 19, Perceval de Cagny and Q V, p. 19.
13. Q V, p. 129.
14. ibid.
15. Q IV, p. 185, *Journal du siège*.
16. Q IV, p. 513, Pope Pius II.
17. Q IV, p. 185, *Journal du siège*.
18. ibid.
19. Q V, p. 189.
20. Q IV, p. 186, *Journal du siège*.
21. ibid.
22. ibid.
23. Q V, p. 189.
24. Q IV, p. 380, Monstrelet.
25. Q V, p. 128.
26. ibid., p. 129.
27. T/L I, pp. 178–9 – T/L II, p. 146.
28. Q IV, p. 186, *Journal du siège*.
29. Q III, pp. 110–111.
30. Q V, p. 129.
31. Q IV, p. 380, Monstrelet.
32. Luce, *Revue bleue*, vol. L, p. 204.
33. T/L I, p. 101 – T/L II, p. 97.
34. Q V, p. 141–7, Q V, p. 266.
35. Q II, p. 445.
36. T/L I, p. 100 – T/L II, p. 97.
37. Q V, pp. 126–7.

CHAPTER 21

1. Q IV, p. 78, Jean Chartier and Q IV, p. 187, *Journal du siège*.
2. Q V, p. 130.
3. Q V, pp. 139–40.
4. *Livre noir de la Rochelle*, op. cit., p. 344.
5. Q IV, pp. 80–2, Jean Chartier.
6. Q IV, p. 21, Perceval de Cagny.
7. ibid., p. 22.
8. ibid., p. 21.
9. Q IV, p. 82, Jean Chartier.
10. Q IV, p. 22, Perceval de Cagny.
11. Q IV, p. 434, Lefèvre de Saint-Rémi.
12. Q IV, p. 21, Perceval de Cagny.
13. Q IV, pp. 82–3, Jean Chartier.
14. Q IV, p. 388, Monstrelet.
15. Q IV, p. 434, Lefèvre de Saint-Rémi.
16. Q IV, pp. 387–8, Monstrelet.
17. ibid.
18. Q IV, p. 190, *Journal du siège*.
19. Q IV, p. 85, Jean Chartier.
20. ibid., p. 83.
21. Q IV, p. 22, Perceval de Cagny.
22. Lafons de Mélicocq, 'Document nouveau sur Jeanne d'Arc', *Bulletin de la société de l'histoire de France*, 1857–8, p. 104.

23. Q IV, p. 23, Perceval de Cagny.
24. Q IV, p. 388, Monstrelet.
25. Q IV, p. 434, Lefèvre de Saint-Rémi.
26. Q IV, p. 389, Monstrelet.
27. ibid., p. 388.
28. Q IV, p. 434, Lefèvre de Saint-Rémi.
29. Q IV, p. 84, Jean Chartier. See also Q IV, p. 196, *Journal du siège.*
30. Q IV, p. 195, *Journal du siège.*
31. Q IV, p. 23, Perceval de Cagny.
32. Q IV, p. 435, Lefèvre de Saint-Rémi.
33. Q IV, p. 23, Perceval de Cagny.
34. Q IV, p. 384, Monstrelet.
35. Q V, p. 126.
36. T/L I, p. 266 – T/L II, p. 190.
37. T/L III, pp. 215–17.
38. T/L II, p. 226 – T/L II, p. 190.
39. T/L I, p. 82 – T/L II, p. 82.
40. ibid.

CHAPTER 22

1. Q IV, p. 24, Perceval de Cagny.
2. ibid.
3. ibid.
4. T/L I, p. 102 – T/L II, p. 98.
5. T/L I, p. 152 – T/L II, p. 131.
6. ibid.
7. Q III, p. 81.
8. Bourgeois de Paris, op. cit., p. 243.
9. Morosini, op. cit., vol. III, pp. 196–8.
10. Q IV, p. 392, Monstrelet.
11. Q IV, p. 24, Perceval de Cagny.
12. Q IV, p. 392, Monstrelet.
13. Q IV, p. 25, Perceval de Cagny.
14. Bourgeois de Paris, op. cit., p. 243.
15. Jean Favier, *Paris au XVᵉ siècle*, Paris, 1974, p. 61.
16. Morosini, op. cit., vol. III, pp. 188–9, 190–91.
17. Q IV, pp. 454–5, de Fauquembergue.
18. Q IV, pp. 25–6, Perceval de Cagny.
19. Bourgeois de Paris, op. cit., p. 243.
20. ibid., n.4.
21. ibid., pp. 243–4.
22. Q IV, p. 86, Jean Chartier.
23. Q IV, p. 26, Perceval de Cagny.
24. Q III, p. 99. See also Q IV, p. 71, Jean Chartier.
25. Q III, p. 73.
26. Q IV, pp. 71–2, Jean Chartier.
27. ibid., p. 93.
28. T/L I, p. 141 – T/L II, p. 124.
29. T/L I, p. 140 – T/L II, p. 124.
30. T/L I, p. 141 – T/L II, p. 124.

31. Bourgeois de Paris, op. cit., pp. 224–5.
32. ibid.
33. Q IV, pp. 86–7, Jean Chartier and Q IV, p. 198, *Journal du siège*.
34. ibid.
35. ibid.
36. Q IV, pp. 26–7, Perceval de Cagny and *Livre noir de la Rochelle*, op. cit., p. 344.
37. Bourgeois de Paris, op. cit., p. 245.
38. Q IV, p. 199, *Journal du siège* and Q IV, p. 457, de Fauquembergue.
39. Q IV, p. 199, *Journal du siège*.
40. Bourgeois de Paris, op. cit., p. 245.
41. Q IV, p. 342, anonymous Norman chronicle.
42. Ayroles, op. cit., vol. III, p. 472, Pierre Cochon.
43. Q IV, p. 457, de Fauquembergue.
44. Q IV, p. 199, *Journal du siège*.
45. Bourgeois de Paris, op. cit., p. 245.
46. T/L I, p. 142 – T/L II, p. 124.
47. Bourgeois de Paris, op. cit., p. 245.
48. Q IV, p. 199, *Journal du siège*.
49. Ayroles, op. cit., vol. III, pp. 227–8, quoting the *Chronique de Tournai*.
50. Bourgeois de Paris, op. cit., p. 246; Ayroles, op. cit., vol. III, p. 442, quoting the *Chronique des cordeliers*.
51. Bourgeois de Paris, op. cit., pp. 245–6.
52. ibid.
53. Q IV, p. 87, Jean Chartier.
54. Q IV, p. 27, Perceval de Cagny.
55. ibid., pp. 27–8.
56. Bourgeois de Paris, op. cit., p. 246.
57. Q IV, p. 28, Perceval de Cagny.
58. Q IV, p. 200, *Journal du siège*.
59. Ayroles, op. cit., vol. III, p. 472.
60. Q IV, p. 200, *Journal du siège*.
61. ibid.
62. Q IV, p. 29, Perceval de Cagny.
63. T/L I, p. 53 – T/L II, p. 57.
64. T/L I, p. 237 – T/L II, p. 199.
65. T/L I, p. 78 – T/L II, pp. 76–7; T/L I, pp. 170–71 – T/L II, p. 141.
66. T/L I, pp. 170–71 – T/L II, p. 141.
67. T/L I, p. 78 – T/L II, p. 77.
68. Q IV, p. 29, Perceval de Cagny.
69. Bourgeois de Paris, op. cit., p. 248.

CHAPTER 23

1. Q III, p. 84.
2. T/L I, p. 100 – T/L II, p. 96.
3. Ayroles, op. cit., vol. III, p. 471, Pierre Cochon.
4. Lafons de Mélicocq, *Bulletin de la société de l'histoire de France*, 1857–8, p. 102.
5. Chastellain, op. cit., vol. II, p. 40.
6. Chastellain, quoted Beaucourt, vol. II, p. 244.
7. T/L I, p. 261 – T/L II, p. 220.

8. Noel Valois, *Un Nouveau Témoignage sur Jeanne d'Arc*, Paris, 1907, pp. 12–13.
9. Pierre Lanéry d'Arc, *Le Culte de Jeanne d'Arc au XVe siècle*, Orleans, 1887, p. 16.
10. Vallet de Viriville, *Revue archéologique*, new series, June 1861, pp. 434–7.
11. T/L I, p. 114 – T/L II, p. 106.
12. Q IV, p. 30, Perceval de Cagny.
13. Vaughan, op. cit., pp. 123–4.
14. Q III, pp. 86–8.
15. Q III, p. 34.
16. Q III, p. 212.
17. Q III, p. 18.
18. Q III, p. 81.

CHAPTER 24

1. Q IV, p. 31, Perceval de Cagny.
2. Beaucourt, op. cit., vol. II, p. 128.
3. Q V, p. 71, Martial d'Auvergne.
4. T/L I, p. 106 – T/L II, p. 100.
5. ibid. and T/L I, p. 141 – T/L II, p. 124.
6. Q V, p. 71, Martial d'Auvergne.
7. Q III, pp. 217–18.
8. Ayroles, op. cit., vol. III, p. 376.
9. Q III, p. 23.
10. Q V, p. 147.
11. ibid.
12. ibid., p. 149.
13. ibid., p. 146.
14. ibid., pp. 268–70.
15. Q IV, p. 91, Jean Chartier.
16. T/L I, p. 106 – T/L II, p. 100; Q IV, p. 49, Le Hérault Berri.
17. Q V, p. 72, Martial d'Auvergne.
18. Q IV, p. 49, Le Hérault Berri; Q IV, p. 91, Jean Chartier.
19. Q IV, p. 49, Le Hérault Berri.
20. ibid.
21. Q IV, p. 31, Perceval de Cagny.
22. Ayroles, vol. III, p. 375–6.
23. Q IV, p. 31, Perceval de Cagny.
24. Q IV, p. 474, Bourgeois de Paris.
25. Lowell, op. cit., p. 191, n.2.
26. T/L I, p. 264 – T/L II, pp. 223–4.
27. ibid.
28. T/L I, p. 105 – T/L II, p. 100.
29. ibid.
30. T/L I, p. 104 – T/L II, p. 99.
31. T/L I, pp. 105–6 – T/L II, p. 100.
32. Q III, p. 219.
33. Bourgeois de Paris, op. cit., p. 271.
34. H. I. F. R. du Motey, *Jeanne d'Arc à Chinon*, Paris, 1927, pp. 109–10, 110, n.1.
35. Bourgeois de Paris, op. cit., pp. 259–60.

CHAPTER 25

1. Q V, pp. 150–53.
2. T/L I, p. 114 – T/L II, p. 106.
3. T/L I, p. 268 – T/L II, p. 228.
4. Q III, p. 67.
5. Quoted by Jules Quicherat, *Livre noir de la Rochelle*, loc. cit., p. 330.
6. *Bulletin de la Société de l'histoire de France*, 1857–8, p. 103.
7. T/L I, pp. 426–7 – T/L II, p. 372.
8. Q V, p. 270.
9. Q V, pp. 154–5.
10. Q V, p. 160.
11. Q IV, p. 299.
12. Andrew Lang, *The Maid of France*, London, 1908, pp. 223–5.
13. Q IV, p. 32, Perceval de Cagny.
14. Q IV, p. 92, Jean Chartier.
15. T/L I, p. 115 – T/L II, p. 107.
16. Bourgeois de Paris, pp. 251–2.
17. Pierre Champion, *Splendeurs et misères de Paris, XIVe–XVe siècles*, Paris, 1934, p. 153.
18. ibid., p. 181.
19. Bourgeois de Paris, op. cit., p. 253.
20. Lowell, op. cit., p. 203, n.1.
21. Q IV, p. 399, Monstrelet.
22. ibid.
23. Q IV, p. 32, Perceval de Cagny.
24. Q IV, p. 399, Monstrelet.
25. Q IV, p. 158, *Journal du siège*; Q V, p. 91, Martial d'Auvergne.
26. Q V, p. 177.
27. Q IV, p. 399, Monstrelet.
28. ibid.
29. ibid., pp. 399–400 and Q IV, pp. 442–3, Georges Chastellain.
30. Q IV, p. 91, Jean Chartier.
31. Q IV, p. 32, Perceval de Cagny.
32. ibid. and Q IV, p. 400, Monstrelet.
33. Q IV, p. 400, Monstrelet.
34. T/L I, p. 150 – T/L II, p. 130.
35. Bourgeois de Paris, op. cit., p. 252.
36. T/L I, pp. 150–51 – T/L II, p. 130.
37. Q IV, p. 443, Georges Chastellain.
38. T/L I, pp. 150–51 – T/L II, p. 130.
39. Q IV, p. 443, Georges Chastellain.
40. Charles Wayland Lightbody, *The Judgements of Joan*, London, 1961, p. 61.
41. T/L I, p. 141 – T/L II, p. 124.
42. T/L I, p. 78 – T/L II, pp. 76–7.
43. T/L I, p. 103 – T/L II, p. 98. For the Virgin of Lagny see Abbé F. A. Denis, *Le Séjour de Jeanne d'Arc à Lagny*, Lagny, 1896, p. 4.

CHAPTER 26

1. T/L I, pp. 111–12 – T/L II, p. 104.
2. Q IV, p. 32, Perceval de Cagny.
3. Charles Jules Flammermont, 'Senlis pendant la seconde partie de la

Guerre de Cent Ans', *Mémoires de la sociéte de l'histoire de Paris et de l'Île de France*, vol. V, 1878, p. 245, n.2.

4. Alexandre Sorel, *La Prise de Jeanne d'Arc devant Compiègne*, Paris/ Orleans, 1889, pp. 144–5.

5. Ayroles, op. cit., vol. III, p. 296.

6. Q IV, p. 372, *Le Miroir des femmes vertueuses*.

7. Vallet de Viriville, *Histoire de Charles VII*, Paris, 1863, vol. II, p. 143.

8. Q IV, p. 397, Monstrelet; Q IV, p. 437, Lefèvre de Saint-Rémi.

9. Q IV, p. 398, Monstrelet.

10. Q IV, p. 437, Lefèvre de Saint-Rémi.

11. Q IV, p. 397, Monstrelet.

12. ibid.

13. T/L I, p. 141 – T/L II, p. 124.

14. Q IV, p. 437, Monstrelet.

15. Pierre Champion, *Guillaume de Flavy*, Paris, 1906, p. 42.

16. Q IV, p. 50, Le Hérault Berri.

17. ibid.

18. ibid.

19. Champion, op. cit., p. 38, quoting the *Chronique de Tournai*.

20. Q IV, p. 50, Le Hérault Berri; T/L II, p. 102, n.1.

21. T/L I, p. 108 – T/L II, p. 102.

22. Q IV, p. 92, Jean Chartier.

23. T/L I, p. 111 – T/L II, p. 104.

24. Q IV, p. 33, Perceval de Cagny.

25. Q IV, p. 400, Monstrelet.

26. ibid.

27. Q IV, p. 445, Georges Chastellain.

28. T/L I, p. 111 – T/L II, p. 104.

29. Q IV, p. 445, Georges Chastellain.

30. T/L I, p. 115 – T/L II, p. 106.

31. Q IV, p. 445, Georges Chastellain.

32. ibid.

33. T/L I, p. 113 – T/L II, p. 105.

34. Q IV, p. 446, Georges Chastellain.

35. T/L I, p. 113 – T/L II, p. 105.

36. Q IV, p. 446, Georges Chastellain.

37. Q IV, p. 459, de Fauquembergue.

38. Ayroles, op. cit., vol. III, p. 536.

39. T/L I, p. 113 – T/L II, p. 105.

40. Q IV, p. 447, Georges Chastellain.

41. T/L II, p. 2, n.1. Tisset and Lanhers give the correct Christian name.

42. Q IV, p. 447, Georges Chastellain.

43. Q IV, p. 34, Perceval de Cagny.

44. T/L I, p. 232 – T/L II, p. 195.

45. Ayroles, op. cit., vol. III, p. 536.

46. Sorel, op. cit., pp. 282–6.

47. Q IV, p. 402, Monstrelet.

48. Q V, p. 167.

CHAPTER 27

1. T/L I, pp. 8–9 – T/L II, pp. 9–10.

2. Morosini, op. cit., vol. III, pp. 232–5.

3. T/L I, p. 7 – T/L II, p. 8.
4. T/L I, p. 7 – T/L II, p. 9.
5. Q II, p. 21.
6. Ayroles, op. cit., vol. II, p. 31.
7. T/L I, p. 10 – T/L II, p. 11.
8. Chastellain, op. cit., vol. I, p. 204.
9. T/L I, p. 10 – T/L II, p. 11.
10. T/L I, p. 10 – T/L II, pp. 11–12.
11. T/L III, p. 9.
12. Henri Debout, *Jeanne d'Arc et les archives anglaises*, Paris, 1895, pp. 19–20.
13. Q III, p. 122.
14. Q IV, p. 262, L'Abréviateur du procès.
15. Q V, p. 179.
16. Q V, p. 191–2.
17. *Chronicles of London*, Kingsford (ed.), p. 73.
18. cf. W. T. Waugh, in *Historical Essays in Honour of James Tait*, Edwards, Galbraith and Jacob (eds.), Manchester, 1933, pp. 387ff.
19. Q II, p. 325.
20. Morosini, op. cit., vol. III, pp. 356–7.

CHAPTER 28

1. Q IV, p. 34, Perceval de Cagny.
2. ibid., p. 35.
3. T/L I, p. 155 – T/L II, p. 133.
4. W. S. Scott, op. cit., p. 84.
5. T/L I, p. 155 – T/L II, p. 133.
6. T/L I, p. 156 – T/L II, p. 133.
7. Holland-Smith, op. cit., p. 103.
8. T/L I, p. 107 – T/L II, p. 101.
9. T/L I, p. 94 – T/L II, p. 92.
10. ibid.
11. T/L I, p. 95 – T/L II, p. 93.
12. T/L I, p. 213 – T/L II, p. 175.
13. T/L I, p. 101 – T/L II, p. 107.
14. Henri Debout, *Jeanne d'Arc, prisonnière à Arras*, Arras, 1894, pp. 14–18.
15. Q V, p. 253.
16. Ayroles, op. cit., vol. I, p. 688.
17. Q V, p. 168.
18. Morosini, op. cit., vol. III, pp. 336–7.
19. Quoted by Beaucourt, op. cit., vol. II, pp. 254–5.
20. Q V, p. 194.
21. Jules Quicherat, *Aperçus nouveaux sur l'histoire de Jeanne d'Arc*, p. 57.
22. Jules Quicherat, 'Supplément aux témoignages contemporaines sur Jeanne d'Arc', *Revue historique*, vol. 19, May–June 1882, pp. 82–3.
23. T/L I, p. 144 – T/L II, p. 126.
24. T/L I, p. 153 – T/L II, p. 131.
25. T/L I, p. 144 – T/L II, p. 126.
26. T/L I, pp. 145–6 – T/L II, p. 127.
27. T/L I, p. 145 – T/L II, p. 127.
28. Jules Quicherat, *Aperçus nouveaux sur l'histoire de Jeanne d'Arc*, p. 56.
29. Q IV, p. 162, L'Abréviateur du Procès.

CHAPTER 29

1. Lomier, op. cit., p. 61.
2. T/L II, p. 12, n.2.
3. T/L I, p. 95 – T/L II, p. 93.
4. T/L I, pp. 98–9 – T/L II, p. 95.
5. T/L I, p. 288 – T/L II, p. 243.
6. T/L I, pp. 12–14 – T/L II, pp. 14–16.
7. T/L I, pp. 11–12 – T/L II, pp. 13–14.
8. Q III, p. 121.
9. T/L I, pp. 17–18 – T/L II, pp. 19–20.
10. Q III, p. 121.
11. Q III, p. 137.
12. T/L I, pp. 15–18 – T/L II, pp. 18–20.
13. T/L I, pp. 14–15 – T/L II, pp. 16–17.
14. T/L I, pp. 18–22 – T/L II, pp. 20–24.
15. T/L I, p. 23 – T/L II, p. 25.
16. T/L III, p. 70.
17. Q III, p. 161.
18. Q II, pp. 462–3.
19. Q II, p. 394.
20. Q III, pp. 192–3.
21. Q III, p. 153.
22. Jules Quicherat, *Aperçus nouveaux sur l'histoire de Jeanne d'Arc*, p. 101.
23. Q III, p. 137.
24. Q III, p. 174; Q V, pp. 196–201.
25. Q III, pp. 56, 161, 166, 253.
26. Q III, p. 56.
27. Q III, p. 174.
28. T/L I, p. 15 – T/L II, p. 17.
29. Q III, pp. 155, 163.
30. Q III, p. 163.
31. Q II, p. 11.
32. Q III, p. 63
33. Q III, p. 180.
34. Q III, p. 154.
35. Q II, p. 186; Q III, p. 140.
36. Q II, p. 186; Q II, p. 154.
37. Q III, p. 140.
38. Q III, p. 155.
39. Q III, p. 346.
40. T/L I, p. 42 – T/L II, p. 42 and n.2
41. Q II, p. 318.
42. Q II, p. 361.
43. Q III, p. 89.
44. Q III, p. 121.
45. Q II, p. 299.
46. Q III, pp. 147–8.
47. Q II, p. 299.
48. Q II, p. 322.
49. Q II, p. 323.
50. Q II, p. 377.

51. Q III, p. 130.
52. Q III, p. 154.

CHAPTER 30

1. Q III, p. 60.
2. Q III, p. 135.
3. T/L I, p. 38 – T/L II, p. 37.
4. T/L I, p. 42 – T/L II, p. 42.
5. Q III, pp. 140–1.
6. J. Fabre, *Procès de réhabilitation*, Paris, 1913, vol. II, p. 31, n.2
7. Q III, p. 60.
8. Q III, p. 141.
9. Q III, p. 136.
10. Q III, p. 162.
11. Q III, p. 173.
12. Q III, p. 181.
13. Q II, pp. 12–13; Q III, p. 146.
14. T/L I, p. 61 – T/L II, p. 62.
15. Q III, p. 136.
16. Q II, p. 16.
17. Q II, p. 322.
18. Q III, p. 155.
19. Q III, p. 51.
20. Q II, p. 357.
21. Q III, p. 153.
22. Q II, p. 326.
23. Q III, pp. 171–2.
24. Q II, p. 329.
25. Q II, p. 322.
26. T/L I, p. 59 – T/L II, p. 60.
27. Q III, p. 175.
28. T/L I, p. 62 – T/L II, p. 63.
29. T/L II, p. 63, n.1.
30. Q III, p. 163.
31. Q III, p. 175.
32. T/L I, p. 75 – T/L II, p. 74.
33. T/L III, p. 29.
34. Q III, p. 34.
35. ibid.
36. Q II, p. 16.
37. T/L I, p. 103 – T/L II, p. 98.
38. T/L I, p. 96 – T/L II, p. 93.
39. Q III, pp. 142, 161.
40. Q III, p. 201.
41. Q III, p. 135.
42. Q II, p. 371.
43. Q III, p. 48.
44. T/L I, pp. 108–9 – T/L II, p. 102.

CHAPTER 31

1. T/L I, p. 110 – T/L II, p. 103.

2. Manchon says the meeting took place 'on a Saturday in Lent', and this is the likeliest date.
3. Q III, pp. 11–12.
4. T/L I, p. 113 – T/L II, p. 103.
5. T/L I, p. 117 – T/L II, pp. 108–9.
6. T/L I, p. 125 – T/L II, p. 114.
7. Q II, p. 326.
8. T/L I, p. 147 – T/L II, p. 128.
9. T/L I, p. 148 – T/L II, pp. 128–9.
10. T/L I, p. 148 – T/L II, p. 129.
11. T/L I, p. 157 – T/L II, p. 134.
12. T/L I, p. 155 – T/L II, p. 132.
13. T/L I, p. 158 – T/L II, p. 134.
14. Q II, p. 4.
15. T/L I, pp. 167–8 – T/L II, pp. 139–40.
16. Q II, p. 14.
17. Q II, pp. 349–50.
18. T/L I, p. 176 – T/L II, p. 144.
19. T/L I, p. 343 – T/L II, p. 298.
20. T/L I, p. 182 – T/L II, p. 149.

CHAPTER 32

1. Q III, p. 142.
2. T/L I, p. 186 – T/L II, p. 153.
3. T/L I, p. 189 – T/L II, p. 156.
4. T/L I, p. 190 – T/L II, p. 157.
5. Q II, p. 9.
6. Q II, p. 325.
7. Q II, pp. 9–10.
8. Q II, p. 166.
9. Q II, p. 13.
10. T/L I, p. 238 – T/L II, p. 243.
11. Q II, p. 341.
12. Q II, p. 13.
13. Q II, p. 242; Q III, p. 136.
14. Q II, p. 22.
15. Q III, p. 232.
16. Jules Quicherat, *Aperçus nouveaux sur l'histoire de Jeanne d'Arc*, p. 126.
17. Q III, p. 143.
18. T/L I, p. 296 – T/L II, p. 251.
19. Q III, p. 145.
20. T/L I, pp. 298–9 – T/L II, p. 254.
21. Q III, p. 49.
22. Q III, p. 162.
23. Q III, p. 51.
24. ibid.
25. T/L I, p. 328 – T/L II, p. 285.
26. T/L I, p. 330 – T/L II, p. 287.
27. T/L I, p. 332 – T/L II, p. 287.
28. T/L I, p. 346 – T/L II, p. 300.
29. T/L I, p. 349 – T/L II, p. 302.

30. T/L I, p. 350 – T/L II, p. 302.
31. ibid.
32. T/L I, p. 351 – T/L II, p. 303.
33. Régine Pernoud, *Jeanne devant les Cauchons*, Paris, 1970, pp. 82–3.
34. T/L I, pp. 381–2 – T/L II, p. 332.
35. T/L I, p. 384 – T/L II, p. 334.
36. Q II, p. 298.
37. Q II, p. 10.
38. Q II, p. 20.
39. Q II, p. 304.
40. Q III, p. 129.
41. Q III, p. 58.
42. Q II, p. 354.
43. Q III, pp. 183–4.

CHAPTER 33

1. Q II, p. 21.
2. Q III, p. 146.
3. Q III, p. 60.
4. Q III, p. 113.
5. John XV: 4; T/L I, p. 386 – T/L II, p. 336.
6. Q III, p. 61.
7. Q II, p. 17.
8. ibid.
9. Q III, p. 168.
10. Q II, p. 17.
11. Q II, p. 353.
12. T/L I, pp. 386–7 – T/L II, pp. 336–7.
13. Q III, p. 123.
14. T/L I, p. 387 – T/L II, p. 337.
15. Q III, p. 123.
16. T/L I, p. 389 – T/L II, p. 337; Q III, p. 146.
17. Q III, p. 52; Q III, p. 146.
18. Q II, p. 17.
19. Q III, p. 156.
20. ibid.
21. Q III, p. 146.
22. Q III, pp. 156–7.
23. Q II, p. 17.
24. Q II, p. 331.
25. Q III, p. 157.
26. Q III, p. 147.
27. Q III, p. 157.
28. Q II, p. 325.
29. Q III, p. 64.
30. Q III, p. 55.
31. Q II, p. 130.
32. Q III, p. 273.
33. Q II, p. 132.
34. Jules Quicherat, *Aperçus nouveaux sur l'histoire de Jeanne d'Arc*, p. 135.
35. Q II, p. 17.

36. Q III, p. 164.
37. T/L I, p. 390 – T/L II, p. 339.
38. T/L III, p. 138, n.4.
39. T/L I, p. 82 – T/L II, p. 82.
40. Q III, p. 55.
41. Q II, p. 338.
42. Q II, pp. 17–18.
43. Q II, p. 376.

CHAPTER 34

1. T/L I, pp. 393–4 – T/L II, p. 343.
2. T/L I, pp. 397–8 – T/L II, p. 345.
3. T/L I, p. 402 – T/L II, p. 349.
4. Q II, p. 21.
5. Q II, p. 18.
6. Q III, p. 55.
7. Q II, p. 21.
8. Q II, p. 14 and Q III, p. 148 conflated.
9. Q II, p. 19.
10. Q III, p. 158. Marguerie himself confirms this, Q III, p. 184.
11. Q II, p. 8.
12. ibid. and Q II, p. 305.
13. Q II, p. 14.
14. Q III, p. 149.
15. T/L I, pp. 305–6 – T/L II, pp. 344–5.
16. Q II, p. 334.
17. T/L I, p. 399 – T/L II, p. 346.
18. ibid.
19. T/L I, p. 398 – T/L II, p. 345.
20. Q III, p. 149.
21. Q II, pp. 5, 8.
22. T/L I, p. 407 – T/L II, p. 353.

CHAPTER 35

1. T/L I, p. 418 – T/L II, p. 364.
2. Q III, p. 191.
3. Q II, pp. 3–4.
4. ibid.
5. T/L I, p. 419 – T/L II, p. 365.
6. Q II, p. 320.
7. Q III, p. 158.
8. T/L I, p. 420 – T/L II, p. 356.
9. Q III, p. 149.
10. T/L I, p. 420 – T/L II, p. 366.
11. Q II, p. 334.
12. Q II, p. 18.
13. Q III, p. 114.
14. Q III, p. 162.
15. Q II, p. 344.
16. Q IV, p. 480 and n.3, Walter Bower.
17. Q II, p. 328.

18. Q IV, pp. 459–60, de Fauquembergue.
19. T/L I, p. 410 – T/L II, p. 356.
20. Q III, p. 114.
21. T/L I, p. 411 – T/L II, p. 356.
22. Q III, p. 159.
23. Q IV, p. 459, de Fauquembergue.
24. Q II, p. 344.
25. Q III, p. 56.
26. Q II, p. 19.
27. Q III, p. 53.
28. Q II, p. 324.
29. Q III, p. 150.
30. Q II, p. 9.
31. Q II, p. 363.
32. Q II, p. 324.
33. Q II, p. 355.
34. Q III, p. 53.
35. Q II, p. 20.
36. ibid.
37. Q II, pp. 6, 20.
38. Q II, p. 9.
39. Q III, p. 159.
40. Q III, p. 194.
41. Q II, pp. 7, 20.

✦⊰| Index |⊱✦

321

322